Emily Brontë Criticism

1900–1982

An Annotated Check List

Emily Brontë Criticism

1900–1982

An Annotated Check List

JANET M. BARCLAY

MECKLER PUBLISHING
520 Riverside Avenue, Westport, CT 06880

3 Henrietta Street, London WC2 8LU, England

Library of Congress Cataloging in Publication Data

Barclay, Janet M.
  Emily Brontë criticism, 1900-1982

  Update of: Emily Brontë criticism, 1900-1968.
  Includes index.
  1. Brontë, Emily, 1818-1848—Bibliography.
I. Barclay, Janet M. Emily Brontë criticism, 1900-1968.
II. Title.
Z8121.98.B38   1983   [PR4173]   016.823'8   83-17433
ISBN 0-930466-63-2

Printed and bound in the United States of America

Contents

INTRODUCTION

W HEN it appeared in 1974, *Emily Brontë Criticism 1900-1968: An Annotated Check List* was critically received as a needed, thoughtful, and indispensable working tool. This bibliography, an update of the *Check List*, retains the first edition's broad coverage and format and provides a survey of twentieth-century criticism for students, scholars, and others interested in Emily Brontë—her biography, poetry, and her novel, *Wuthering Heights*.

The first section, "Books and Parts of Books," includes chapters and sections of books on Emily Brontë; introductions and prefaces to editions of *Wuthering Heights* and the poems; bibliographies; anthologies of essays, with reprintings cross-referenced throughout the list; and books on a general subject (e.g., the nineteenth-century English novel) that contain comments on Emily Brontë's work. The second section, "Articles," includes all periodicals, both popular and scholarly, with reprintings of articles cross-referenced throughout the list. The references in the first two sections, comprising the major portion of the *Check List*, are in English. "Books and Articles in Foreign Languages," the third section, were found in the course of research for the English sections. Although they are neither verified nor annotated, the sources listed in the third section could prove of value to students in the United States, Canada, and the United Kingdom as indicators of foreign critical opinion, as well as to students in the foreign countries themselves.

Each work is annotated from an examination of the original text, except for those unavailable for verification. In these instances, the work is listed exactly as it appears in the original footnote, reference, or bibliography and is marked with an asterisk to indicate that it was not read. If the item has been reprinted (in an anthology, for example), it is annotated from the reprinting although the original was not seen.

Since the *Check List* is an effort to record only criticism, general reviews of books about Emily Brontë and her work are not included, nor are general accounts such as those in encyclopedias. No works of fiction—in the form of novels, plays, poems, television and radio productions, motion pictures, readings, or juvenile treatments—are included, whether adaptations of *Wuthering Heights* or versions of Emily Brontë's life. Books and articles concerning the topography of the Haworth area, the parsonage, and the Brontë Museum have been excluded unless they are relevant to Emily Brontë's biography or to collections that could be of interest to the Emily Brontë scholar. A more complete listing of topographical works may be found in Yablon and Turner, noted below. Moreover, the *Check List*, although not exhaustive, is as complete as possible within the boundaries outlined above. Suggestions and critical comments will be gratefully received.

BRONTË BIBLIOGRAPHY

Since the publication of *Emily Brontë Criticism 1900-1968* in 1974, several other Brontë bibliographies with the goal of extensive coverage have appeared. Each of these bibliographies, included in the *Check List*, has a purpose and scope different from the one here, as indicated in their annotations. *A Brontë Bibliography* by G. Anthony Yablon and John R. Turner (1978) is an excellent descriptive bibliography restricted to books and parts of books about the Brontë family; it covers 122 years, but is not annotated. Also covering 122 years, Anne Passel's *Charlotte and Emily Brontë: An Annotated Bibliography* (1979) contains books, periodicals, and sources of primary material, annotated in most cases. It includes somewhat less twentieth-century coverage, however, than does the 1974 edition of the *Check List*. A third Brontë bibliography is restricted to American nineteenth-century periodicals: "The Brontës in the American Periodical Press of Their Day," *Brontë Society Transactions* 16:5 (1975), 383-99. The only bibliography devoted to Emily Brontë exclusively is an unpublished doctoral dissertation limited to criticism of *Wuthering Heights*, "An Annotated Bibliography of the Criticism on Emily Brontë's *Wuthering Heights*" by David M. Byers (1973). The most recent bibliography to appear is *Charlotte and Emily Brontë, 1846-1915: A Reference Guide* (1982) by Rebecca W. Crump. Competently annotated, the entries include—in addition to books and articles—sketches, reminiscences, and memorials. Although the avalanche of material covered in the Brontë family bibliographies makes the task of the Emily Brontë student a difficult one, all of these works constitute useful complements to this 1900-1982 *Check List* in that they contain literary criticism excluded here, i.e., sources of primary material, nineteenth-century secondary material, and criticism on the other Brontës.

Although Emily Brontë is an eminent author, very few attempts were made before 1970 to compile extensive and annotated check lists of items about her. One of the best, needing no annotation because of discussion within the book, is "An Emily Brontë Reading List," an appendix to *Emily Brontë: A Critical and Biographical Study* by John Hewish (1969). Another of merit—though it includes Charlotte Brontë and is not annotated—is Joseph Henry Dugas' bibliography for his "The Literary Reputation of the Brontës: 1846-1951" (a dissertation)(1951). Mary Visick's *The Genesis of* Wuthering Heights (1958) contains a selected annotated bibliography. Mildred G. Christian's chapter in *Victorian Fiction: A Guide to Research*, edited by Lionel Stevenson (1964), is a selected bibliography in chronological form, confined to the preceding thirty years of work on Emily Brontë. It is a model of bibliographic scholarship. *Victorian Fiction: A Second Guide to Research*, edited by George H. Ford (1978), is designed as a sequel to the Lionel Stevenson *Guide*, covering the years 1962-1974. The chapter on the Brontës by Herbert J. Rosengarten contains an excellent and comprehensive survey of recent criticism on Emily Brontë and includes sections on manuscripts, editions, translations, and dramatic adaptations.

PRIMARY AND SECONDARY MATERIAL

A listing of Brontë manuscript material accessible to students in the United States and England has been compiled by Mildred G. Christian in her "Guide to Research Materials on the Major Victorians: The Brontës" in *Victorian Newsletter* 13 (Spring 1958). For locating Emily Brontë's manuscripts of poems in this country, Dr Christian's "A Census of Brontë Manuscripts in the United States" in *The Trollopian* 2 (Dec 1947)—3 (Dec 1948) is invaluable. John Hewish, in *Emily Brontë: A Critical and Biographical Study* (1969), describes the complex problems surrounding Brontë primary source material and includes an appendix, "A Location List of Manuscripts."

C. W. Hatfield's *The Complete Poems of Emily Jane Brontë* (1941) is the definitive edition of the poems, and the Clarendon edition of *Wuthering Heights* (1976) edited by Hilda Marsden and Ian Jack, based on the 1847 edition, is generally accepted as the most accurate edition of the novel. Among others also based on the 1847 edition are the W. W. Norton edition (1963) edited by William M. Sale, Jr, and the Harcourt, Brace edition (1962) edited by Thomas C. Moser.

Primary source material, such as Charlotte Brontë's letters, may be found in Mrs Gaskell's *The Life of Charlotte Brontë* (1857) and Clement Shorter's *The Brontës: Life and Letters* (1908). It should be stressed that very little of Emily Brontë's own writing is extant; there are a few letters to Ellen Nussey, some diary papers, and several essays in French. Two of the diary papers and two letters to Ellen Nussey are in Clement Shorter's *The Brontës and*

Their Circle (1917?); four diary papers are in Fannie E. Ratchford's *Gondal's Queen* (1955). Essays are translated by Lorine W. Nagel and introduced by Fannie E. Ratchford in *Five Essays in French by Emily Jane Brontë* (1948); another essay is translated and discussed by Margaret Lane in *The Listener* 52 (Nov 11 1954). Seven essays are reproduced in Winifred Gérin's biography (1971).

Descriptive bibliography of primary material, the first editions of *Wuthering Heights*, and *Poems by Currer, Ellis and Acton Bell* are thoroughly covered by M. L. Parrish in *Victorian Lady Novelists* (1933). M.R.D. Seaward's introduction to a reproduction of the Smith, Elder 1848 edition of the poems (1978) discusses the problems involved in the authentication of the original binding.

Twentieth-Century Criticism

Literary criticism of Emily Brontë's work during the nineteenth century has specialized value and has received attention in recent years in studies by Miriam Allott in *The Brontës: The Critical Heritage* (1974) and Burton R. Pollin in "The Brontës in the American Periodical Press of Their Day" (1975), among others. It was in the twentieth century, however, that Emily Brontë's work came to be recognized as classic literature and extensive study was applied to it. For these reasons, the *Check List* is limited to criticism in this century.

In an effort to classify them, some of the twentieth-century approaches to literature have been variously described as impressionist, genetic, New Criticism, myth-and-symbol, psychoanalytic, socio-economic, comparative, and linguistic. These constitute only one arbitrary classification of criticism; another, for example, is Jean-Pierre Petit's temporal division of criticism into "Contemporaneous Criticism," "The Developing Debate," and "Modern Views" in *Emily Brontë: A Critical Anthology* (1973). For the purposes of this introduction, however, the twentieth-century approaches to literature offer a convenient format for a discussion of some of the criticism.

In the early 1900s, the impressionist approach, in which the critic simply recorded his personal response to a work, became popular. Arthur Symons sees "pain and the ineradicable sting of personal identity" in Emily Brontë's poems in 1906, and George Saintsbury in 1913 dismisses *Wuthering Heights* as "an ornament in novel history." A few more recent critics have modified this approach somewhat, basing their criticism on the literary work alone. Herbert Dingle, for example, in 1974 tries to determine from Emily Brontë's writings alone her quality of mind, and Tom Winnifrith (1977) is wary of too much critical emphasis on the Brontë juvenilia.

Genetic scholarship searches for earlier literature which may have influenced a particular work. Byron is one choice as a source for Emily Brontë's poems, and Scott and Shakespeare are seen as sources for *Wuthering Heights*, e.g., Florence S. Dry's *The Sources of* Wuthering Heights (1937), and A.J. Tough's "*Wuthering Heights* and *King Lear*" (1972).

Whereas the genetic approach explores literature preceding Emily Brontë's work, the comparative critic often sees in her work a genesis of later English literature or compares certain aspects of *Wuthering Heights* with those of other novels. Michael Black in 1975 examines love, marriage, and fidelity in *Wuthering Heights*, *David Copperfield*, and *Madame Bovary*; Jacqueline Viswanathan in 1974 compares unreliable narrators in *Under Western Eyes*, *Doktor Faustus*, and *Wuthering Heights*; and Jeanne Delbaere-Grant investigates "The Divided Worlds of Emily Brontë, Virginia Woolf and Janet Frame" (1979).

Some of the most discerning criticism has been generated since 1940 by the literary approach of the so-called New Criticism School. Under this approach, literary work is closely read, then judged solely as a work of art. The aspects of *Wuthering Heights* deplored by earlier critics—the cruelty depicted in the novel and the double narrative—were discovered by the New Critics to be ingeniously contributory to its art. Mark Schorer, evaluating the metaphors, epithets, and verbs in *Wuthering Heights* in 1949, concludes that it was no cruel tragedy but a "moral teething" for both Heathcliff and Emily Brontë. Benjamin H. Lehman in 1955, Carl Woodring in 1957, and Peter K. Garrett in 1977 applaud the multiple narration of the story.

The psychoanalytic and the socio-economic approaches, which seem to lead to combining the biography of a writer with his writings, have produced some studies with erratic conclusions. A few illuminating investigations have been based on these approaches, however. Among the psychoanalytic, "Romances, Novels and Psychoanalysis" by Patrick Brantlinger (1975) and "Visionary Experience in *Wuthering Heights*" by Joan Carson (also 1975) are notable. As for the socio-economic approach, neither the nature of Emily Brontë's work nor her isolated existence seems to have brought forth much of this kind of criticism. Nevertheless, David Wilson in his "Emily Brontë: First of the Moderns" (1947) convincingly takes exception to the idea that Emily Brontë was isolated from her local West Riding social history, and in 1940 Martin Turnell wrote an analysis in which *Wuthering Heights* is seen as an "indictment of contemporary civilization."

Myth-and-symbol interpretation applies readily to Emily Brontë's work: Dorothy Van Ghent's explication of "The Window Figure and the Two-children Figure in *Wuthering Heights*" (1952) is credible and well-supported by instances in the novel. "The Image of the Book in *Wuthering Heights*" by

Robert C. McKibben (1960) complements this and other myth-and-symbol studies and those focusing on imagery, such as Elisabeth van de Laar's *The Inner Structure of* Wuthering Heights: *A Study of an Imaginative Field* (1969).

An example of the more recent structural linguistics approach and an outstanding scholarly addition to literary criticism of *Wuthering Heights* is *Emily Brontë and the Haworth Dialect* (published by the Yorkshire Dialect Society in 1970) by K. M. Petyt, Lecturer in Linguistic Science, University of Reading. Another is Jeremy Cott's analysis of the last sentence in *Wuthering Heights* (1964).

Two literary approaches appearing within the last decade or so are unquestionably in keeping with their time; they can imprecisely be termed the philosophic/search for self, and the feminist. In an example of the first, *Wuthering Heights* and other literary works are seen to "explore metamorphoses of the self" in Leo Bersani's *A Future for Astyanax: Character and Desire in Literature* (1976); Wayne Burns examines the prophetic and archetypal aspects of *Wuthering Heights* in "In Death They Were Not Divided: The Moral Magnificence of Unmoral Passion in *Wuthering Heights*" (1973); and Walter L. Reed finds a historical basis for comparison of Emily Brontë with Lermontov (1974) and goes beyond these parallels into the philosophical ideas of Dostoyevsky and Kierkegaard, among others. Some of the feminist approaches emphasize Emily Brontë as an author, e.g., Margaret Homans' *Women Writers and Poetic Identity: Dorothy Wordsworth, Emily Brontë and Emily Dickinson* (1980). Others concentrate on *Wuthering Heights* or the poems. For instance, Christine Gallant discusses "The Archetypal Feminine in Emily Brontë's Poetry" (1980), and Helene Moglen perceives the theme of *Wuthering Heights* as the maturation of the female self in "The Double Vision of *Wuthering Heights*: A Clarifying View of Female Development" (1971).

ACKNOWLEDGMENTS

Invaluable assistance has been given me during my work on the *Check List* by Dr Jackson R. Bryer, Department of English, the University of Maryland.

I also appreciate the assistance of the staffs of the libraries where I have worked on this material: The Library of Congress, Washington, D.C.; the McKeldin Library, the University of Maryland, College Park, Md.; the Pratt Library and the Milton S. Eisenhower Library at the Johns Hopkins University, Baltimore, Md.; the McFarlin Library, the University of Tulsa, Tulsa, Okla.; and the Prince Georges Memorial Library, Greenbelt, Md.

Thanks are especially due my editors, Evamarian S. Brubaker and Arthur S. Barclay.

I am grateful to have had access to the *Publications of the Modern Language Association*; *Abstracts of English Studies*; *The Year's Work in English Studies*; and the *Brontë Society Transactions*. These publications have been of great help in compiling the *Check List*.

Bracketed pagination identifies those pages which focus more specifically on Emily Brontë and her work. In Section A, pagination is added for the critical works wholly on Emily Brontë or on *Wuthering Heights* or the poems. For convenience, I have abbreviated—in my own comments in the *Check List*—"Emily Brontë" as "EB" and "*Wuthering Heights*" as "WH." *Dissertation Abstracts International* has been abbreviated as *DAI*, and three serial titles have also been abbreviated: (London) *Times Literary Supplement* as *TLS*, *Brontë Society Transactions* as *BST*, and *Nineteenth Century Fiction* as *NCF*.

JANET M. BARCLAY
JUNE 1984

THE CHECK LIST

A Books and Parts of Books
Anonymous

A1 *The Brontës Then and Now* (Shipley [England]: Outhwaite Brothers 1947)
A symposium of eleven articles (ten of which pertain to EB) reprinted from *BST* and published as a *WH* and *Jane Eyre* centenary tribute. Annotated under the individual entries, the contents are as follows:
"The Three Sisters" by William Haley (B220)
"The Misses Brontë—Victorians" by Donald Hopewell (B253)
"The Haworth Tradition" by Ernest Rhys (B421)
"Influence of the Moorlands on Charlotte and Emily Brontë" by Butler Wood (B521)
"Ups and Downs of Celebrity" by W. L. Andrews (B35)
"Brontës through Foreign Eyes" [Originally "Through Foreign Eyes"] by Prince D. S. Mirsky (B351)
"Americans and the Brontës" by Helen H. Arnold (B37)
"Causes of Death in the Brontë Family" [Originally "Causes of Death of the Brontës"] by C. Mabel Edgerley (B160)
"Our Greatest Woman" by W. L. Andrews (B34)
"The Burial Place of the Brontës" by J. C. Hirst (B244)

A2 "Emily Brontë: 1818-1848" *Wuthering Heights* (Boston: Houghton Mifflin 1965) xv–xviii
A brief sketch of EB's life attributing the intensity of her emotions to a tubercular constitution.

A3 "*Wuthering Heights*, Emily Brontë" *Wuthering Heights* (New York: Airmont Books 1963) [1–4]
A short discussion of the novel and EB's life; the two Catherines give *WH* unity.

*   *   *

A4 ABERNETHY, Peter L., Christian J. W. Kloesel, and Jeffrey R. Smitten *English Novel Explication Supplement I* (Hamden, Conn: Shoe String Press 1976) 24–25
Created to supplement and update *English Novel Explication: Criticisms to 1972* (A277), itself a supplement to *The English Novel 1578–1956: A Checklist of Twentieth–Century Criticisms* (A20), this bibliography covers major books and articles written from 1972 through 1974 on the English novel from 1578 through 1956. See A20, A277.

*A5 AKIHO, Shinichi and Takashi Fujita *A Concordance to the Complete Poems of Emily Jane Brontë* (Tokyo: Shohakusha Pub Co Ltd 1976) 229 p

A6 ALLEN, Walter "The Early Victorians" *The English Novel* (New York: E. P. Dutton 1955) 153–252 [223–29]

WH is an "intensely individual apprehension of the nature of man and life," and Heathcliff is "a primordial figure of energy" rather than a monster. The double narrative is especially effective because it forces a role on the reader. EB anticipates Conrad.

A7 ALLOTT, Kenneth "Introduction" in Kenneth and Miriam Allott, eds *Victorian Prose 1830–1880* (Harmondsworth, Middlesex [England]: Penguin Books Ltd 1956) xvii–xliii and *passim*
The last sentence in *WH* is characterized by the "true voice of feeling."

*A8 ALLOTT, Miriam "The Brontës" in A. E. Dyson, ed *The English Novel: Select Bibliographical Guides* (London: Oxford University Press 1969) 218–45
A selective survey of studies on the novel, including some modern studies on EB not in Allott's 1970 *Casebook*. [From mention in *Emily Brontë: 'Wuthering Heights': A Casebook*, A10.]

A9 ———, ed *The Brontës: The Critical Heritage* (London and Boston: Routledge and K. Paul 1974) *passim*
"It is hoped that the present collection will set the record straight for the Brontës' early reviewers and also represent the movement of opinion among their successors in the later years of the nineteenth century." A finely detailed review of the literary criticism of the Brontës through 1900. The book is divided into sections of nineteenth–century reviews of the various Brontë novels and poems. The reviews are reprinted and discussed separately, with information about the reviewer supplied in most instances. Section I, "The Critical Reputation of the 'Brothers Bell,' 1846–1853," includes reviews of the poems and of the 1847 edition of *WH*. Section II, "The Brontës in the 1850's," includes Dobell's review on 'Currer Bell' and *WH* in 1850. Section III, "Judgments and Opinions, 1858–1899," includes Swinburne and A. Mary F. Robinson on EB and *WH*. The selected bibliography, p 461–63, is annotated.

A10 ——— "Introduction" and ed *Emily Brontë: 'Wuthering Heights': A Casebook* (London: Macmillan 1970) 11–36
Allott's introduction provides a comprehensive survey of the entire body of criticism on *WH*. She discusses the historical context of the criticism and the influences brought to bear as opinion and the criticism developed. Parts 1 and 2 are concerned with criticism in the 1800s. Part 3 is titled "Some Opinions and Criticism 1873–1949," and Part 4 consists of "Recent Studies." Each section is accompanied by useful notes. The essays and other material are partially reprinted except for the studies since 1949. See individual entries for annotation in most cases.
    "Introduction" by Mrs Humphry Ward (A385)
    "Charlotte and Emily Brontë" by Alice Meynell (A250)
    "The Brontës Today" by Lascelles Abercrombie (B23)
    "*Jane Eyre* and *Wuthering Heights*" by Virginia Woolf (A419)
    The Structure of Wuthering Heights by C. P. Sanger (A324)
    "Prophecy" by E. M. Forster (A110)
    "Introduction" by H. W. Garrod (A116)
    Fiction and the Reading Public by Q. D. Leavis (A215)
    Early Victorian Novelists by David Cecil (A51)
    The Authorship of Wuthering Heights by Irene Cooper Willis (A402)
    "Fiction and the Matrix of Analogy" by Mark Schorer (B439)
    ("Recent Studies" which follow are reprinted in their entirety except for the book excerpts.)

"*Wuthering Heights* after a Hundred Years" by Derek Traversi (B487)

"Dark 'Otherness' in *Wuthering Heights*" (Originally "On *Wuthering Heights*") by Dorothy Van Ghent (A374)

"The Rejection of Heathcliff?" by Miriam Allott (B30)

The Genesis of Wuthering Heights by Mary Visick (A377)

"Literary Influences on *Wuthering Heights*" from *Emily Brontë: Expérience Spirituelle et Création Poétique* by Jacques Blondel (C13)

> Allott notes in her Introduction, "It is to be hoped that [Jacques Blondel's] book—which is the most substantial study of Emily Brontë to have appeared—will eventually find a worthy English translator...." Allott translates this chapter here: Blondel examines influences on WH, which include Sir Walter Scott, the Gothic novel, Byron, Hoffmann's *Das Majorat*, tales in *Blackwood's Magazine*, and Shakespeare. See also A262, A283.

"Charlotte Brontë as a Critic of *Wuthering Heights*" by Philip Drew (B152)

There is a select bibliography on p 262–65.

A11 ——— *Novelists on the Novel* (New York: Columbia University Press 1959) 169–70 and *passim*

The place of WH in the evolution of the novel is discussed, and EB's work is briefly compared to that of Stendhal.

A12 ALTICK, Richard D. *The Scholar Adventurers* (New York: Macmillan 1950) 316–17

In a chapter on the way that scholars have added to literary works, there is a brief discussion of the manuscript history of EB's poems and their Gondalan context.

A13 ANDERSON, Quentin "Introduction" *Wuthering Heights* (New York: Collier Books 1962) v–viii

"*Wuthering Heights* exhibits the realities of human life more clearly than any other English novel of the century." It has a moral order and a conventional order.

APPLEBEE, Roger K. *see* A183.

APTER, T. E. *see* A344g.

ASTIN, Marjorie *see* A242.

A14 AUERBACH, Nina "This Changeful Life: Emily Brontë's Anti–Romance" in Sandra M. Gilbert and Susan Gubar, eds *Shakespeare's Sisters: Feminist Essays on Women Poets* (Bloomington: Indiana University Press 1979) 49–64

The Gondal saga is the subject of this essay. An investigation of A.G.A., EB's "child" in her poetry, finds that A.G.A. "celebrates mutability as wholeheartedly as Blake's and Wordsworth's children struggled against it...." Change is the essence of life for A.G.A. "In releasing her queen from the dungeon of memory and permanence, [EB] allows her to live...as a consciousness of motion and a pledge to 'changeful dreams' ...."

BAIRD, Donald *see* A20.

A15 BAKER, Ernest A. "The Brontës—Emily and Anne" *The History of the English Novel* VIII (New York: Barnes and Noble 1936) 64–77

EB's personality is revealed through her poetry and *WH*. A full discussion of *WH* includes some possible sources for the novel such as Methodist magazines and the religious controversy in and around Haworth at the time the Brontës lived there, and the possibility that Branwell Brontë wrote part of it. The author says of the structure: "If it was clumsy to take the last events first, it was assuredly the clumsiness of genius." Reprinted: A220.

A16 BALD, Marjory A. "The Brontës" *Women Writers of the Nineteenth Century* (New York: Macmillan 1923) 28–99 [77–99]
The part of this discussion concerning EB centers on the effects her poems and *WH* have on readers, with special attention to objectors to the novel and their reasons for objecting.

A17 BARCLAY, Janet M. *Emily Brontë Criticism 1900–1968: An Annotated Check List* (New York: The New York Public Library & Readex Books 1974) 76 p
A bibliography of the criticism on EB appearing from 1900 through 1968 including that of *WH* and the poetry, general criticism, biography, and bibliography. Each work is annotated from an examination of the original text, with annotations reflecting the content of the work. The material is divided into three sections: "Books and Parts of Books," "Articles," and "Books and Articles in Foreign Languages," with the works listed alphabetically by author's name. Reprintings are cross–referenced throughout the *Check List*.

A18 BASCH, Françoise "The Countervailing Criticism" *Relative Creatures: Victorian Women in Society and the Novel 1837–67* trans Anthony Rudolf (New York: Schocken Books 1974) 89–93; see also *passim*
The *WH* heroines Cathy and Isabella pass between two antagonistic worlds symbolized in the two houses: from Nature to Culture for Cathy, and from Culture to Nature for Isabella, both journeys ending with death. [The chapter titled "Revolt and Duty in the Brontës" in this book is concerned with the role of governess for Charlotte and Anne Brontë.]

A18A BATAILLE, Georges "Emily Brontë" *Literature and Evil* trans Alastair Hamilton (London: Calder and Boyars 1973) 3–17
This essay investigates the philosophy of evil as it appears in *WH*. EB "had an anguished knowledge of passion. She had the sort of knowledge which links love not only with charity, but also with violence and death—because death seems to be the truth of love, just as love is the truth of death. . . ." The fundamental theme of *WH* is childhood, when the love of Catherine and Heathcliff originated. The subheadings in the essay reflect Bataille's concerns: "Eroticism is the approval of life up until death," "Childhood, reason, and evil," "Emily Brontë and transgression," "Literature, liberty and the mystical experience," and "The significance of evil." Reprinted A283.

A19 BAUGH, Albert C. "The Brontës" *A Literary History of England* (New York: Appleton–Century–Crofts Inc 1948) 1370–78 [1375–78]
A short, perceptive account of EB—biography, poetry, and *WH*. Her work is more like Blake's than Wordsworth's.

A20 BELL, Inglis F. and Donald Baird *The English Novel 1578–1956: A Checklist of Twentieth–Century Criticisms* (Denver: Alan Swallow 1958) 9–11
Conceived as a companion work to George Arms' and Joseph M. Kuntz's *Poetry Explication* (1950), this checklist of criticism of the novel lists the major books and articles written about *WH* since 1900 to date. For supplements after 1957, see A4 and A277.

A21 BELL, MacKenzie "Emily Brontë" *Representative Novelists of the Nineteenth Century* I (London: MacVeagh 1927) 285–91
Most of this chapter is an excerpt from *WH*; a brief biographical sketch of EB and a short summary of *WH* is added.

A22 BENSON, Arthur C. "Introduction" *Bronte Poems* (New York: G. P. Putnam's Sons 1915) iii–xx
EB's poetry is evaluated on p x–xvii. Her genius is "instantly apparent" and her poetry is clearly superior to that of the other Brontës. The interest the Brontë children had in writing poetry is attributed to Mr Brontë's writing poetry and to the books the young Brontës probably read.

A23 BENSON, E. F. "The Brontës" in Derek Verschoyle, ed *The English Novelists* (New York: Harcourt, Brace 1936) *passim*
The traditional Brontë story with little about EB and *WH*.

A24 —— *Charlotte Brontë* (London: Longmans, Green 1932) 168–79
The evidence presented here that Branwell Brontë wrote the first two chapters of *WH* is based mainly on the style of writing; the style in these two chapters is compared with that at the end of the book. Both the beginning and the end of *WH* consist of Lockwood's narrative, and this fact is considered pertinent to Branwell's probable authorship. A section of this book is reprinted in A220.

A25 BENTLEY, Phyllis *The Brontë Sisters* (London: Longmans, Green 1950)
This short book touches on the qualities of the Brontë works which attract a wide range of readers, and is a brief factual account of the Brontë sisters' lives. It also contains a 4–page bibliography. (Reissued in 1967 with additions to the bibliography.)

A26 —— *The Brontës* (London: Home and Van Thal 1947) 83–102
The Brontës are investigated as to the material and equipment available to them (i.e., heredity, environment, inter–family influence, and education) enabling them to become novelists and poets. There is a perceptive treatment of EB's poetry and a short treatment of *WH* from the point of view that "the story of Heathcliff. . .is a cuckoo's story." See B58.

A27 —— *The Brontës and Their World* (New York: Viking Press 1969) *passim*
The Brontë story is retold, illustrated with numerous photographs, sketches, and reproductions of title pages of the Brontë novels. EB's birthday note dated 30 July 1845 is reproduced; there are notes on the illustrations, and a Brontë family chronology.

A28 —— *The English Regional Novel* (London: Allen and Unwin 1941)
On p 17 Dr Bentley notes that her selection of *Shirley* by Charlotte Brontë rather than *WH* by EB as the "first great English regional novel" may cause some surprise, but points out that *WH* is not regional, except in setting.

*A29 —— "Introduction" *The Heather Edition of the Works of the Brontë Sisters* (London: Wingate 1949)
"Highly interesting for its anticipations and psychological importance." [From an abstract in *The Year's Work in English Studies*.]

A30 ——— "Yorkshire and the Novelist" in Richard Church, ed *Essays by Divers Hands, Being the Transactions of the Royal Society of Literature* n s 33 (London: Oxford University Press 1965) 145–57 [*WH passim*]
The diversity of the Yorkshire landscape and the characteristics of its inhabitants give impressive features to novels by Yorkshire authors which are set in Yorkshire.

*A31 ——— and John Ogden *Haworth of the Brontës* (Lavenham, Suffolk [England]: Terence Dalton Ltd 1977)

A31A BENVENUTO, Richard *Emily Brontë* (Boston: Twayne Publishers 1982) 148 p
EB's life and literary work are treated separately in this modern and thorough study of both. As his purpose is to present her life and all her work fully and fairly, Benvenuto includes chapters on Gondal, the poetry, the essays in French, EB's biography, and *WH*. In the French essays, EB comes "as close as she ever does to speaking in her own voice and to revealing the person behind the artist." There are full, clear notes and an 8–page annotated bibliography.

A32 BERSANI, Leo "Desire and Metamorphosis" *A Future for Astyanax: Character and Desire in Literature* (Boston: Little, Brown 1976) 189–229 [197–223]
In this enlightening study of "the correlations between different ways of conceiving desire and different ways of conceiving character in literature," *WH* and other literary works explore "metamorphoses of the self, as well as the possibility of an almost unthinkable and yet compelling identity between the self and the other." Bersani investigates *WH* and Lautreamont's *Les Chants de Maldoror:* "Both works have a kind of ontological slipperiness; being is always somewhere else, and human utterance tends to make personality problematic rather than to express it. . . ."

A33 BLACK, Michael "*Wuthering Heights:* Romantic Self–commitment" *The Literature of Fidelity* (London: Chatto and Windus 1975) 125–51
In this investigation of the love themes and interaction of the characters in *WH*, Heathcliff is seen as "reflecting a reality onto Dickens" when compared to *David Copperfield*, as a "humanly conceivable evolution." Catherine's psyche is compared to that of Emma Bovary; after the scene in which an angry Catherine shakes Hareton, then strikes Edgar Linton, she says revealingly, "I did nothing deliberately." This powerful truth limns her nature: direct, uninhibited, powerful and dangerous, yet bound up with her vitality and attraction. *WH* is about "life seen as. . .a fight to the death between wills. Racine saw the same vision, and reacted with dread and horror. Emily Brontë sees it as perfectly natural, inevitable and potentially heroic. . . ."

A34 BLACKBURN, Ruth H. *The Brontë Sisters: Selected Source Materials for College Research Papers* (Boston: D. C. Heath 1964)
This is a bibliography of source materials for study of the Brontës. Section III, "Papers and Poems of Emily Jane Brontë and Anne Brontë," contains the diary papers and some of EB's poems. Section IV, "Contemporary Reviews of the Brontë Novels," in addition to the reviews of *WH*, contains "Two Nineteenth Century Estimates of Emily Brontë," those of Algernon Charles Swinburne and Angus M. Mackay.

A34A BLONDEL, Jacques "Emily Brontë and Emily Dickinson, A Study in Contrasts" in Jacques Blondel and Jean–Pierre Petit, eds *Études Brontëenes* (Paris: Editions Ophrys 1970) 19–29

EB's "poetic creation appears closer to the Coleridgean conception of 'the shaping power' of the imagination; Emily Dickinson opens vistas towards Imagism and not to poetry as 'a criticism of life.' " Their poetry is compared and contrasted; aspects of their lives and work compared are religious backgrounds, types of poetic creation, and abstractions.

———— *see* A10, A262, A283.

*A35 BLOOR, R. H. U. "The Brontë Sisters" *The English Novel from Chaucer to Galsworthy* (London: Ivor Nicholson and Watson Ltd 1935) 226–31

A36 BLUNDEN, Edmund "Foreword" in Mary Visick *The Genesis of* Wuthering Heights [3rd Edition] (England and Conn: Ian Hodgkins & Co Ltd and Meckler Books 1980) 3 p
A. Mary F. Robinson, writing in 1883, was attempting to discover in the available EB poems more about the author of *WH*. She did not have, as we do now, the Gondal poems. Blunden cites the work of Fannie Ratchford and Rebecca West in the area of the Gondal poems–*WH* relationship and adds that there is yet room for Visick's interpretation (A377) which he calls "the apotheosis of the Gondal people into the immortals of *Wuthering Heights*."
A36a "Author's Note to the 1980 Edition" by Mary Visick, 5 p
Mrs Visick briefly reviews and comments on some of the EB criticism which has appeared since the initial publication of *The Genesis of* Wuthering Heights, including that of Ewbank (A105) and Winnifrith (A410). See A377.

A37 BOWEN, Elizabeth *English Novelists* (London: Collins 1946) 33–36
WH, a book of "fire and ice," bearing no feminine stamp, is compared with *Jane Eyre* which "gains force by being woman from beginning to end."

A38 BRADBY, Godfrey Fox "Emily Brontë" and "Brontë Legends" *The Brontës and Other Essays* (London: Oxford University Press 1932) 23–36, 37–50
The first essay is a reprinting of Item B66. In the second essay, the veracity of some of the legends related by A. Mary F. Robinson in her biography of EB (1883) is questioned.

A39 BRAITHWAITE, William S. *The Bewitched Parsonage* (New York: Coward–McCann 1950) *passim*
This is a logical, objective, and intelligent account of the Brontë story, taking into account previous biographer's opinions.

A40 BRIDGES, Robert "The Poems of Emily Brontë" *Collected Essays* 9 (London: Oxford University Press 1932) 259–68
Referring to Clement Shorter's *Complete Works of Emily Brontë*, the author discusses the editions of EB's poetry to date. This is a fresh and perceptive evaluation of EB's poetry, but slightly distracting because it is written in a phonetic alphabet. See B141. Partially reprinted: A283.

A41 BROWN, Helen and Joan Mott "Introduction" *Gondal Poems by Emily Jane Brontë* (Oxford: Basil Blackwell 1938) 5–8
EB's notebook which she herself entitled "Gondal Poems" was presented to the British Museum in 1933. This introduction to them discusses their history and significance. The value of the notebook itself lies in new poems and variants, new information on the Gondal story,

new dates, and clues to EB's earlier poems. This edition of the poems was the first published from the manuscript in the British Museum.

A42 BURNS, Wayne "In Death They Were Not Divided: The Moral Magnificence of Unmoral Passion in *Wuthering Heights*" in Melvin Goldstein, ed *Metapsychological Literary Criticism—Theory and Practice: Essays in Honor of Leonard Falk Manheim. Hartford Studies in Literature* V (Hartford, Conn: University of Hartford 1973) 135–59
The central argument is that *WH* is not Panzaic, but prophetic in the sense suggested by E. M. Forster in *Aspects of the Novel. WH* does not achieve its end "by means of the Panzaic Principle, by using the real to undercut the ideal; rather what it does is to carry a particular ideal—the ideal of immaculate love—to such uncompromising extremes that it not only becomes magnificent in itself but also serves to undercut the pretensions of nearly all our other ideals." See B84, B167.

A43 BURTON, Richard *Masters of the English Novel: A Study of Principles and Personalities* (New York: Holt 1909)
WH is very briefly dealt with (p 259) as "strangely unrelated to the general course of the nineteenth century."

A44 BUTLER, Lord "The Prevalence of Indirect Biography" in Robert Speaight, ed *Essays by Divers Hands, Being the Transactions of the Royal Society of Literature of the United Kingdom* n s 37 (London: Oxford University Press 1972) 17–30
On autobiography: "The ideal autobiographer needs poetic subjectivity combined with ruthless objectivity." Referring to EB, Butler concludes that "high genius does not need to depict personal experience literally in order to create great literature. . . ."

*A45 BUTTERFIELD, Mary A. *The Heatons of Ponden Hall and the Legendary Link with Thrushcross Grange in Emily Brontë's* Wuthering Heights (Keighley [England]: Roderick and Brenda Taylor 1976) 23 p

*A46 BYERS, David *Emily Brontë's* Wuthering Heights (New York: Barrister Pub Co 1966) 139 p
Bar Notes literature study and examination guides series.

A47 CALDER, Jenni "The Perils of Independence" *Women and Marriage in Victorian Fiction* (London: Thames and Hudson 1976) 56–67; see also *passim*
Like Mrs Gaskell's *Sylvia's Lovers*, *WH* "cannot be assessed in terms of conventional expectations. It establishes its own values. . . ."

A47A CAUDWELL, Christopher, pseud [Christopher St. John Sprigg] *Romance and Realism: A Study in English Bourgeois Literature* (Princeton: Princeton University Press 1970) *passim*
The Brontës are seen as "characteristic of the final phase of bourgeois culture, in which woman revolts against her subjection. . .*Wuthering Heights* has . . . a kind of quintessence of masculinity as seen by woman. . . ." (Written in 1936, unpublished until 1970.)

A48 CANNON, John *The Road to Haworth: A Family Saga of the Brontës in Ireland* (New York: Viking Press 1981) *passim*

Patrick Brontë's father, Hugh Brunty, was a famous teller of tales. One of them was about the life of his adoptive father, Welsh Brunty, who was adopted into the family after being found as a child abandoned aboard a ship sailing from Liverpool. Presumably, EB heard this story from her father and it could have formed the basis for her creation of Heathcliff. A Brontë family tree 1776–1855 is included.

*A49 CARRINGTON, Norman T. *Notes on Chosen English Texts: Emily Brontë's* Wuthering Heights (London: James Brodie Ltd 1961) 76 p
"Notes on Chosen English Texts" series.

A50 CAZAMIAN, Louis "The Idealistic Reaction" *A History of English Literature, Modern Times* (London: J. M. Dent and Sons 1927) 345–68 [360–61]
This chapter contains a brief and concise comment which credits *WH* with realizing "the ideal of independence in thought, and freedom in spiritual life, which the emancipation of Romanticism had set forth."

A51 CECIL, David "Emily Brontë and *Wuthering Heights*" *Early Victorian Novelists: Essays in Revaluation* (London: Constable, 1934) 147–93
This is one of the best analyses of *WH*: the famous "storm and calm" interpretation. The theme of the novel is the destruction and re–establishment of cosmic harmony. "The conflict is not between right and wrong, but between like and unlike." The individuality of *WH* comes from intensity, solidity, and spontaneity. The basis of this essay is that cosmic harmony contains elements of both storm (Heathcliff, and Catherine's separation from him) and calm (the Lintons and the love between the second Catherine and Hareton Earnshaw). Reprinted: A52, A220, A283, A322, A379. Partially reprinted: A10. See B504.

A52 ——— "Emily Brontë and *Wuthering Heights*" *Victorian Novelists: Essays in Revaluation* (Chicago: University of Chicago Press 1958) 136–82
This is a reprinting of Item A51. The edition contains a new preface in which the author re–evaluates some of the Victorian novelists. He does not change his interpretation of *WH* and EB except to say that she is, instead of "the most poetical of all English novelists," "*among the most poetical...*" (italics are his).

A53 CHADWICK, Mrs Ellis H. *In the Footsteps of the Brontës* (London: Sir Isaac Pitman and Sons, Ltd 1914)
This is an encyclopedic study of the Brontës. Many details concerning their lives not mentioned or barely mentioned by other authors are included here. For example, the first five chapters give the ancestry and history of Rev Patrick Brontë, and Chapter XVII gives the history of M Heger. Of special interest to EB students are Chapters X and XXIV which deal with her career at Southowram and with *WH* respectively. Law Hill and the Southowram area are related to *WH*. The author gives careful evidence that EB stayed at Law Hill from 1836 to 1839 and discusses the poems she wrote while there. The authorship of *WH* is discussed at great length, and the conclusion is that EB is the only possible author. The idea that M Heger was the model for Heathcliff is lengthily supported by excerpts from Charlotte Brontë's novels and letters and EB's poems.

A54 CHAPMAN, Raymond "The Brontës" *The Victorian Debate, English Literature and Society, 1832–1901* (London: Weidenfeld and Nicolson 1968) 159–70; see also *passim*

The Brontës were not, as often depicted, isolated from the world; they were fully involved in it. EB created her own values, neither for nor against the social norms. "She is dealing with affections and enmities that spring from primitive existence, not from any institutional grouping. . . ."

A55 CHASE, Richard "The Brontës, or Myth Domesticated" in William Van O'Connor, ed *Forms of Modern Fiction* (Minneapolis: University of Minnesota Press 1948) 102–19
This is a reprinting of Item B96.

A56 CHESTERTON, Gilbert K. "Great Victorian Novelists" *The Victorian Age in Literature* (London: Williams and Norgate 1913) 90–155 [110–16]
Both Charlotte Brontë and EB had a false view of men, but Emily was "further narrowed by the broadness of her religious views."

*A57 CHILDE, Wilfred Rowland "The Brontës as Poets" in William L. Andrews, ed *The Enduring Brontës* (Shipley [England]: Outhwaite Bros 1951) 25–31

A58 CHRISTIAN, Mildred G. "The Brontës" in Lionel Stevenson, ed *Victorian Fiction: A Guide to Research* (Cambridge: Harvard University Press 1964) 214–44
This is an excellent and thorough discussion of the background and history of the Brontës and one of the best surveys of Brontë manuscripts, editions, and criticism. See A319.

A59 CHURCH, Richard *The Growth of the English Novel* (London: Methuen 1951) 179–82
This is a very short treatment in which WH and EB are yet enigmas, and EB's poems are as "stark" as Blake's.

A60 CHURCHILL, R. C. *English Literature of the Nineteenth Century* (London: University Tutorial Press Ltd 1951) 115–19
A brief biography of EB and short appreciation of WH.

A61 CLARKE, Graham " 'Bound in Moss and Cloth': Reading a Long Victorian Novel" in Ian Gregor, ed *Reading the Victorian Novel: Detail into Form* (New York: Harper and Row 1980) 54–71; see also *passim*
WH is used as one example of a long Victorian novel.

A62 CLARKE, Isabel C. *Haworth Parsonage: A Picture of the Brontë Family* (London: Hutchinson 1927) *passim*
The author states that this is an "attempt to present, in the form of biographical narrative, the tragic lives of the inmates of Haworth Parsonage." Some parts of the narrative are somewhat conjectural, but for the most part, it presents the traditional view of EB. Isabel Clarke was one of the first to suggest that EB was influenced toward mysticism by reading Ruysbroeck at Brussels.

CLAY, Henry *see* A422.

A63 CLUTTON–BROCK, A. "The Brontës" *Essays on Books* (London: Dutton 1920) 92–103

The author is primarily concerned with May Sinclair's *The Three Brontës* (see A341) with which he takes issue, with emphasis on Charlotte Brontë.

A64 COLLARD, Millicent *Wuthering Heights—The Revelation* (London: Regency Press 1960) 106 p

Subtitled "A Psychical Study of Emily Brontë," this is an imaginative, symbolical interpretation of *WH*. The characters all have counterparts in the Brontë family, and in its symbolic detail the novel is shown to be very closely related to the Bible.

A65 COLLINS, Norman "The Independent Brontës" *The Facts of Fiction* (London: Gollancz 1932) 174–88

In working with the Brontës, "Mrs. Gaskell is...a critical necessity" because their biography is so bound up with their books. *WH* is childish and the tale "leaps like a frog."

A66 COLUM, Mary M. "Genius to Squander" in H. S. Canby, ed *Designed for Reading* (New York: Macmillan 1934) 103–11

EB and Charlotte Brontë are considered together. EB especially has "intensity which is one of the Celtic contributions to literature."

A67 COMPTON–RICKETT, Arthur "The Brontës" *A History of English Literature* (London: T. C. & E. C. Jack Ltd 1918) 518–26

EB's sheer force of imagination in *WH* is greater, and her verse finer, than Charlotte Brontë's.

A68 COOKE, John D. and Lionel Stevenson "The Brontë Sisters: Charlotte (1816–1855), Emily (1818–1848), Anne (1820–1849)" *English Literature of the Victorian Period* (New York: Appleton–Century–Crofts Inc 1949) 266–73

The traditional Brontë story is told with brief evaluations of the Brontë novels. *WH* "has come to be recognized as a great poetic tragedy rather than what is conventionally regarded as a novel...."

*A69 CORR, Patricia *Emily Brontë*, Wuthering Heights (Gill and Macmillan 1972) 55 p

One of a study guide series.

A70 CRAIK, Wendy A. "The Brontës" in Arthur Pollard, ed *The Victorians* (London: Barrie and Jenkins 1970) 140–68 [159–66]

Heathcliff is clearly the topic of *WH*: "The known span and compass of Heathcliff's life at Wuthering Heights is the span and compass of the novel. When he is not there there is no story...." Furthermore, the novel is neither as violent not as cruel as it seems. "Much of the violence is of expression and interpretation, not action...."

A71 ———— *"Wuthering Heights" The Brontë Novels* (London: Methuen and Co 1968) 5–47

"Religious references (in contrast to principles) are frequent, because some theory of right and wrong and salvation is clearly being worked out," but EB is only using Christian references as a narrative method. What is required by EB of her characters in *WH* is "that they experience the full consequences of their actions." Dr Craik is primarily concerned with the characters in *WH*—their motivations, personalities, and effects on each other. Catherine's rejection of Heathcliff turns him from a passive person into a destructive force. Catherine and Heathcliff as characters are explicated in detail; they set themselves apart from the other characters and outside convention by contrast to brother and sister—Edgar and Isabella Linton, to husband and wife—Hindley and Frances Earnshaw; and they reject, separately, conventional Christian concepts. There is also a full discussion of the minor characters and EB's utilization of time in *WH*.

A72 CRANDALL, Norma *Emily Brontë: A Psychological Portrait* (Rindge, N H: R. R. Smith 1957) 160 p

Because EB had few friends and no proven lovers, "understanding the members of her family is not only the only certain method of portraying Emily, but is . . . essential in interpreting her writing." The author draws psychological conclusions such as: Patrick Brontë must have seemed "inhuman if not repellent" to EB, and when Aunt Branwell died EB's feelings were probably "tinged with scorn." There is a 4–page bibliography at the end of the book.

CRAUFORD, Emma *see* A79.

A73 CREHAN, T., ed Wuthering Heights: *With a Critical Commentary* (London: University of London Press 1962) ix–xlii

The force of *WH* lies "in the writing, in the presentation, and in the author's steady vision of her subject matter." In this well–detailed essay Crehan deals with the credibility of three elements in the novel: the misanthropy of Heathcliff, the love of Catherine and Heathcliff, and the characteristics of these two. EB uses the children, Catherine and Heathcliff, to make the adults more credible, and in her poetry we find anticipations of both of them. Crehan also discusses fully the chronology and law in *WH*.

A73A CRUMP, Rebecca W. *Charlotte and Emily Brontë, 1846–1915: A Reference Guide* (Boston: G. K. Hall & Co 1982) 194 p

This annotated bibliography of writings about Charlotte and EB begins in 1846 with the earliest reviews of the Brontës' work and extends to the 1916 centennial studies on Charlotte Brontë. Entries include reminiscences, memorials, sketches, essays, articles, book–length studies, chapters of books, reviews of the Brontës' work, introductions to editions, and reviews of works about the Brontës in which the reviewer adds comments concerning them. The entries are arranged chronologically in order to reflect the changing attitudes toward the Brontës and their work, and to reveal the main strands of criticism that developed in the nineteenth century. The order within each year is alphabetical by author. The index lists names of authors and titles of books; entries are also indexed by genre.

A74 CUNLIFFE, J. W. "Charlotte and Emily Brontë" *Leaders of the Victorian Revolution* (New York: Appleton–Century 1934) 102–13

The author claims that, of the two sisters, Charlotte is the superior novelist; *WH* is barely mentioned.

A75 ——— et al "Charlotte and Emily Brontë," in J. W. Cunliffe et al, eds *The Columbia University Course in Literature* (New York: Columbia University Press 1928) 218–41

In this critical essay the stress is on Charlotte Brontë. As for *WH*, "it is a ghastly and gruesome creation. Not one bright ray redeems it. It deals with the most evil characters and the most evil phases of human experience."

A76 CUNNINGHAM, Valentine "The Brontës" *Everywhere Spoken Against: Dissent in the Victorian Novel* (Oxford: Clarendon Press 1975) 113–26
This book is an examination of "a set of fictional accounts...of religious Nonconformity, within real historical contexts...." Methodism was demonstrably a strong influence upon the Brontës' works, and EB had heard Tabby's stories, her father's tales, and probably stories Branwell brought home from Luddenden–Foot railway station. Some of these may have been the basis for parts of *WH*, e.g., "Grimshaw's passion for his wife...his insistence on being buried 'in the same grave with my deceased wife' at Luddenden, make him curiously like Heathcliff...."

A77 DAICHES, David "Introduction" *Wuthering Heights* (Middlesex: Penguin 1965) 7–29
A thorough review and discussion of differing modern interpretations of *WH*, and a listing of some explicit points that anyone discussing *WH* should consider. The introduction is accompanied by notes and a selected bibliography. Dr Daiches' edition of *WH* is based on the 1847 edition of the novel, although it does incorporate some corrections from the Shakespeare Head Edition (1931), in an effort to retain EB's punctuation and paragraphing throughout. "A Note on the Text" is appended. Reprinted: A379.

A78 ——— "The Victorian Novel" *A Critical History of English Literature Vol. II* (New York: Ronald Press 1960) 1064–66
WH "represents the one impressive prose example in English of induced emotion creating its own 'objective correlative' by the sheer force and conviction of its expression."

A79 DANIEL–ROPS, Henry, pseud [Jules Charles Henri Petiot] "Emily Brontë, Poetry and Solitude" *Where Angels Pass* trans Emma Crauford (London: Cassell and Co Ltd 1950) 70–89
There is always a close relationship between author and work, and in the case of EB, the death and tragedy in her life as well as the moorland was the strong influence which produced *WH*. Her poems support the dramatic tone found in *WH*.

A80 DAVENPORT, Basil "Emily Brontë" *Wuthering Heights* (New York: Dodd, Mead 1942) 3–4
In this brief sketch of EB's life it is mentioned that Heathcliff may have been modeled on M Heger. *WH* may have been narrated by the heroine's nurse because Charlotte Brontë was ill when she returned from Brussels, and EB was her nurse.

A81 DAWSON, William J. "The Brontiës" *The Makers of English Fiction* (New York: Revell 1905) 124–44
The heredity and environment of EB and Charlotte Brontë are considered. The task of criticism is made difficult by (1) the influence of their personal lives on their work, and (2) the progress made by the art of fiction since they wrote. "The reading world" does not yet understand *WH*, but it is a classic. Reprinted: A85.

A82 DAY–LEWIS, C[ecil] "Emily Brontë and Freedom" *Notable Images of Virtue* (Toronto: Ryerson Press 1954) 1–25

EB's work illuminates the idea of freedom, and is "a classic example of the way poetry moves from the particular to the universal." Reprinted: A322.

A83 DEACON, Lois *The Poetic Fervour of Emily Brontë and Thomas Hardy* (St Peter Port, Guernsey: Toucan Press 1971)

A brief, popular comparison of the poetry of EB and Thomas Hardy, in a sentimental vein, e.g., "...the music of the spheres sounded eternally for Emily and Thomas...."

A84 DELAFIELD, E. M., pseud [Edmée Elizabeth Monica De La Pasture] ed and intro *The Brontës: Their Lives Recorded by Their Contemporaries* (London: Leonard and Virginia Woolf at the Hogarth Press 1935) *passim*

Excerpts from contemporary nineteenth–century books, publications, collections of letters, and essays are placed in chronological order to reveal the lives of the Brontës. The section on EB is made up entirely of excerpts from Mrs Gaskell's *Life of Charlotte Brontë* (1857) and two of Clement Shorter's works: *The Brontës: Life and Letters* (A335) and *Charlotte Brontë and Her Circle* (1896). In the editor's preface, *WH* is criticized for lack of construction and a confusing double narrative.

A85 DELLO BUONO, Carmen Joseph, ed *Rare Early Essays on the Brontës* (Darby, Pa: Norwood Editions 1980)

Of the ten essays, four pertain to EB. See individual entries for annotation.
"The Brontës" by William J. Dawson (A81)
"Charlotte and Emily Brontë by E. M. Wilmot–Buxton (A406)
"Reactions in Haworth Parsonage" by G. Elsie Harrison (A152)
"The Brontës in Ulster" by W. A. Osborne (A275)

A86 DIMNET, Ernest *The Brontë Sisters* trans L. M. Sill (London: Cape 1927)

This is a detailed, sympathetic study of the lives of the three sisters. Chapter VIII is an account and discussion of the stay in Brussels; Chapter XIV contains a perceptive investigation of the nature of *WH*—as a novel and as a work of art.

A87 DINGLE, Herbert *The Mind of Emily Brontë* (London: Martin Brian & O'Keefe 1974) 128 p

"The purpose of this book is to see what can be determined, from [EB's] writings alone, concerning the type of mind necessary to produce" the judgments which have been made about EB and her work. All external events of her life are "largely irrelevant." If one had to choose one word to express the character of her mind, it would be "positive." In the poems, her single expression of a thing is usually intense, but in keeping with her positiveness, she does not supplement the intensity by extension or any repetition. Moreover, EB does not use metaphor or simile in the way other poets do, nor abstraction and generalization. EB is preeminently interested in individual persons: abstractions, to become real, have to be personified. Drawing from these cornerstones, Dingle proposes that *WH* is far from being a novel of the moors; EB was writing for publication when she created *WH* and was wise enough to write of an environment she knew. Also, since "she has told us nothing of Heathcliff's parentage, we are therefore free to suppose that he is a son of Earnshaw, and therefore Catherine's half–brother," which gives greater plausibility to the events. Dingle's essay on EB's poetry (B135) is added as an appendix.

DIXON, Canon W. T. *see* A223.

*A88 DOBRÉE, Bonamy "Introduction" *Wuthering Heights* (New York: Collins Classics Edition 1953)
In this thorough examination of the flaws and excellences of Nelly Dean's role of narrator, her function is seen as not merely mechanical but also emotional because she is a part of the emotional texture of *WH*. Reprinted: A104.

A89 DOBRÉE, Valentine "Introduction" *Wuthering Heights* (New York and London: Knopf 1927) xiii–xxxv
WH is related to EB's poetry, and the grand scale of *WH* is attributed to her "preoccupation with metaphysical problems." EB "embraces her characters in a larger truth."

DONALDSON, Betty *see* A89A.

A89A DONALDSON, Norman and Betty Donaldson "The Brontës" *How Did They Die?* (New York: St Martin's Press 1980) 45–46
A short account of the deaths of each of the Brontës, according to fact mixed with traditional folklore.

A90 DONOGHUE, Denis "Emily Brontë: On the Latitude of Interpretation" in Morton W. Bloomfield, ed *The Interpretation of Narrative: Theory and Practice. Harvard English Studies I.* (Cambridge: Harvard University Press 1970) 105–33
Donoghue looks at EB's work as a whole, a network of relationships—thereby studying her poems in detail—before he is ready to "settle upon her fiction." *WH* is of a mixed genre, the novel under stress of romance. Catherine and Heathcliff are of merged identities and thus leagued against all the other characters "by living in terms of nature...consanguinity...clearly destructive of any code or pattern of society...the aura of incest which surrounds their relationship is a mark of this destructive power. Society cannot bear such a relationship; so it must live in the cellar, until it transcends society in death...." Reprinted: A283.

——— *see* A136.

A91 DOOLEY, Lucile "Psychoanalysis of the Character and Genius of Emily Brontë" in H. M. Ruitenbeek, ed *The Literary Imagination* (Chicago: Quadrangle Books 1965) 43–79
This is a reprinting of Item B147.

A92 DRABBLE, Margaret "Introduction" in Philip Henderson, ed Wuthering Heights *with Selected Poems* (New York: Dutton 1978) v–xxii
Although the poems may reveal EB as a mystic, they do not reveal her as a novelist. Various critical approaches to *WH* are discussed at length. The volume includes sixty–four poems with an index of first lines.

A93 ——— *A Writer's Britain: Landscape in Literature* (New York: Knopf 1979) *passim*
This account of English literature, history, and criticism, as seen in the context of literary landmarks in England, includes the traditional Brontë story told with some psychological explanations.

A94 DREW, Elizabeth A. "Emily Brontë: *Wuthering Heights*" *The Novel: A Modern Guide to Fifteen English Masterpieces* (New York: Norton 1963) 173–90

This essay contains a brief review of modern criticism, which has rated EB's genius far above that of Charlotte Brontë. *WH*, however, remains mysterious; EB's own voice interprets nothing. Heathcliff loses the sympathy of the reader because of his inhuman cruelty. The fascination of *WH* is defined in Virginia Woolf's "unfinished sentence" evaluation (see A419).

A95 DRINKWATER, John "The Brontës as Poets" *Prose Papers* (London: Mathews 1917) 118–30 [121–27]
The author questions the fairness of EB's genius as a poet having to carry with it the "dead weight" of Charlotte's, Anne's, and Branwell's poetry. He traces the development of EB as a poet, and he analyzes her poetry in order to separate the wheat from the chaff.

A96 DRY, Florence Swinton *The Sources of* Wuthering Heights (Cambridge: Heffer 1937) 48 p
This short book is an effort to delineate the sources of *WH*. The author points out the parallels between *WH* and Scott's *The Black Dwarf*; there are similarities of names, characters, revenge theme, and plot. There are also minor similarities to other Scott novels and to Shakespearean plays.

A97 DU MAURIER, Daphne "The Brontë Heritage" in *Vanishing Cornwall* (London: Victor Gollancz Ltd 1967) 156–65
The Cornish individuality of Maria Brontë, the mother of the Brontës, is discussed and Penzance, her girlhood home, is described.

A98 —— *The Infernal World of Branwell Brontë* (New York: Doubleday and Co 1961) *passim*
The author surmises that the germ of the idea for *WH* could have come from Branwell Brontë. She points out the Brontës' childhood habit of collaboration, but adds that the full credit for *WH* belongs to EB.

*A99 —— "Introduction" *Wuthering Heights* (New York. Coward–McCann 1955)

A100 DURRELL, Lawrence "Lawrence Durrell" in E. W. Tedlock, ed *Dylan Thomas: The Legend and the Poet* (London: Heinemann 1960) 34–40 [38–39]
The author mentions in a short paragraph that EB's physical characteristics and her handwriting resemble those of Dylan Thomas. Reprinted: B156.

A101 EAGLETON, Terry *Myths of Power: A Marxist Study of the Brontës* (London: Macmillan 1975) 97–121
"I am concerned in this study to identify in the Brontës' fiction a recurrent 'categorical structure' of roles, values and relations...distinctly ideological...." The novels of Charlotte, Emily, and Anne are studied in terms of ideology, world–view, and myth, among other things.

A102 EDGAR, Pelham "The Brontës" *The Art of the Novel* (New York: Macmillan 1933) 136–45
This is a reprinting of Item B158.

A103 ELTON, Oliver "Emily Brontë" *The English Muse* (London: Bell and Sons 1933) 365–66
This is a very brief analysis of EB's poetry.

A104 EVERITT, Alastair "Preface" and ed Wuthering Heights: *An Anthology of Criticism* (London: Frank Cass 1967) vii–viii
Criticism of *WH* is marked by dissent about the essential meaning of the novel. Everitt notes in his preface that the various essays reprinted here reflect the complexity of *WH*, but they will not provide a solution to it. The collection includes:
"The Origin of *Wuthering Heights*" by A. Mary F. Robinson (1883)
"The Growth of *Wuthering Heights*" by Leicester Bradner (B67)
"*Wuthering Heights* and the Critics" by Melvin R. Watson (B504)
"Thoughts on *Wuthering Heights*" [Originally "*Wuthering Heights*"] by F. H. Langman (B290)
"Nelly Dean and the Power of *Wuthering Heights*" by John K. Mathison (B332)
"The Narrator in *Wuthering Heights*" [Originally "Introduction"] by Bonamy Dobrée (A88)
"Charlotte Brontë as a Critic of *Wuthering Heights*" by Philip Drew (B152)
"Infanticide and Sadism in *Wuthering Heights*" by Wade Thompson (B476)
"The Implacable, Belligerent People of *Wuthering Heights*" [Originally "Books in General"] by V. S. Pritchett (B398)
"On *Wuthering Heights*" by Dorothy Van Ghent (A374)
"The Style of *Wuthering Heights*" [From her book, *The Authorship of* Wuthering Heights] by Irene Cooper Willis (A402)
"The Structure of *Wuthering Heights*" by C. P. Sanger (A324)

A105 EWBANK, Inga–Stina "Emily Brontë: The Woman Writer as Poet" *Their Proper Sphere: A Study of the Brontë Sisters as Early–Victorian Female Novelists* (Cambridge: Harvard University Press 1966) 86–155
This very thorough treatment, which is of unusual depth, evaluates EB as "a Maker as well as a Seer." In *WH* her vision is a moral one. Miss Ewbank disagrees with David Cecil's contention (see A51) that *WH* exemplifies EB's philosophy of nature, made up of calm and storm; EB is primarily investigating the human condition, and the characters in the novel are moral beings showing the exploration of that condition. EB's sex does not matter because she is, above all, a poet. There is also a thorough review of nineteenth– and twentieth–century criticism and a bibliography. Partially reprinted: A283.

———— *see* A238a, A238g, A238h

A106 EWBANK, Jane M. *The Life and Works of William Carus Wilson, 1791–1859* (Kendal [England]: T. Wilson & Son 1960)
This is an attempt to reveal the true personality of the Reverend William Carus Wilson, founder of the Clergy Daughters' School which EB attended at age six. An authentic copy of the prospectus (the proposed objectives of the school) is reproduced on p 27–30.

A107 FADIMAN, Clifton "Afterword" *Wuthering Heights* (New York: Macmillan 1963) 347–48
This is a brief and popular description of *WH* in which the author generalizes that the novel is "a nightmare that makes perfect sense."

*A108 FELTHAM, Irene M. Wuthering Heights; *with Reader's Guide* (Amsco School Publications 1970)

*A109 FLAHIFF, Frederick T. "Introduction" and ed, *Wuthering Heights* (New
York: Macmillan 1968)

A109A FLEISHMAN, Avrom "*Wuthering Heights*: The Love of a Sylph and a Gnome"
Fiction and the Ways of Knowing: Essays on British Novels (Austin: University of
Texas 1978) 37–51
"Emily Brontë supplies no system of cosmic spheres . . . comparable to those of the alchemical
and astrological traditions . . . but she does adumbrate concepts allied to these. . . ." Taking into
account all the commentaries written on *WH*, there should be "room for a statement on the
alchemical processes engaged in the dramatic action." There is "spiritual alchemy" or "re-
transformation" in the mystic marriage of Heathcliff—of the earth, heath, and rocks, and
Catherine—of the air, breath, and wind. Fleishman supports his reading admirably with
references to the French essays and, to a lesser degree, EB's poems.

A110 FORSTER, E. M. "Prophecy" *Aspects of the Novel* (New York: Harcourt Brace
1927) 181–212 [209–11]
After carefully constructing her *WH* on a time chart and genealogical table, EB introduced
"muddle, chaos, tempest" because she was a prophetess, and "what is implied is more important to her than what is said." Reprinted: A262. Partially reprinted: A10, A283.

*A111 FOSTER, Amy G. *Analytical Index of the Contents of the* Brontë Society
Transactions *Volume I (1895)–Volume XV (1967) and Index of Authors* (Keighley
[England]: Keighley Printers Ltd 1968)
The Index is in two parts: (1) by subject, and (2) by author, with a list of their contributions.
[From an abstract in *The Year's Work in English Studies*.] See B181, B182.

A111A FOX, Ralph "The Victorian Retreat" *The Novel and the People* (New York:
International Publishers 1945) 52–61 [59–61]
WH is a cry of despairing agony wrung by life itself from EB. Lockwood's nightmare is an
example of this agony which no other age but mid–Victorian England could have tortured
from the author.

A112 FRANKENBERG, Ronald "Styles of Marxism: Styles of Criticism: *Wuthering
Heights*: A Case Study" Diana Laurenson, ed *The Sociology of Literature* (Keele
[England]: University of Keele 1978) 109–44
As a way of charting the changes in Marxist criticism as history has changed, this study
examines "changing analyses of Emily Brontë's *Wuthering Heights* from Caudwell's brief but
extremely perceptive and revealing comments (1936) . . . through the alleged reductionism of
Wilson . . . in 1947 and then Kettle 1951. . . ." and on by way of Q. D. Leavis 1969, Raymond
Williams 1973, Eagleton 1975, Musselwhite 1976, and Kermode 1975.

FUJITA, Takashi *see* A5.

A113 FULCHER, Paul M. "The Brontë Sisters" *Foundations of English Style* (New
York: Crofts 1927) 267–70
This is simply a reprinting of the part of Charlotte Brontë's "Biographical Notice" concerning
EB's death, with no comment.

BOOKS AND PARTS OF BOOKS

A114 —— "Introduction" *Wuthering Heights* (New York: Macmillan 1929) v–xvii
EB's reputation has steadily grown for the last forty years. *WH* is compelling, but "the faults of craftsmanship are as obvious as their corresponding merits." Nelly Dean is too literary and the narrative method is complicated, but Fulcher praises the way the characters are mirrored in one another. There are perhaps in *WH* some minor incidents of EB's life; certainly the moors are reflected in it. Although it is transformed, Hoffmann's *The Entail* is the source of the plot. When one returns to *WH* a second time "its full power appears."

A115 GARRETT, Peter K. *The Victorian Multiplot Novel: Studies in Dialogical Form* (New Haven: Yale University Press 1980) 18–22
In this study of the multiple narrative in Dickens, Thackeray, G. Eliot, and Trollope, the double plot of *WH* is used as a preliminary example of some of the effects produced by dialogical form.

A116 GARROD, H. W. "Editor's Introduction" *Wuthering Heights* (London: Humphrey Milford 1930) v–xiv
WH is a "novel of edification" for Mr Lockwood. He is the instrument of the moral of the story: to teach the reader what love is. As for the scope of *WH*, "human nature cannot be interpreted. . .out of anything less than *all* nature." The story, however, is "ill–constructed, and in its detail often complicated and obscure." Partially reprinted: A10.

A117 GÉRIN, Winifred "The Authorship of *Wuthering Heights*" *Branwell Brontë* (London: Thomas Nelson and Sons 1961) 307–14
This modern, scholarly approach to the question of Branwell Brontë's possible authorship of *WH* explores the evidence connecting him with the novel. The conclusion that he had no part in creating *WH* is supported by examples of his prose and poetry and by an analysis of his personality.

A118 —— *The Brontës. I: The Formative Years* (Harlow: Longman for the British Council 1973) *passim*
Precocious as they were, the Brontë children also shared a strong creative urge; these qualities fostered an extremely early literary beginning. As the Brontës evolved into adulthood, they had already finished their adolescent literary apprenticeship and were thus able to "transmute their experience into the abiding truth of art." Shaping influences were Patrick Brontë, their education, and environment.

A119 —— *The Brontës. II: The Creative Work* (Harlow: Longman for the British Council 1974) *passim*
The life experiences of the Brontës as adults are related to the novels and poems they created. Emily's experiences at Halifax and Law Hill were a strong influence in the creation of *WH*.

A120 —— "Byron's Influence on the Brontës" in Robert Speaight, ed *Essays by Divers Hands, Being the Transactions of the Royal Society of Literature of the United Kingdom* n s 37 (London: Oxford University Press 1972) 47–62
The Reverend Mr Brontë possessed the 1853 edition of the *Complete Works of Lord Byron*, edited by Thomas Moore, Esq. Evidence of Byron's influence on the Brontë children abounds, not only in their writing, but in their drawing too. One aspect of Byron which appealed to EB was his love of animals. The essay discusses similarities between Byron's work and *WH*,

one of which is Heathcliff's crying out to the dead Catherine as Byron's Manfred cries out to the dead Astarte.

A121 ———— "The Effects of Environment on the Brontë Writings" in Mary Stocks, ed *Essays by Divers Hands, Being the Transactions of the Royal Society of Literature of the United Kingdom* n s 36 (London: Oxford University Press 1970) 67–83

The Brontës derived a lifelong stimulus from their environment: ". . .from the situation of their father's parish 1,000 ft. up on the Yorkshire moors. . .the swift passage of careering clouds from coast to coast. . .a spectacle made more dramatic, changeful and sudden from the proximity of the seas. . . ." EB's sources of inspiration came from her natural environment.

A122 ———— *Emily Brontë: A Biography* (London: Oxford University Press 1971) 290 p

The object of this biography is to seek the truth between two biographical extremes: the school viewing EB's life as romantic and emotionally charged, and the scholars seeking to eliminate all biographical content from EB's work. Another purpose is to "correct the image of a girl who has been thought and spoken of as being always, at all ages, the woman she eventually became in the last three years of her life—a kind of Athena sprung complete from the head of Zeus. . . ." Appendix A contains the original text of seven French devoirs signed and dated by EB. See A303, B17, B109, B288, B289.

A123 GEROULD, Gordon H. "Interpreters: I. Hawthorne, Melville, and the Brontës" *The Patterns of English and American Fiction; A History* (Boston: Little, Brown 1942) 341–66 [361–63]

WH is clumsy in structure and has technical defects. Nelly Dean keeps it rational, but the "mad" characters are hard to believe. Nevertheless, EB accomplished what Melville "was to attempt less successfully in *Pierre* only a few years later. No one has pictured better the dubious battle of good and evil. . . ."

A124 GETTMANN, Royal A. "Introduction" *Wuthering Heights* (New York: Random House 1950) v–xvi

This is a discussion of the position of *WH* as a Victorian novel. Nelly Dean is the prism for the story; her purpose is "to control passions, bring out their meanings, and make them beautiful." There are no set descriptions of nature in *WH*, for nature is "felt on every page. . .in phrases and figures of speech." The theme of *WH* is found in Heathcliff.

*A125 GILBERT, E. L. *Review Notes and Study Guide to Brontë's* Wuthering Heights (New York: Monarch 1966)

A126 GILBERT, Sandra M. and Susan Gubar "Looking Oppositely: Emily Brontë's Bible of Hell" in *The Madwoman in the Attic: The Woman Writer and the 19th Century Literary Imagination* (New Haven, Conn: Yale University Press 1979) 248–308

This chapter appears within Part III titled "How Are We Fal'n? Milton's Daughters." *WH* is compared to Mary Shelley's *Frankenstein*. Both have a tension between dramatic surfaces and metaphysical depths, but ". . .the most serious matter *Wuthering Heights* and *Frankenstein* share is the matter of *Paradise Lost*, and their profoundest difference is in their attitude toward Milton's myth. Where Shelley was Milton's dutiful daughter, retelling his story to clarify it, Brontë was the poet's rebellious child, radically revising (and even reversing) the terms of his mythic narrative. . . ." EB appears, like Blake in his *The Marriage of Heaven and Hell*, to be insisting in *WH*, "I have also the Bible of Hell, which the world shall have whether they will or no."

A127 GILLIE, Christopher "The Heroine Victim" *Character in English Literature* (New York: Barnes and Noble 1965) 124–34
Catherine Earnshaw is the focal point in this comparative criticism. Emma Woodhouse of Jane Austen's *Emma* and Catherine Earnshaw of *WH* are considered separately, then the two are compared as their authors' central characters. Heathcliff's credibility and five styles of "sexual emotion" in *WH* are also discussed.

*A128 GLEAVE, J. J. *Emily Brontë: An Appreciation* (Manchester: Marsden & Co Ltd 1904)

A129 GOODRIDGE, Jonathan Francis *Emily Brontë*: Wuthering Heights (*Studies in English Literature* xx) (London: E. Arnold 1964) 72 p
This is an assessment of *WH* as fiction, not as other things. Heathcliff is the pivotal character as every facet of the novel is examined—craft, structure, detail, dramatic movement, pace, perspectives, and use of time, to name a few. Of special value are a graph of the novel's time structure and a map of the geography of the two houses, the Kirkyard, the Road to Gimmerton, and the moor. This work is an excellent starting point for a study of *WH*. Two chapters, "Nelly as Narrator" and "The Circumambient Universe," are reprinted and annotated in A274 and A379. Partially reprinted: A283.

———— *see* A344e.

A130 GOSE, Elliott B., Jr "Introduction" and "*Wuthering Heights*" *Imagination Indulged: The Irrational in the Nineteenth–Century Novel* (Montreal: McGill–Queen's University Press 1972) 13–18, 59–71 and *passim*
The subject of this insightful study is not the history of an idea, but rather "a concern with the possibilities of imaginative perception." Dickens, EB, Hardy and Conrad employed "the irrational" or "Fantasy, Romance, Fairy Tale, Dream and Ritual" toward solving the artist's problem of ". . . how best to embody the tensions, concerns, and insights which he finds in his psychic self. . . ." The authors are all concerned with dramatization and exaggerated emotion. Fairy tale patterns are important in *WH*. The first we encounter is the Beauty–and–Beast tale when Earnshaw returns from Liverpool bearing, not the presents Hindley, Cathy, and Nelly requested, but Heathcliff instead. Oppositions and resolutions in *WH* work in the same subtle way as they do in a fairy tale. Besides their concern with dramatization and exaggerated emotion which these authors share, ". . .the important characters in *Wuthering Heights*, *Bleak House*, *The Return of the Native*, and *Lord Jim* aim also at establishing some sort of archetypal identity. . . ."

A131 GOSSE, Edmund "The Challenge of the Brontës" *Selected Essays* (London: William Heinemann 1928) 91–102
This is a reprinting of Item B202.

A132 ——— "The Challenge of the Brontës" *Some Diversions of a Man of Letters* (London: William Heinemann 1919) 139–50
This is a reprinting of Item B202.

A133 GRABO, Carl H. "Technical Characteristics of *Wuthering Heights*" *The Technique of the Novel* (New York: Gordian Press 1928) 139–51
"Nature" in *WH* is more effective than "Nature" in Thomas Hardy's *The Return of the Native*. Lockwood intrudes and "is of no value whatsoever." Although the reader identifies with Nelly Dean, the devices which allow her narration of the story are thin. However, "the structural inadequacies are insignificant when weighed with its great merits."

*A134 GREEN, John Albert *Brontë Collection, Public Library, Moss Side, Manchester, List of Additions, 1907–1916* (Picadilly: 1916)

A135 ——— *Catalogue of the Gleave Brontë Collection* (Manchester: Moss Side 1907)
This is a valuable source for bibliography of Brontë works and nineteenth–century criticism.

A136 GREGOR, Ian "Introduction" and ed *The Brontës: A Collection of Critical Essays* (Englewood Cliffs, N J: Prentice–Hall 1970) 1–6
In introducing these essays on the novels of Charlotte and EB, and one essay on EB's poetry, Ian Gregor addresses two concerns: the relationship of the artist to his material, and the latitude of interpretation any particular work can stand. A discussion of some of the critical history of *WH* follows, in which the elusiveness of the reader–engaging power of *WH* is stressed. See individual entries for annotation in most cases.
The Structure of Wuthering Heights by C. P. Sanger (A324)
"The Brontës: A Centennial Observance" by Richard Chase (B96)
"The Image of the Book in *Wuthering Heights*" by Robert C. McKibben (B319)
"Charlotte Brontë as a Critic of *Wuthering Heights*" by Philip Drew (B152)
"Control of Sympathy in *Wuthering Heights*" by John Hagan (B215)
"The Place of Love in *Jane Eyre* and *Wuthering Heights*" by Mark Kinkead–Weekes. (This essay is printed here for the first time.)
> Love is more passionate and more central in the Brontës' works than it is in earlier novels such as those of Jane Austen. To explore the "radical differences in the place of 'love' within the 'story' " in the two Brontë novels, we need a way of relating the different ways of looking at love to the structures of the novels. Kinkead–Weekes chooses the metaphor, "house," which can be an expression of self, relationship, or both.
"The Other Emily" by Denis Donoghue. (This essay is printed here for the first time.)
> We should distinguish between EB's autobiographical poems and the Gondal poems, but "we should not push them too far apart." They, and *WH*, all share "a landscape of feeling." EB's imagination, as shown in the poems, occupies a position almost impossible to define, somewhere between the two extremes of soliloquy and drama. Donoghue attempts a definition using examples of the imagination of Shakespeare, Yeats, Proust, and T. S. Eliot.

A137 ——— "Reading a Story: Sequence, Pace, and Recollection" and ed *Reading the Victorian Novel: Detail into Form* (New York: Harper and Row 1980) 92–110 [92–98]
Chapter Nine of *WH* is "a good instance of the importance of tempo in reading." EB is

involving the reader in a highly concentrated suspension of judgment, by use of timing and reading pace.

A138 GRIERSON, Herbert J. C. and J. C. Smith "Early Victorians: Mrs. Browning and Others" *A Critical History of English Poetry* (New York: Oxford University Press 1946) 463–75 [467–68]
In this discussion of EB's poetry the authors conclude that she is "a more intense, if less variously accomplished, poet than Mrs. Browning."

A139 GROOM, Bernard "The Brontës" *A Literary History of England* (London: Longmans, Green 1929) 345–48
There is a very brief reference to EB on p 346–47: "Emily's nature was more tragic than her sister's [Charlotte's], but it was also less rich," for Charlotte was the one who "usually kept her balance."

GROVE, Robin *see* A344a.

GUBAR, Susan *see* A126.

A140 GUERARD, Albert J. "Preface" *Wuthering Heights* (New York: Washington Square Press 1960) v–xix
WH is a possible compensation for a life not lived, and is "a dark, splendid, imperfect novel." As an author, EB oscillates about the portrait of Heathcliff the reader receives; her treatment of Heathcliff, which is erratic and uncertain, is the novel's most disturbing structural weakness. Reprinted: A262, A379.

A141 HALDANE, Elizabeth *Mrs. Gaskell and Her Friends* (London: Hodder and Stoughton 1931) *passim*
On p 164 Charlotte Brontë's personality is compared with EB's.

*A142 HALL, Henry C. *Emily Brontë and Her Genius: Selected Poems and Appreciations* 93 p

A143 HALPERIN, John, and Janet Kunert *Plots and Characters in the Fiction of Jane Austen, the Brontës, and George Eliot* (Hamden, Conn: Shoe String Press 1976) 192–203
One of the "Plots and Characters" series, the book summarizes the plot of *WH* and lists the characters.

HAMILTON, Alastair *see* A18A.

*A144 HANNAH, Barbara *Striving Towards Wholeness* (New York: G. P. Putnam's Sons 1971) 105–257
An examination of *WH* and the Brontës as children from a Jungian psychological viewpoint. [From an abstract in *BST*.]

*A145 ——— *Victims of the Creative Spirit: A Contribution to the Psychology of the Brontës from the Jungian Point of View* (1951)

HANSON, E. M. *see* A146.

HANSON, Elisabeth *see* A147.

A146 HANSON, Lawrence and E. M. Hanson *The Four Brontës: The Lives and Works of Charlotte, Branwell, Emily and Anne Brontë* (London: Oxford University Press 1949)
This detailed history, well–documented, of the lives of all four Brontës is a good starting point for any student of Brontë biography because it shows the effects the family members had on each other. Of particular interest to EB students are the chapters "Branwell and Emily," "*Wuthering Heights*," and "The Death of Emily." The major influence Branwell had on EB was her eventual reaction against his romanticization of life, which led to her own mystical belief that the final contentment of the soul is not found on earth. This belief is borne out in *WH* because the love of Catherine and Heathcliff is not an earthly love. In a thorough analysis of *WH*, the authors explore the role of Heathcliff, but determine that the two Catherines provide the vitality and human interest in *WH*, and indeed both give reality to Heathcliff. There is also a discussion of the prose and poetry of *WH*. From her letters concerning EB's illness and death, we can see that Charlotte Brontë understood neither *WH* nor Emily. There are careful notes and a 10–page bibliography.

A147 HANSON, Lawrence and Elisabeth Hanson "Corrections to the First Impressions of *The Four Brontës: The Lives and Works of Charlotte, Branwell, Emily and Anne Brontë with a New Preface by the Authors* (New York: Archon Books 1967) xvii–xxxiv
As the new preface explains, this is a reprinting of the first impressions published in 1949, with errata which "consists in the main of corrections of style and psychological judgments...."

A148 HARDWICK, Elizabeth "The Brontës" *Seduction and Betrayal: Women and Literature* (New York: Random House; London: Weidenfeld & Nicolson 1974) 3–29
The Brontë story is told with emphasis upon the social and economic situation of the sisters. They "seized upon the development of their talents as an honorable way of life and in this they were heroic."

A149 HARDY, Barbara Wuthering Heights (*Emily Brontë*) (New York: Barnes and Noble 1963) 94 p
This book was written to be used as a teaching aid. *WH* gives the reader both physical adventure and "inner adventure." The inner adventure is effected by the reader's being required to sift evidence and make judgments. *WH* consists of two storytellers, two generations, and two worlds (supernatural and natural). Chapter XVII of *WH*, a transitional chapter, is analyzed in detail as an example of analysis and because the structure of *WH* can be seen in it.

———— *see* A344c.

A150 HARRISON, G. Elsie *The Clue to the Brontës* (London: Methuen 1948) *passim*
The clue is "that the home of Thomas Tighe, who was Patrick Brontë's patron, was the Mecca...for Wesley's travelling preachers in Ireland." EB "could toss off the old childhood's tale [*WH*]" easily when Charlotte said the three sisters should all write books. It all came

from Methodism lore. (See B15 and B228 for discussions of Methodist influence on the Brontës.)

A151 ——— *Haworth Parsonage: A Study of Wesley and the Brontës* (London: Epworth Press 1937) *passim*
"Emily Brontë achieved her reputation on her Methodist background. . . ." An entry in John Wesley's journal is quoted mentioning the names "Lockwood," "Grimshaw," and "Sutcliffe," and the conclusion is that these names were the inspiration for the ones EB used in *WH*.

A152 ——— *Methodist Good Companions* (London: Epworth Press 1935)
Chapter III, "Jabez Bunting," is about the man who has been suggested as the real–life model for Jabes Branderham in *WH*. Chapter V, "Reactions in Haworth Parsonage," alleges Bunting actually to be the model. The author says, "Methodism was Emily Brontë's nursery. . .her university also." She also finds parallels between Branderham's sermon and the character Joseph and the William Grimshaw legend. Chapter V reprinted: A85.

*A153 HARTHILL, Rosemary *Emily Brontë: Poems* (London: Tom Stacy 1973) 150 p

A154 HARTLEY, L. P. "Emily Brontë in Gondal and Gaaldine" *The Novelist's Responsibility* (London: Hamish Hamilton 1967) 35–53
A reprinting of B229.

A155 HARVEY, W. J. *Character and the Novel* (Ithaca, N Y: Cornell University Press 1965) *passim*
WH is nearly a contemporary novel along with *Vanity Fair* and *Dombey and Son*, "yet they differ considerably in their mimetic relationship to life." *WH* is used as an example of narrative technique and novelistic structure.

A156 HATFIELD, C. W. "Introduction" *The Complete Poems of Emily Jane Brontë* (New York: Columbia University Press 1941) 3–13
In this introduction to the definitive edition of EB's poems, Hatfield assumes the Gondal poems to be those in EB's notebook which she herself entitled "Gondal Poems," and he assumes that the poems in the other untitled notebook do not relate to Gondal. He says that the poems identify the mind of the genius who wrote *WH*. There is also a discussion of the ascription of poems not hers to EB. This work also contains sources from which the text of the poems has been derived, a list of books and magazines in which the manuscripts of EB have been printed in facsimile, and a list of words found in the manuscripts which have been altered to agree with ordinary spelling. See B409.

A157 ——— "Preface" in Clement Shorter, ed *The Complete Poems of Emily Jane Brontë* (London: Hodder and Stoughton 1923; New York: Doran 1924) v–vi
". . .[I]t is believed that we have now as accurate a transcript of the words written by Emily Brontë as it is possible to obtain." Hatfield's 1941 edition, however, is the definitive one to date.

A158 HEILBRUN, Carolyn G. "The Woman as Hero" *Toward a Recognition of Androgyny* (New York: Alfred A. Knopf 1973) 49–112 [79–82]
The view of *WH* as a pure, androgynous novel is meant to accompany other interpretations

of it, not to supplant them. Catherine and Heathcliff, whose love represents the androgynous ideal, betray that ideal.

*A159 HENDERSON, Philip "Introduction" *The Complete Poems of Emily Brontë* (London: The Folio Society 1951)
    EB's punctuation of the poems is retained throughout. [From mention in M. R. D. Seaward, A329.]

A160 ―――― "Introduction" *Emily Brontë: Selected Poems* (London: Lawson and Dunn 1947) ix–xxviii
    This is an explication of themes in EB's poems. Her poetry is compared to Byron's, briefly; although her poems contain the same satanism as Byron's, EB's poetry "explores those regions known to readers of St. John of the Cross as the Dark Night of the Soul."

*A161 HERVEY–BATHURST, Pamela *An Account of Emily Brontë. Born July 30, 1818, Died Dec. 19, 1848, Aged 30* (Stanbury, Yorkshire [England]: Brontë Booklets Ltd 1971) 34 p

A162 HEWISH, John *Emily Brontë: A Critical and Biographical Study* (London: Macmillan 1969) 204 p
    The integrity to be found in this thorough study of EB is foreshadowed in the "Introduction: The Sources," wherein Hewish comes to grips with the many problems concerning primary source material. The work comprises three books: "The Life," "*Wuthering Heights*," and "Public and Critics: 1846–1968." EB's life story is reconstructed on the foundation of primary sources. *WH* is investigated in the same manner, with great attention to the Gondal poems, although EB "did not work *from* Gondal, but *away* from it. . ." and ". . .no other Victorian novel (perhaps no other novel) is related to the author's work from childhood in quite this way." Two excellent appendices are "A Location List of Manuscripts," and "An Emily Brontë Reading List." Partially reprinted: A283.

A163 HEWITT, Douglas "Interpretation and Over–interpretation" *The Approach to Fiction: Good and Bad Readings of Novels* (Totowa, N J: Rowman and Littlefield 1972) 105–26 [123–26]
    Hewitt includes *WH* in a discussion of particular novels having additional meaning through their symbols, metaphors, and imagery. It is possible, however, to over–interpret symbolic patterns.

A164 HINKLEY, Laura L. *The Brontës: Charlotte and Emily* (New York: Hastings House 1945)
    The author presents the facts, and her opinions based on these, in this careful recounting of the Brontë sisters' life story. EB is discussed on p 164–97, *WH* on p 318–49. Possibly a German story and a tale in *Blackwood's Magazine*, "The Bridegroom of Barna," influenced the creation of *WH*. Heathcliff could have been modeled on Joshua Taylor. EB's poems are seen as the Gondal story, except for twenty of them, which are designated as personal. There is also a full bibliography.

A165 ―――― "Emily" *Ladies of Literature* (New York: Hastings House 1946) 175–211
    This treatment of EB's life is similar to that in the author's *The Brontës: Charlotte and*

Emily (A83). The treatment of *WH* differs in that it takes up the question of Branwell Brontë's influence on *WH*: the character of Lockwood was modeled on Branwell.

*A166 HOCHMAN, Baruch "Afterword" *Wuthering Heights by Emily Brontë, with a Critical Supplement and an Afterword* (London: Bantam 1974)

*A167 HODGE, Alan "Introduction" *Wuthering Heights* (London: Hamish Hamilton 1950)

*A168 HOLDERNESS, Graham *The Nineteenth–Century Novel and its Legacy: A Study Guide to* Wuthering Heights (London: The Open University Press 1973) 40 p

A169 HOMANS, Margaret "Emily Brontë" *Women Writers and Poetic Identity: Dorothy Wordsworth, Emily Brontë and Emily Dickinson* (Princeton, N J: Princeton University Press 1980) 104–61
"The book's purpose is to define the special challenges faced by women who aspired to be poets and thereby to illuminate both their failures and their successes." Homans discusses EB's authorial character as a poet and novelist, beginning with the thesis that EB's muse is a masculine one. As the investigation of EB as author of the poetry and *WH* reveals, EB, in writing *WH*, freed herself of the idea that nature is feminine or maternal—an idea found in the poetry—so that "the novel succeeds where the poetry breaks down."

A170 HOPKINS, Annette B. *The Father of the Brontës* (Baltimore: Johns Hopkins University Press for Goucher College 1958) *passim*
This is a scholarly and sympathetic treatment of Mr Brontë. EB's "practical vein," shown in her skill at housekeeping, was probably derived from her father. On p 157–58 the author mentions the lesson in marksmanship Mr Brontë was supposed to have given EB.

*A171 HOPKINS, Marie M. *Emily Brontë* (Chicago 1903) 25 p

A172 HOWE, Bea "Triumvirate of Governesses. The Brontës" *A Galaxy of Governesses* (London: Derek Verschoyle 1954) 93–111 [99–105]
"The brief interlude Emily Brontë spent as governess at Miss Patchett's Academy for Young Ladies at Law Hill, near Halifax, was of great importance to her as a creative writer...." Although Charlotte wrote to Ellen Nussey that Emily's labor at Law Hill was slavery and that she feared Emily would never stand it, according to Howe, EB not only stood it but emerged from it "stronger in health and imaginatively far the richer for her gruelling experience."

A173 HOWELLS, William Dean "The Two Catherines of Emily Brontë" *Heroines of Fiction* (New York: Harpers 1901) 228–39
This is a reprinting of Item B256.

A174 HUDSON, William Henry "Emily Brontë" *A Short History of English Literature in the Nineteenth Century* (London: G. Bell and Sons Ltd 1918) 238–39
"The grim and ghastly story is difficult to appraise. Its construction is almost incredibly bad.... Yet there is something stupendous about its sustained and undiluted horror...."

HUGHES, H. S. *see* A226.

A175 HUISH, Marcus B. *Samplers and Tapestry Embroideries* (London: Longmans, Green and Co 1900)
The sampler reproduced on Plate 36 is assumed to have been embroidered by EB.

A176 IRWIN, Michael *Picturing: Description and Illusion in the Nineteenth–Century Novel* (London: George Allen and Unwin 1979) 109–10, 138–39 and *passim*
Concerned with mental pictures of people and places evoked by the author for the reader in the nineteenth–century novel, Irwin points out that EB was careful not to let the reader visit Gimmerton where her characters would have to mingle with ordinariness and thus possibly appear strange by contrast.

*A177 JACK, Ian "Introduction" *Wuthering Heights* (London: Oxford University Press 1981)
The World's Classics Series.

———— *see* A238, A238b, A238c, A238e, A238f.

A178 JAMES, Henry *The Question of Our Speech, The Lesson of Balzac: Two Lectures* (Boston and New York: Houghton Mifflin and Co 1905) 62–65 and *passim*
"The romantic tradition of the Brontës. . .has been. . .helped. . .by the attendant image of their dreary, their tragic history, their loneliness and poverty of life. That picture has been made to hang before us as insistently as the vividest page of *Jane Eyre* or of *Wuthering Heights*. . . ." Reprinted: A283.

A179 JAMES, Janet C. *Brontë's* Wuthering Heights (Lincoln, Neb: Cliffs Notes 1979) 73 p
The Cliffs Notes series.

A180 JENNINGS, Elizabeth "Introduction" Wuthering Heights *and Selected Poems* (London: Pan Books 1967) 5–13
WH "does almost all the forbidden things as far as nineteenth–century fiction is concerned," but EB brings them off by a force of vision. We learn more of EB's personality from her poetry than from *WH*.

*A181 JENNINGS, John *Inscapes 10: Wuthering Heights* (Dublin: The Educational Co 1975) 40 p
Part of the "Inscapes" series.

A182 JOAD, C. E. M. "The Brontës" *The Bookmark* (London: John Westhouse 1945) 40–45
Authors of genius who are women are the exception; nevertheless *Jane Eyre* and WH by Charlotte Brontë and EB are remarkable, especially when considered in the light of their biography.

JOHNSON, Hamish *see* A296.

*A183 JOHNSON, James William "Introduction, with Suggestions for Reading and

Discussion by Roger K. Applebee" *Wuthering Heights* (Boston: Houghton Mifflin 1966)

A184 ——— "Nightmare and Reality in *Wuthering Heights*" *Wuthering Heights* (Boston: Houghton Mifflin 1965) vi–xiv
Physical nature and human nature are both stormy in *WH*. EB is concerned with the irrational, "that vast body of emotion which cannot be tested by logic or 'common sense.'" She uses dreams and ghosts to show the irrational. The elements of continuity in *WH* are landscape, weather, genealogy of the families, and a repetition of events. The characters, however, are the central nucleus.

A185 JOHNSON, R. Brimley " 'Jane Eyre' to 'Scenes of Clerical Life' (1847–1858)" *The Women Novelists* (London: Collins 1918) 179–84
WH is seen as "unique for the passionate intensity of its emotions." This critique reflects some of the ideas prevalent in the early twentieth century concerning *WH*: Heathcliff is an arch–fiend, and Edgar, Isabella, and Linton are "weak, good people."

A186 KARL, Frederick R. "The Brontës: The Outsider as Protagonist" *An Age of Fiction* (New York: Farrar, Straus, and Giroux 1964) 77–103 [77–90]
WH, a novel without hero or heroine, is held together by the doubling of structure and character and the counterpointing of themes. There are many levels and contrasts in this novel. Also discussed is the place of *WH* in the history of the English novel, and it is compared with the novels of Austen, Conrad, Dickens, Lawrence, and Scott.

A187 ——— "The Brontës: The Self Defined, Redefined, and Refined" in Richard A. Levine, ed *The Victorian Experience: The Novelists* (Athens: Ohio University Press 1976) 121–50 [138–44]
This study of "the literature of enclosure" explores the way certain novelists are preoccupied with the unfolding of the self and the protean self, which is usually associated with Kafka, Proust, and Beckett. The most famous example of enclosure is the red room of *Jane Eyre*, but one of its counterparts is "the hothouse atmosphere of Wuthering Heights (the house itself as well as the novel)." Karl discusses all seven Brontë novels and finds much in common in them and their authors, e.g., parentless protagonists, and characters forced to look deep within for their best selves.

A188 KAVANAGH, Colman *The Symbolism of* Wuthering Heights (London: John Long 1920) 30 p
This original treatment sees EB as a "Celtic genius . . . stimulated by keen domestic sorrow." In *WH*, Mr Earnshaw is father to Heathcliff and a hypocrite who leaves his family "a legacy of woe" in Heathcliff. Hindley, after Mr Earnshaw's death, proceeds on the principle of "an eye for an eye. . ." and Heathcliff reciprocates in the same manner. Hindley, for the unpardonable sin of despair, incurs the heaviest punishment of all, and Catherine Earnshaw commits the sin of pride, for which her daughter suffers humiliation. Edgar Linton, buried beside Catherine and Heathcliff, is their "good angel, unrecognized by them in mortal life, no longer between but for ever beside them."

A189 KENNEDY, Alan "The Thread in the Garment" *Meaning and Signs in Fiction* (New York: St Martins Press 1979) 51–56
This stimulating essay points out that the theme of education is important in nineteenth–

century literature because education is the process of realization for the soul. The aspect of the proper direction of flow—from inner to outer—makes a consideration of *WH* appropriate in this chapter. *WH* is "perhaps the profoundest study of permanence and change that our literature has produced." Heathcliff is the central figure, and "his final change is one that brings him around finally to a righting of the relationship of inner to outer; a relationship which he has perverted by enslaving himself to an external condition and then trying to enforce other lives to follow his pattern by creating a determinist situation for them. In modern terms, Heathcliff attempts to apply a behaviorist or mechanistic conception of identity and finally learns that man is spiritual."

A190 KEPPLER, C. F. *The Literature of the Second Self* (Tucson: The University of Arizona Press 1972) 135–38, 148–49 and *passim*
Keppler is using relevant works of literature to shed light on the figure of the Double, instead of the other way around. Heathcliff, among other literary characters such as Poe's Ligeia, possesses all the attributes of the second self, whereas Catherine does not.

A191 KERMODE, Frank *The Classic: Literary Images of Permanence and Change* (New York: Viking Press 1975) 117–41
"These reflections had their origin in T. S. Eliot's paper 'What Is a Classic?' (1944)." Kermode is considering the extreme variety of response characteristic of the modern reading of the classic and chooses *WH* as a means to approach this and other topics "by way of a single familiar text." "The survival of the classic must. . .depend on its possession of a surplus of signifier; as in *King Lear* or *Wuthering Heights* this may expose them to the charge of confusion, for they must always signify more than is needed by any one interpreter or any one generation of interpreters."

A192 KETTLE, Arnold "Emily Brontë *Wuthering Heights* (1847)" *An Introduction to the English Novel* (London: Hutchinson House 1951) 139–55
WH is "concrete and yet general, local and yet universal." EB works not in ideas but in symbols, and *WH* is compared with *Oliver Twist* in this respect. This is an analysis of *WH* that leads logically to the conclusion that the "feeling that binds Catherine and Heathcliff. . . is an expression of the necessity of man, if he is to choose life rather than death, to revolt against all that would destroy his inmost needs and aspirations. . .to become. . .more fully human." Reprinted: A220, A262, A379.

A193 KIELY, Robert "*Wuthering Heights*: Emily Brontë 1847" *The Romantic Novel in England* (Cambridge: Harvard University Press 1972) 233–51
EB's craftsmanship is the subject of this chapter. ". . . [A]long with *Emma*, *Wuthering Heights* is one of the few perfect novels in 19th century English [conveying] the impression of an utterly self–sufficient world where style and content really are the same. . . ." *WH* has no "literary" aura, i.e., EB does not have her characters quote or recite, allude to chivalric romance, or discover old letters, as did many of her predecessors. The views of authors and critics on *WH* are considered and discussed.

KINKEAD–WEEKES, Mark *see* A136.

A194 KINSLEY, Edith E. *Pattern for Genius: A Story of Branwell Brontë and His Three Sisters, Charlotte, Emily and Anne, Largely Told in Their Own Words* (New York: E. P. Dutton 1939) *passim*

The influence of Branwell Brontë on his sisters is narrated in the words and sentences of the Brontë novels; the characters in the novels are given the name Charlotte, Branwell, Emily, or Anne, but their words are the fictitious ones in the novels. The author says, "no apology is offered for transference in the following narrative of superb and well–known passages of prose from one setting to another, if such passages seem to have biographic verity." However, this biographical method is indefensible. *WH* and EB's poetry are used principally in Chapters V, VIII, XII, XVI, XXXII, XXXIII, and XXXIV.

A195 KLINGOPULOS, G. D. "The Literary Scene" in Boris Ford, ed *From Dickens to Hardy; Pelican Guide to English Literature* VI (Baltimore: Penguin Books 1958) 59–116
EB is mentioned several times in this very general discussion of the Victorian literary world, e.g., "the novelists most free of the general dampness of the age are Emily Brontë and George Eliot." EB's poetry is compared with George Meredith's on p 95–96

KLOESEL, Christian J. W. *see* A4.

A196 KNIGHT, Grant C. "The Brontës" *The Novel in English* (New York: Richard R. Smith Inc 1931) 204–15
To the typical literary mid–Victorian the world was a well–ordered place, so that the very novelty of *WH*, when it appeared, eclipsed its merit. Nevertheless, Knight sees it in 1931 as too electric and lacking restraint.

A197 ——— "The Most Terrible" *Superlatives* (New York: Alfred A. Knopf 1925) 20–39
Written for the potential reader of *WH*, this is a colorful and enthusiastic description of the novel and of Heathcliff in particular.

A198 KNOEPFLMACHER, U. C. "*Wuthering Heights*: A Tragicomic Romance" *Laughter and Despair: Readings in Ten Novels of the Victorian Era* (Berkeley: University of California Press 1971) 84–108
"*Wuthering Heights* relies on the resemblances between opposites and the disjunction of alikes." For example, Heathcliff in oppressing Hareton eventually matches the Hindley who oppressed Heathcliff. EB fused pessimism and hope, tragedy and comedy, and thereby controlled the polarities upon which her vision was built.

*A199 KRESLIN, John B. *Notes on* Wuthering Heights: *Brontë* (Canada: Forum House Publishing Co 1968) 96 p

KUNERT, Janet *see* A143.

A200 LAAR, Elisabeth Th. M. van de *The Inner Structure of* Wuthering Heights: *A Study of an Imaginative Field* (The Hague: Mouton 1969) 262 p
In this study, "the inner structure will be seen as the pattern made by the literary imagination, i.e., by that spiritual mobility which is characterized by the ability to transform sights and sounds, forms and colours, suggested by the perception or memory, into a new sequence of living images which has the power to open up new worlds of experience and thereby to enrich the language." "Image" in this study is that vehicle of the literary imagination which

unfolds a world existing entirely apart from the material world. The imagery forming the inner structure of WH is that of the elements: air, water, earth, and fire; and further components, e.g., weather; dreams, visions, omens; windows, keys, gates; animal and vegetable life; books and the Bible; and light and darkness.

*A201 LAING, James W. B. "*Wuthering Heights*, Emily Brontë" *English Literature: Getting to Know Them, Notes on Great Writers and Their Works* (Leven Dale 1974) 57–63

*A202 LAMONT, William H. F. *An Analysis of Emily Brontë's* Wuthering Heights (New Brunswick 1938)

A203 LANE, Margaret *The Brontë Story: A Reconsideration of Mrs. Gaskell's Life of Charlotte Brontë* (London: Heinemann 1953) *passim*
This narrative story uses long quotes from Mrs Gaskell's *Life of Charlotte Brontë*. The author updates this valuable biography, using new material (e.g., the juvenilia) which was not available to Mrs Gaskell in 1857.

A204 ——— "Emily Brontë in a Cold Climate" *The Drug–Like Brontë Dream* (London: Murray 1980) 57–80
A reprinting of B287.

A205 ——— "Introduction" in Philip Henderson, ed Wuthering Heights *with Selected Poems* (London: J. M. Dent and Sons 1907) v–x
Most of the poems are of no great worth; a few, however, are as beautiful as anything in our language. WH is a "long, intoxicating poem in itself," and its power lies in the ruthless love of Catherine and Heathcliff, made memorable by EB's own intense conviction of their existence.

A206 ——— "The Mysterious Genius of Emily Brontë" *Purely for Pleasure* (London: Hamish Hamilton 1966) 139–51
A reprinting of B289.

A207 LANGMAN, Fred "*Wuthering Heights*" in John Colmer, ed *Approaches to the Novel* (Adelaide [Australia]: Rigby Ltd 1966) 39–58
A discussion of different critical approaches to WH, asserting that criticism should be reasonable, attend to the novel, ask basic questions, and go some way in answering them.

*A208 LAW, Alice *Emily Jane Brontë and the Authorship of* Wuthering Heights (Altham, Accrington: The Old Parsonage Press 1925)

A209 ——— *Patrick Branwell Brontë* (London: A. M. Philpot Ltd 1923)
The case for Branwell Brontë's authorship of WH is carefully and calmly constructed in Chapter V, "*Wuthering Heights*—By Emily?" p 103–40, a collection of evidence for EB's not writing WH, and in Chapter VI, "*Wuthering Heights*—By Branwell?" p 141–84, a presentation of the evidence for Branwell's authorship.

A210 LAWRENCE, Margaret "The Brontë Sisters Who Wrestled with Romance" *School of Femininity* (New York: Stokes 1936) 60–88

An apt subtitle would be "The Brontës and Their Men," because, according to this author, Charlotte Brontë and EB had a romantic attachment to almost all the men they knew. Reprinted: A211.

A211 ——— "The Brontë Sisters Who Wrestled with Romance" *We Write as Women* (London: Michael Joseph Ltd 1937) 62–87
A reprinting of A210.

*A212 LAYCOCK, John W. *Methodist Heroes of the Great Haworth Round, 1734–1784* (Keighley [England]: Wadsworth & Co 1909)

A213 LEAVIS, F. R. "Note: 'The Brontës' " *The Great Tradition* (New York: George W. Stewart 1949) 27
A short note explains why he did not mention *WH* in his book: it seems to him "a kind of sport." Nevertheless, *WH* may have had some "influence of an essentially undetectable kind" on English literature.

A214 LEAVIS, Q. D. "A Fresh Approach to *Wuthering Heights*" in F. R. Leavis and Q. D. Leavis, eds *Lectures in America* (New York: Random House 1969) 84–152
Q. D. Leavis asserts that *WH* should be read as a realistic novel in the context of the Yorkshire environment, at home in its Victorian era with antecedents in Scott and Shakespeare. It is flawed because EB "...had some trouble getting free of a false start," and "the favorite Romantic theme of incest...must have been the impulsion behind the earliest conception of *Wuthering Heights....*" Nelly Dean, Joseph, and Zillah assume more importance in Leavis' new approach. To support her contentions, she includes four appendices: "The Northern Farmer, Old Style," "Violence," "Superstitions and Folklore," and "*Wuthering Heights* and 'The Bride of Lammermoor.' " Reprinted: A283.

A215 ——— "Living at the Novelists' Expense" *Fiction and the Reading Public* (New York: Russell and Russell 1932) 235–73
On p 238 there is a very brief evaluation of *WH* as it looks to the book market: it belongs to the classroom. Partially reprinted: A10.

A216 LECLAIRE, Lucein *A General Analytical Bibliography of the Regional Novelists of the British Isles, 1800–1950* (Paris: Les Belles Lettres 1954) 76–80
The bibliography lists chronologically all the editions of *WH* published through 1950, noting publisher, a preface, introduction or memoir (with author), type of illustration (with artist), whether limited edition or reissue, and whether the edition includes the poems. The regional note reads, "The atmosphere is that of West Riding of Yorkshire moors...." "Collected Editions" is a separate list of the works of the Brontë sisters with the same information about each edition. Fold–out maps of the British Isles are included.

A217 LEEMING, Glenda "Who's Who in the Brontës" *Who's Who in Jane Austen and the Brontës* (London: Elm Tree Books 1974) 83–164
A comprehensive and accurate list of all the characters created by the Brontë sisters.

A218 LEHMAN, Benjamin H. "Of Material, Subject, and Form: *Wuthering Heights*" in B. H. Lehman et al, eds *Image of the Work: Essays in Criticism* (Berkeley and Los Angeles: University of California Press 1955) 3–17

WH is not a Gothic novel; it is too universal. The material is nature and life; the subject is life renewing itself; and the form centers on Nelly Dean's character in the novel and her role as double–narrator. Reprinted: A283.

A219 LEMON, Lee T. "The Hostile Universe: A Developing Pattern in Nineteenth–Century Fiction" in George Goodin, ed *The English Novel in the Nineteenth Century: Essays on the Literary Mediation of Human Values* (Urbana: University of Illinois Press 1972) 1–13
Lemon surveys a number of classic nineteenth–century novels, characterizing the forces against which the authors pitted their heroes. As the survey moves from early to late nineteenth century, the pattern "will be one of increasing complexity, of the growing complication of those fate–determining forces...." Although admittedly a large generalization, he says, "If we can take *Wuthering Heights* as a symptom of its time, we can say that the best mid–nineteenth–century English fiction was beginning to reflect the multi–dimensioned complexity of the factors involved in human destiny...." *WH* is compared in some ways to Jane Austen's *Pride and Prejudice*, and in viewing the early part of the century, it can be said that the step from Richardson's or Fielding's world to Austen's is much smaller than the step from Austen's to Emily Brontë's. Some of the other novels examined in this context are *Jude the Obscure*, *Vanity Fair*, and some of Dickens' works.

A220 LETTIS, Richard, and William E. Morris "Introduction" and eds *A Wuthering Heights Handbook* (New York: Odyssey Press 1961) v–viii
There are several possible approaches to *WH*: the characters in the novel offer a serious challenge to the reader, and other challenges are the action of the story, the point of view, the style, the symbolism, and the imagery. The essays (see individual entries for annotation) reprinted are as follows:
"*Jane Eyre* and *Wuthering Heights*" by Virginia Woolf (A419)
"The Structure of *Wuthering Heights*" by C. P. Sanger (A324)
"*Wuthering Heights*" [From his book *Charlotte Brontë*] by E. F. Benson (A24)
"Emily Brontë and *Wuthering Heights*" by David Cecil (A51)
"*Wuthering Heights*" [From his book *The History of the English Novel*] by Ernest A. Baker (A15)
"The Dramatic Novel: *Wuthering Heights*" [From his book *Representative English Novelists*] by Bruce McCullough (A230)
"Implacable, Belligerent People of Emily Brontë's Novel *Wuthering Heights*" [Originally "Books in General"] by V. S. Pritchett (B398)
"The Brontës, or, Myth Domesticated" [Originally "The Brontës: A Centennial Observance"] by Richard Chase (B96)
"Tempest in the Soul: The Theme and Structure of *Wuthering Heights*" by Melvin R. Watson (B503)
"Introduction to *Wuthering Heights*" [Originally "Introduction"] by Mark Schorer (A327)
"Emily Brontë: *Wuthering Heights* (1847)" [From his book *An Introduction to the English Novel*] by Arnold Kettle (A192)
"On *Wuthering Heights*" [From her book *The English Novel, Form and Function*] by Dorothy Van Ghent (A374)
"Nelly Dean and the Power of *Wuthering Heights*" by John K. Mathison (B332)
"The Narrators of *Wuthering Heights*" by Carl Woodring (B523)
"Emily Brontë's Mr. Lockwood" by George J. Worth (B525)
"*Wuthering Heights*: The Land East of Eden" by Ruth M. Adams (B25)

"The Villain in *Wuthering Heights*" by James Hafley (B214)
"The Incest Theme in *Wuthering Heights*" by Eric Solomon (B455)
"Lockwood's Dreams and the Exegesis of *Wuthering Heights*" by Edgar F. Shannon, Jr (B445)
"*Wuthering Heights*: Narrators, Audience, and Message" by Allan R. Brick (B72)
"The Image of the Book in *Wuthering Heights*" by Robert C. McKibben (B319)

A221 LEVINE, George *The Realistic Imagination: English Fiction from Frankenstein to Lady Chatterley* (Chicago: University of Chicago Press 1981) 215–16 and *passim*
More or less outside the area of this study since it is closer to romance than realism, *WH* is one of the few Victorian novels which treats "the dangers of energies that lie outside the social norms"—as Heathcliff's do—not in social terms, but as a force of nature. "The space Emily Brontë finds for him is on the heights, and its accommodation to the realist's 'actual' comes only in a later generation with a tamer and more sexual sort of love."

A222 [LIVINGSTON, Luther S.] "Prefatory Note" *Poems by Charlotte, Emily, and Anne Brontë Now for the First Time Printed* (New York: Dodd, Mead 1902) v–vi
Most of these poems are EB's, and all of them are printed exactly as written with no effort made to edit them. Some are from the manuscripts written in a tiny script by the Brontës during their childhood.

A223 LOCK, John, and Canon W. T. Dixon *A Man of Sorrow: The Life, Letters and Times of the Rev. Patrick Brontë 1777–1861* (London: Nelson 1965) 367–72
EB is supposed to be her father's favorite according to this well–written, but conjectural, account.

A224 LONGFORD, Elisabeth "The Brontës" *Eminent Victorian Women* (New York: Alfred A. Knopf 1981) 29–60
The traditional Brontë story, attractively illustrated, with emphasis on family life at the parsonage, and including some conjecture.

A225 LORD, Walter Frewen "The Brontës" *The Mirror of the Century* (New York: John Lane 1906) 97–116
WH suffers in comparison to the other Brontë novels because it relies on harsh language and characters for realism. Lord has trouble "making out the story and who is telling it."

A226 LOVETT, Robert M., and H. S. Hughes "Thackeray, Trollope, The Brontës" *The History of the Novel in England* (Boston: Houghton Mifflin 1932) 256–92
There is a short discussion of *WH* on p 283–85. It is yet a mysterious novel, "clumsily introduced" and told in a "style which is Emily Brontë's own." The story is "remote from human society." EB had a "tortured spirit" that is reflected in the love of Catherine and Heathcliff; their love is "both more and less than human."

A227 LOXTERMAN, Alan S. "*Wuthering Heights* as Romantic Poem and Victorian Novel" in Frieda Elaine Penninger, ed *A Festschrift for Professor Marguerite Roberts* (Richmond: University of Richmond 1975) 87–100
WH has a dual form in that it has two plots: the love of Catherine and Heathcliff expressed in myth and symbol, and the love of Cathy and Hareton expressed in "moral terms more appropriate to the pragmatic love ethic of a Victorian novel." This essay follows these two

parallel plots which "develop contradictory philosophies of love." At the end of WH, "they perpetuate thematic ambiguity by giving the reader his choice between a Romantic apotheosis and a Victorian denouement."

*A228 LUCAS, Peter D. *An Introduction to the Psychology of* Wuthering Heights (London: Guild of Pastoral Psychology 1943)

A229 MACAULAY, Rose "Introduction" *Wuthering Heights* (New York: Modern Library 1926) v–x
A factor contributing to EB's personality and authorship of WH was the Brontë ancestry, having in it Celtic mysticism and imagination and also the conflict engendered by mixed marriages of Catholics and Protestants in North Ireland. Nelly Dean's language in WH is sometimes too literary, but Joseph's is superb. Catherine and Heathcliff are "false men and women," but the author praises EB's "effortless power for creating atmosphere."

A230 McCULLOUGH, Bruce "The Dramatic Novel" *Representative English Novelists: Defoe to Conrad* (New York: Harper and Brothers 1946) 184–96 [190–91]
To its credit, WH did not fit the conventions for a novel of its time. This author investigates the major techniques used by EB in WH and the novel's major themes. Reprinted: A220.

A231 ———— "Introduction" *Wuthering Heights* (New York: Harper and Brothers 1950) v–xix
This is an expanded and slightly altered version of Item A230, with a good survey of criticism of WH.

A232 McILWRAITH, Jean N. "Introduction" *Wuthering Heights* (New York: Doubleday, Page and Company 1907) v–xi
"WH is Shakespearean in its impersonality...." EB worked with a limited locale because "she could not paint a large canvas; her experience of life was too limited." The "taste for horrors" in WH is attributed to EB's reading the romances of Hoffmann.

A233 MAGNUS, Laurie *English Literature in the 19th Century: An Essay in Criticism* (London: Andrew Melrose 1909) 254–56
WH is merely "a forceful romance"; *Jane Eyre* is the most notable book written by the Brontë sisters.

A234 MAIS, S. P. B. *"Wuthering Heights" Why We Should Read —* (London: Richards 1921) 25–31
Catherine's unforgivable sin in marrying Edgar Linton is "the attempt to sunder the body from the soul." EB was unerring in her psychology: her minor characters, Joseph and Nelly Dean, retain their individuality, and she could depict civilized over–refined people like Edgar and Isabella as well as the half–savages at Wuthering Heights.

A235 MALHAM–DEMBLEBY, John *The Confessions of Charlotte Brontë* (Bradford [England]: Mrs. Leah Malham–Dembleby 1954) *passim*
This author contends that Charlotte Brontë wrote the poems ascribed to EB and wrote WH, principally because he finds many similarities to Charlotte Brontë's novels in WH. Charlotte Brontë also wrote everything attributed to the other Brontë children.

*A236 ———— *The Key to the Brontë Works* (London: Walter Scott 1911)
Among other allegations in this book is the one that Charlotte Brontë wrote *WH* as well as *Jane Eyre*. [Annotated from mention in *NCF*.]

A237 MARGESSON, Maud *The Brontës and Their Stars* (London: Rider 1928)
Viewed from strictly an astrological vantage point, EB is discussed on p 111–58. The planets and stars underscore EB's genius, introversion, and strong–willed individualism. The text is illustrated with astrological charts.

A238 MARSDEN, Hilda and Ian Jack, eds *Wuthering Heights* [Clarendon Edition] (Oxford [England]: Clarendon Press 1976) 513 p
A238a "Introduction" [Part 1] by Inga–Stina Ewbank, xiii–xxiv
    A discussion of the probable, possible, and actually known dates and circumstances of the writing and publication of *WH*, with a thorough history of Thomas Newby's reputation and publishing practices. The second part of the Introduction is by Ian Jack, A238b.
A238b "Introduction" [Part 2] by Ian Jack, xxiv–xxxii
    In this second section of the Introduction, Jack explicates the complex textual problems confronted by an editor attempting to produce a text of *WH* based on the 1847 Newby edition. He also discusses some of the differences between the 1847 edition and the 1850 edition and outlines the criteria employed in the production of this Clarendon edition. The first part of the Introduction is by Inga–Stina Ewbank, A238a.
A238c "Descriptive List of Editions" by Hilda Marsden and Ian Jack, xxxiii–xxxix
    The early English, American, and German (Tauchnitz) editions of *WH* are described.
A238d "Appendix I," 435–46
    This appendix consists of: "Biographical Notice of Ellis and Acton Bell," "Editor's Preface to the New Edition of *Wuthering Heights*," and "Extract from the Prefatory Note to 'Selections from Poems by Ellis Bell' " [all by Charlotte Brontë].
A238e "Selected Textual Variants from the Second Edition" by Hilda Marsden and Ian Jack, 447–77
    These are "...*1850* readings which are not recorded in the textual footnotes but which differ from *1847* (a) in substantives, or (b) in accidentals in a manner which significantly affects the sense, or the emphasis...." Also recorded are: all differences in paragraphing, a few differences in spelling, and no differences in hyphenization.
A238f "Marginal Alterations in the Clement K. Shorter Copy of *Wuthering Heights*" by Hilda Marsden and Ian Jack, 478–79
    Although it seems unlikely to the editors, there has been some conjecture that these marginal notes were written by EB or Charlotte Brontë. They are listed here with references, in brackets, to the Clarendon edition.
A238g "*Wuthering Heights* and Gondal" by Inga–Stina Ewbank, 480–86
    A brief discussion of the lost prose narrative of Gondal and the Gondal poems.
A238h "The Chronology of *Wuthering Heights*" by Inga–Stina Ewbank, 487–96
    A survey and discussion of some of the scholarly work done on the chronology in *WH*, with a chronology in list form based on C. P. Sanger's work, but incorporating the findings of A. Stuart Daley (A324 and B122).
A238i "Land Law and Inheritance in *Wuthering Heights*" by Professor E. F. J. Tucker, 497–99
    An essay describing the legal strategies employed by Heathcliff to gain his revenge, as delineated by C. P. Sanger (A324). This elaboration cites the laws and practices used in *WH* and demonstrates how they operated in the novel.

A238j "The Dialect Speech in *Wuthering Heights*" by K. M. Petyt, 500–13
   This is an excellent condensation of K. M. Petyt's *Emily Brontë and the Haworth Dialect: A Study of the Dialect Speech of* Wuthering Heights (A284), including brief sections on morphology, syntax, semantics, and vocabulary.

MARSDEN, Hilda *see* A238, A238c, A238e, A238f.

A239 MARSHALL, William H. *"Wuthering Heights" The World of the Victorian Novel* (New York: A. S. Barnes and Co 1967) 225–45
   The problem of the re–establishment of fallen order is the primary concern of *WH*, "...in effect, the central problem of the 19th century intellectual...." There are three commitments finally resulting in the ordering of disorder: (1) Mr Earnshaw's taking up Heathcliff in Liverpool, (2) Heathcliff and Catherine's invading the "strange cosmos" at Thrushcross Grange, and (3) the younger Catherine's escaping from Thrushcross Grange to the alien world of Wuthering Heights. "The relation between good and evil is thus analogous to that between insulation and commitment...." An enlightening essay, especially in regard to Hareton's position in the novel.

MARTIN, R. B. *see* A279.

A240 MASEFIELD, Muriel "The Lives of the Brontë Sisters" and "Emily Brontë's Novel" *Women Novelists from Fanny Burney to George Eliot* (London: Ivor Nicholson and Watson, Ltd 1934) 95–128, 146–52
   The first chapter stresses the importance of Mrs Gaskell's *Life of Charlotte Brontë* in any study of the Brontë sisters. The kitchen vignettes in *WH* and in Charlotte Brontë's novels are a reflection of the kitchen as a family center at Haworth Parsonage. The second chapter contains a review of *WH* criticism. Two features have made *WH* live: "the saturation of its characters...in the spirit of the moorland," and "the passion...which owes nothing to sensuality."

A241 MASSON, Flora *The Brontës* (London: T. C. and E. C. Jack 1912) *passim*
   The focus is on Charlotte Brontë.

A242 MATTHEWS, Thomas S. *The Brontës: A Study* I (Dawlesh [England]: Channing Press 1934) *passim*
   The story of the Brontë children is told, up to the end of the Brussels period, with particular attention to their endurance of financial hardships, their continual planning to better their lives, and their natural shyness which made it difficult for them to make friends. The appendix contains an essay, "The Brontë Parsonage Museum," by Marjorie Astin, p 115–18, which is a short description of the museum.

A243 MAUGHAM, W. Somerset "Emily Brontë and *Wuthering Heights*" *Great Novelists and Their Novels* (Philadelphia: Winston 1948) 115–34
   This is a reprinting of Item B333.

A244 ——— "Emily Brontë and *Wuthering Heights*" *Ten Novels and Their Authors* (London: Heinemann 1954) 204–33
   This is a slightly revised and enlarged version of Item B333.

A245 —— "Emily Brontë and *Wuthering Heights*" *Wuthering Heights* (Philadelphia: Winston 1949) vii–xxii
This is a reprinting of Item B333.

A246 MAURAT, Charlotte "A Summary of *Gondal's Queen* (taken from Fannie Ratchford's reconstruction)" *The Brontës' Secret* trans Margaret Meldrum (London: Constable 1969) 258–63 and *passim*
The essential passages of Charlotte Brontë's extant prose juvenilia and the Brontë juvenilia are the secret. The traditional Brontë story is retold, with Charlotte Brontë as the central character.

MELDRUM, Margaret *see* A246.

A247 MEWS, Hazel "Emily Brontë" *Frail Vessels: Woman's Role in Women's Novels from Fanny Burney to George Eliot* (London: The Athlone Press 1969) 80–81
The young women in *WH* are "...immature, cruel, impersonal, and neither love nor marriage softens them...." *WH* does not readily lend itself to the women's roles discussed here.

A248 MEYNELL, Alice "The Brontës" *Prose and Poetry* (London: J. Cape 1947) 97–108
This is a reprinting of Item A250.

A249 —— "Charlotte and Emily Brontë" *Essays of To–day and Yesterday* (London: George C. Harrap and Co Ltd 1926) 44–57
A reprinting of A250.

A250 —— "Charlotte and Emily Brontë" *Hearts of Controversy* (New York: Scribner's 1917) 77–99 [94–99]
A few passages in *WH* are briefly discussed, and EB's poetic art of expression in the novel is evaluated. A possible source for the disinterment in *WH* is suggested. Reprinted: A248, A249, B345, B346. Partially reprinted: A10.

MILES, Rosalind *see* A344b.

A251 MILLER, J[oseph] Hillis "Emily Brontë" *The Disappearance of God: Five Nineteenth–Century Writers* (Cambridge: Harvard University Press 1963) 157–211
This chapter is one of the best modern interpretations of EB and her work. The author explains his point of view: "Post–medieval literature records...the gradual withdrawal of God from the world," and the five writers discussed represent the culmination of the process. For EB a "God of Vision" brought about a duality of feeling: wanting to be controlled by and yet control her "God." Her view of the world derived from her reading of Romantic literature and, to a greater extent, from her childhood religious training. EB's poems, her French essay "The Butterfly," and *WH* are investigated and compared. EB's philosophy is similar to William Blake's and John Wesley's. The other writers discussed are Arnold, Browning, DeQuincey, and Hopkins. Reprinted: A379; partially reprinted: A274, A283. See B79.

A252 ———— *"Wuthering Heights:* Repetition and the 'Uncanny' " *Fiction and Rep-etition: Seven English Novels* (Cambridge: Harvard University Press 1982) 42–72; see also *passim*

A novel is interpreted in part through the identification of recurrences. "This book is an exploration of some of the ways they work to generate meaning or to inhibit the too easy determination of a meaning based on the linear sequence of the story." *WH* is permeated with "reading." Lockwood, unreliable and shallow, must "read" dead rabbits, the sermon by Jabes Branderham, Cathy's diary, Heathcliff, and Nelly's version of what happened. In her 1850 Preface to *WH*, Charlotte Brontë gives at least four incompatible readings of *WH*. Miller's argument is that the best critical readings of *WH* "will be ones which best account for the heterogeneity of the text, its presentation of a definite group of possible meanings which are systematically interconnected, determined by the text, but logically incompatible." The nar-ration manages to involve the reader's innocence or guilt because ". . .any repetitive structure of the 'uncanny' sort. . .tends to generate a sense of guilt in the one who experiences it." He is guilty if he fails to penetrate to the core of the mystery, and guilty if he reveals that which ought to remain secret. But the secret, the core of truth in *WH*, is forever elusive as EB designed it and meant it to be.

*A253 MILLER, Margaret J. *Emily: The Story of Emily Brontë* (London: Lutterworth Press 1969) 144 p

One of the "Famous Lives" series.

A254 MILLMORE, Royston *Brief Life of the Brontës* (Bradford [England]: W. R. Millmore 1947) *passim*

The traditional Brontë story, briefly told.

A255 MOERS, Ellen "Female Gothic" *Literary Women* (Garden City, N Y: Dou-bleday & Co Inc 1976) 90–110 [99–107 and *passim*]

WH is briefly compared to Christina Rosetti's *Goblin Market*, a poem about the erotic life of children. *WH* is a very serious statement about "a girl's childhood and an adult woman's tragic yearning to return to it." Catherine's childhood was brutal, but she wishes—as she is dying—to return to it.

A256 MOORE, Geoffrey "Foreword" *Wuthering Heights* (New York: New American Library 1959) v–viii

It is because EB's "romantic imagination was ballasted by a shrewd grasp of human realities" that the book has such a powerful effect."

A257 MOORE, Virginia "Emily Brontë" *Distinguished Women Writers* (New York: E. P. Dutton 1934) 109–21

A dramatic and traditional biography of EB.

A258 ———— *The Life and Eager Death of Emily Brontë* (London: Rich and Cowan 1936) 383 p

This biography of EB is somewhat histrionic and quite conjectural. One question raised is whether or not EB was lesbian, and it is answered by the possibility that she was in love with a "Louis Parensell" (now generally agreed among most scholars to be "Love's Farewell" misread on a manuscript). In addition to this, EB, because of her unhappiness, was a "virtual suicide." The author suggests that EB had an early jealousy of Branwell Brontë and assumes as fact that EB read certain books and magazines. The emphasis is on EB's introversion, loneliness, and unhappiness. However, in spite of inferences that are not supported by any known fact, the author quotes many primary sources such as Charlotte Brontë's and Ellen Nussey's letters. EB's poems are all seen as personal, even if they were written in the context of Gondal, and three new poems are printed here. One of the items in the book is a facsimile of the "Louis Parensell" manuscript. See also B231.

A259 MORGAN, Charles "Emily Brontë" in H. J. Massingham and Hugh Massingham, eds *The Great Victorians* (London: Nicholson and Watson 1932) 63–79
This is a reprinting of Item B359.

A260 ——— "Emily Brontë" *Reflections in a Mirror* (London: Macmillan 1944) 130–55
This is a reprinting of Item B359.

MORRIS, William E. *see* A220.

A261 MORTON, A. L. "Genius on the Border" *The Matter of Britain: Essays in a Living Culture* (London: Lawrence & Wishart 1966) 122–36
The Brontë children lived on a frontier, geographically as well as in time. The Brontë story is told from a socialistic point of view. For EB in *WH*, love is not purely personal as it is for most novelists, but akin to solidarity, "...like the force which binds members of a clan—or a class...."

MOSER, Mary C. *see* A262.

A262 MOSER, Thomas C. "Introduction" and ed Wuthering Heights: *Text, Sources, Criticism* (New York: Harcourt, Brace 1962) v–vi
WH has modern appeal because the technique used is extremely intricate; moreover, it deals with subjects that are of interest in our century: the problem of evil and the power of the unconscious. In addition to the text of *WH*, this book contains thirty–five of EB's poems designated as those pertaining to *WH*, and a number of critical essays, as follows:
"Biographical Notice of Ellis and Acton Bell" by Charlotte Brontë (1850)
"Editor's Preface to the New Edition of *Wuthering Heights*" by Charlotte Brontë (1850)
"Prophecy in *Wuthering Heights*" by E. M. Forster (A110)
"Introduction to *Wuthering Heights*" by Mark Schorer (A327)
"Emily Brontë: *Wuthering Heights*" by Arnold Kettle (A192)
"On *Wuthering Heights*" by Dorothy Van Ghent (A374)
"The Minor Characters" and "Eros" [From his book *Emily Brontë: Expérience spirituelle et création poétique* trans Mary C. Moser] by Jacques Blondel (C13)
> The first essay deals with the method of narration in *WH* and with the characters. The narrative keeps the reader's attention on two levels which oppose each other: that of moral, everyday people and that of abnormal people whose actions are justified by passion. The characters can be placed in three categories: actors, victims, and witnesses. These, however, are far from rigid, and a character may change from one to the other. The second, shorter essay perceptively analyzes the passion in *WH*. Passion is self–affirmative, yet paradoxically it wishes to destroy its object. (*See* A10, A283.)
"Preface to *Wuthering Heights*" by Albert J. Guerard (A140)

"What Is the Matter with Emily Jane? Conflicting Impulses in *Wuthering Heights*" by
Thomas Moser (B361)
At the end of the book are suggestions for papers and a selected bibliography.

MOTT, Joan *see* A41.

A263 MUIR, Edwin "Time and Space" *The Structure of the Novel* (New York:
   Harcourt, Brace 1929) 62–87
An excellent classification of *WH* as a novel. As *WH* relates to the author's definition of
Time and Space, it is a dramatic novel rather than a character novel, and it is a mode of seeing
life in Time personally. There follows a good discussion contrasting *WH* to *Vanity Fair* and
Tom Jones and comparing it with *The Return of the Native, Moby Dick*, and other novels.

A264 MUSSELWHITE, David "*Wuthering Heights*: The Unacceptable Text" in
   Francis Barker, John Coombes, Peter Hulme, David Musselwhite and Richard
   Osborne, eds *Literature, Society and the Sociology of Literature* (Colchester [Eng-
   land]: University of Essex 1977) 154–60
This provocative essay asserts that *WH* is about reading and mis–reading. Lockwood con-
stantly seeks to mediate the threatening and violent atmosphere at Wuthering Heights, but
fails, because he cannot accept the unacceptable. It is Nelly Dean, however, who is "the
figure of that bland literacy that prevents all reading of the self and all knowledge of the
Other. . . ." Furthermore, Joseph's speeches are quite intentionally unreadable. Musselwhite
notes that the novel is, in a sense, written three times; and ". . . the repeated story is just as
much a device for the allaying and the exorcising of the unacceptable as Nelly's blind
narration. . . ."

NAGEL, Lorine W. *see* A303.

A265 NEILL, S. Diana "Passions Spin the Plot" *A Short History of the English
   Novel* (New York: Macmillan 1952) 164–203 [171–77]
WH has something in common with a morality play because EB saw evil not as a positive
force, but as energy misdirected. The symbolism in *WH* centers on the two houses: one is
passion, the other reason.

A266 NEWSHOLME, Sir Arthur *Fifty Years in Public Health* (London: Allen and
   Unwin 1935)
Background on the Brontës is given on p 17–22. The author, whose father was a church-
warden to the Rev Patrick Brontë in Haworth, relates stories of the Brontës he heard in his
childhood. He also comments on the tuberculosis in the Brontë family.

A267 NEWTON, A. Edward "Brontë Country; My First Visit" and "Brontë Country;
   My Second Visit" *Derby Day and Other Adventures* (Boston: Little, Brown 1934)
   297–306, 307–42
The first chapter is a first–person account, written for a popular audience, of the transfer
of the Bonnell Brontë Collection to the Brontë Society and the establishment of the Brontë
Museum in Haworth Parsonage, with personal descriptions. The second chapter is an account,
in a popular vein, of the author's education about the Brontës.

A268 NICHOLSON, Norman "Introduction" *Wuthering Heights* (London: Paul Elek [Camden Classics] 1947) 5–12
WH is a poet's novel, and only in the greatest Elizabethan drama can be found such a soliloquy as Catherine's concerning the lapwing. EB made "the first great change in the substance and texture of the English novel.... she established a new form for the English novel...."

A269 NICOLL, William Robertson "The Brontës" *People and Books, from the Writings of W. Robertson Nicoll* (New York: George H. Doran Co 1926?) 255–58 [257]
A brief, appreciative personal response to *WH*.

A270 ———— "Introductory Essay" in Clement Shorter, ed *The Complete Works of Emily Brontë* I *Poetry* (London: Hodder and Stoughton 1910) xv–xlviii
Excerpts from letters and diaries by Charlotte Brontë and EB help make up the substance of a simple, condensed biography of EB. In addition, there are a review and discussion of criticism of *WH*, consideration of possible sources for *WH*, a discussion of Branwell's influence on his sisters, a contrast of the work of Charlotte, Emily, and Anne, and a discussion of EB's genius and her "personal faith or unfaith."

A271 NICOLL, William Robertson and Thomas Seccombe "The Brontës" *A History of English Literature* (New York: Dodd, Mead 1907) 1165–71 [1166–67]
"*WH*...by reason of its sincerity, its freedom from affectation, triviality, or verbiage of any kind, is, despite its imperfect or embryonic art, an almost unique book." There is also a reprinting of Henry James' short comment on the Brontës.

A272 O'BYRNE, Cathal *The Gaelic Source of the Brontë Genius* (Edinburgh and London: Sands and Company 1933) *passim*
This is a reprinting, in book form, of Item B373.

OGDEN, John *see* A31.

*A273 OLDFIELD, Jenny Jane Eyre *and* Wuthering Heights: *A Study Guide* (Exeter, N H: Heinemann Educational Books 1976)

A274 O'NEILL, Judith "Introduction" and ed *Critics on Charlotte and Emily Brontë: Readings in Literary Criticism* (London: George Allen and Unwin 1968) 7–9
The introduction briefly traces the critical history of Charlotte Brontë's novels and EB's *WH* and poems. The essays and other material pertaining to EB are only partially reprinted (see individual entries for annotation in most cases).
    "The Early Reviews" by Sydney Dobell, Lady Eastlake, and G. H. Lewes (1846, 1848, and 1850)
    "*Wuthering Heights*" [Originally "Editor's Preface to the New Edition of *Wuthering Heights*"] by Charlotte Brontë (1850)
    "*Wuthering Heights*" [From "*Jane Eyre* and *Wuthering Heights*"] by Virginia Woolf (A419)
    "The Structure of *Wuthering Heights*" by C. P. Sanger (A324)
    "The Style of *Wuthering Heights*" [From her book *The Authorship of* Wuthering Heights] by Irene Cooper Willis (A402)

"Emily Brontë's Romanticism" [From "*Wuthering Heights* after a Hundred Years"] by Derek Traversi (B487)

"The Metaphors in *Wuthering Heights*" [From "Fiction and the Matrix of Analogy"] by Mark Schorer (B439)

"The Window Image in *Wuthering Heights*" [From "On *Wuthering Heights*"] by Dorothy Van Ghent (A374)

"Nelly as Narrator" [From his book *Emily Brontë*: Wuthering Heights] by J. F. Goodridge (A129)

> Nelly's narrative has not only energy, but also a sense of reality because she uses concrete details. Goodridge explicates one passage from *WH*—Catherine's homesickness for Wuthering Heights when she is ill—to show how emphatic speech rhythms and plainness of language convince the reader of Nelly's veracity.

"The Rejection of Heathcliff?" [From "*Wuthering Heights*: The Rejection of Heathcliff?"] by Miriam Allott (B30)

"An Analysis of *Wuthering Heights*" [From "*Wuthering Heights*"] by Boris Ford (B180)

"Passion and Control in *Wuthering Heights*" by Vincent Buckley (B81)

"Infanticide and Sadism in *Wuthering Heights*" by Wade Thompson (B476)

"Themes of Isolation and Exile" [From his book *The Disappearance of God: Five Nineteenth–Century Writers*] by J. Hillis Miller (A251)

"Emily Brontë's Poetry" [From her book *The Genesis of* Wuthering Heights] by Mary Visick (A377)

A275 OSBORNE, W. A. "The Brontës in Ulster" *Essays and Literary Sketches* (Adelaide: Lothian Publishing Co 1943) 25–32; see also *passim*
This essay gives the Ulster background and the Brontë antecedents in County Down and discusses Irish, English, and Scots blood in the Brontës. Reprinted: A85.

A276 PADEN, William D. *An Investigation of Gondal* (New York: Bookman Associates 1958) 85 p
This is another version of the Gondal story, with credit given to F. E. Ratchford's work on Gondal (A301) although Paden disagrees with her. A genealogical diagram accompanies this careful, well–documented treatment of the puzzle.

A277 PALMER, Helen H. and Anne Jane Tyson *English Novel Explication: Criticisms to 1972* (Hamden, Conn: Shoe String Press Inc 1973) 22–26
Designed to supplement the checklist by Inglis F. Bell and Donald Baird, *The English Novel 1578–1956: A Checklist of Twentieth–Century Criticisms*, which covered published criticisms through 1957, this book covers English novel criticisms from 1958 to 1972. See A4 and A20.

A278 PARRISH, M. L. "The Brontë Sisters" *Victorian Lady Novelists. George Eliot, Mrs. Gaskell, The Brontë Sisters. First Editions in the Library at Dormy House, Pine Valley, New Jersey, Described with Notes* (London: Constable 1933) 79–96
This chapter contains a description of the first editions of *WH* and of *Poems by Currer, Ellis and Acton Bell*. There are 1847 and 1850 editions of *WH* and two 1846 editions of *Poems*.

A279 PARROTT, T. M., and R. B. Martin "Charlotte Brontë; Emily Jane Brontë" *A Companion to Victorian Literature* (New York: Scribner's 1955) 159–63
In this short account of both sisters' lives and works the authors say that *WH* and *Jane Eyre*

"brought to the novel an introspection and an intense concentration on the inner life of emotion which before them had been the province of poetry alone."

A280 PASSEL, Anne "Emily Brontë" *Charlotte and Emily Brontë, An Annotated Bibliography* (New York: Garland Publications 1979) 99–197; see also *passim*
A well–organized bibliography covering 122 years of Brontë criticism, and annotated for the most part, this study includes sources of primary material, nineteenth–century secondary material, and criticism on the entire Brontë family. Following a listing of primary material on EB, books and articles are categorized as: Nineteenth–Century Reviews, Criticism of *Wuthering Heights*, Criticism of Poetry, Criticism of Other Writings, General Criticism of the Writer, Textual Criticism, and Biography—Emily Brontë as a Person. The length of the annotation is indicative of the value of the work in the area of EB scholarship.

A281 PATTERSON, Charles I., Jr "Empathy and the Daemonic in *Wuthering Heights*" in George Goodin, ed *The English Novel in the Nineteenth Century: Essays on the Literary Mediation of Human Values* (Urbana: University of Illinois Press 1972) 81–96
Patterson endorses David Cecil's view of WH as neither moral nor immoral, but pre–moral containing a duality of modes; empathy is the aspect of one mode and the daemonic the aspect of the other. The power of WH lies in its success in merging the two opposites.

A282 PETERS, Maureen "Emily Alone" and "*Wuthering Heights*" *An Enigma of Brontës* (New York: St. Martin's Press 1974) 54–61, 126–34 and *passim*
This biography of the Brontës quotes from the Brontë letters owned by Mrs Jean Lewens and the manuscripts in the Haworth Parsonage Museum. "Emily Alone" describes EB as a mystic and her philosophy as "a creed which denied creed, a pantheistic view of eternal life. . . ." "*Wuthering Heights*" deals with the circumstances, as far as they are known, surrounding the writing and publication of the novel.

A283 PETIT, Jean–Pierre "Introductions" and ed *Emily Brontë: A Critical Anthology* (Harmondsworth, Middlesex: Penguin Books Ltd 1973) 344 p; 19–25, 51–59, 101–10
The anthology is divided into three sections, "Contemporaneous Criticism," "The Developing Debate," and "Modern Views," each containing selected criticism of the period on WH and the poems, and each prefaced by an introduction. Of the early reviewers, Petit says they had "sensed the novelty of *Wuthering Heights* and the natural rhythm of the poems" but refused to "yield to the spell, on grounds of taste and ethics." For "The Developing Debate," he chooses three particular writers to represent the different attitudes towards EB at the end of the century: Angus M. MacKay, William Davies, and Mrs Humphry Ward. The introduction to "Modern Views" discusses three critics, besides Mark Schorer, who influenced later studies: Richard Chase (B96), G. D. Klingopulos (B280), and Dorothy Van Ghent (included below). The following twentieth–century works are included in the anthology; some of the longer ones are abridged. See the individual entries for annotation.
"Introduction" *Wuthering Heights* by Mrs Humphry Ward (A385)
The Lesson of Balzac by Henry James (A178)
A review of *The Complete Poems of Emily Brontë* by Robert Bridges (A40)
The Three Brontës by May Sinclair (A341)
The Common Reader by Virginia Woolf (A419)
The Structure of Wuthering Heights by C. P. Sanger (A324)

Aspects of the Novel by E. M. Forster (A110)
"Emily Brontë and *Wuthering Heights*" by Lord David Cecil (A51)
The Authorship of Wuthering Heights by Irene Cooper Willis (A402)
"Fiction and the Analogical Matrix" by Mark Schorer (B439)
The English Novel: Form and Function by Dorothy Van Ghent (A374)
"Of Material, Subject, and Form: *Wuthering Heights*" by B. H. Lehman (A218)
Emily Brontë: Expérience Spirituelle et Création Poétique by Jacques Blondel trans Carole
Sherwood 135–50
> The larger part of this excerpt from the book discusses the role of nature in EB's poems
> and the sense of wonder and shattered harmony in them. Shorter sections address them-
> selves to EB's mysticism and to the role of nature in *WH*. See A10, A262, C13.

"Emily Brontë and Evil" by Georges Bataille (A18A)
The Genesis of Wuthering Heights by Mary Visick (A377)
"*Wuthering Heights*: The Rejection of Heathcliff?" by Miriam Allott (B30)
"*Wuthering Heights*: Narrators, Audience, and Message" by Allan R. Brick (B72)
Studies in the Narrative Technique of the First–Person Novel by Bertil Romberg (A317)
"Infanticide and Sadism in *Wuthering Heights*" by Wade Thompson (B476)
The Disappearance of God by J. Hillis Miller (A251)
"*Wuthering Heights*" by Frank Goodridge (A129)
"A Note on the Pattern of *Wuthering Heights*" by Ingeborg Nixon (B372)
Their Proper Sphere by Inga–Stina Ewbank (A105)
"Emily Brontë and the Metaphysics of Childhood and Love" by Irving H. Buchen (B78)
Lectures in America by Q. D. Leavis (A214)
Emily Brontë, A Critical and Biographical Study by John Hewish (A162)
"A Reading of *Wuthering Heights*" by Cecil W. Davies (B125)
"Emily Brontë: On the Latitude of Interpretation" by Denis Donoghue [with a Note on
Gondal by Jean–Pierre Petit] (A90)
"*Wuthering Heights*" by Sylvia Plath (a poem)
Included are a select bibliography and index.

——— see C17.

A284 PETYT, Keith M. *Emily Brontë and the Haworth Dialect: A Study of the
    Dialect Speech in* Wuthering Heights (Keighley, Yorkshire [England]: Yorkshire
    Dialect Society, 1970) 53 p
In *WH*, EB was recording the dialect she knew better than any other, that of Haworth.
Petyt's aim is "to examine in detail the picture of the Haworth dialect emerging from Joseph's
speech and try to assess its accuracy and consistency and the way Emily employed the English
orthography to record it." This is an extremely careful, scholarly linguistics study, probably
the most thorough one of dialect in *WH* to date. An appendix of Joseph's dialogue in *WH* is
added, from the original 1847 edition, along with a bibliography. See B281. Partially reprinted:
A238j.

——— see A238j.

A285 PHELPS, William Lyon "The Mid–Victorians" *The Advance of the English
    Novel* (New York: Dodd, Mead 1916) 104–32
This is a reprinting of Item B392.

A286 PINION, F. B. *A Brontë Companion: Literary Assessment, Background, and Reference* (London: Macmillan 1975) 55–62, 190–229 and *passim*
This illustrated compilation of Brontë material includes EB's biography, but the greater part of the book is devoted to literary assessment. EB's poems and *WH* are discussed, and of *WH*, "Emily Brontë's judgment is seen in the coherence and proportioning of her novel. She moves rapidly over less important intervals, does not hesitate to jump twelve years, and introduces nothing irrelevant."

*A287 POLLARD, A. L. "The Brontë Sisters" *Great European Novels and Novelists* (Peiping: Henri Vetch 1933) 203–10

A288 POWYS, John Cowper "Emily Brontë" *Suspended Judgments, Essays on Books and Sensations* (New York: C. Arnold Shaw 1916) 311–34
An appreciation of EB written in a dramatic manner. She is briefly compared to Walt Whitman, in that passion, in a sexual sense, in her work is carried so far that it becomes a disembodied, sexless passion.

*A289 ———— "Emily Brontë" *Essays on Emily Brontë and Henry James* (Girard, Kansas: Haldeman–Julius Co 1923) 3–23
A reprinting of A288.

A290 ———— "Emily Brontë, *Wuthering Heights*" *One Hundred Best Books with Commentary and an Essay on Books and Reading* (New York: C. Arnold Shaw 1916) 46–47
A short, appreciative account of *WH*.

*A291 PRICE, M. A. F. "The Brontë Illustrations" *Amy Morgan Price and Her Drawings* (London: The Author's Advisory Service 1927) (Privately published) 22–29

A292 PRIESTLEY, J. B. *The English Novel* (London: Ernest Benn Ltd 1927) 85
"*Wuthering Heights*. . .is a tragic prose poem on the one hand and sheer nightmare on the other. . . ." Yet, it is judged to be a work of art.

A293 PRITCHETT, V. S. "Introduction" *Wuthering Heights* (Boston: Houghton, Mifflin 1956) v–xiii
WH is the product of a mind which merged the blunt taciturnity and self–reliance of the moorland village people with their innate goodness. These are people who do not easily feel emotion, but when they do, they feel it for their lifetime. EB was unafraid to depict cruelty and torture: the elements of cruelty exist in the human soul, and the subject of *WH* is the self alone, or the soul. *WH* is Elizabethan in its intensity.

A294 QUENNELL, Peter "The Brontës" *Casanova in London and Other Essays* (London: Weidenfeld and Nicolson 1971) 81–95
A consideration of the literary works of the Brontës in relation to the lives they led. A large part of the essay is devoted to the question, "How did Emily Brontë write *Wuthering Heights*?" with some speculation about the influence Branwell may have had on its creation.

A295 ———— "Foreword" *Novels by the Brontë Sisters* (London: Pilot Press 1947) vii–xvii

If Branwell Brontë did not write part of *WH*, he certainly had much influence over its author, and the Brontës from their childhood were experienced collaborators. In *WH* the human and superhuman are merged; details of setting and lighting are appropriate and unlabored.

A296 QUENNELL, Peter and Hamish Johnson *A History of English Literature* (London: Ferndale Editions 1973) 352–57

Among the few comments on *WH*, "...the perverse and destructive passion of Catherine and Heathcliff seems more mystical than physical...."

A297 RALLI, Augustus J. "Emily Brontë: The Problem of Personality" *Critiques* (New York: Longmans, Green 1927) 1–16

This is a reprinting of Item B404.

A298 RATCHFORD, Fannie E. "Biography" *Wuthering Heights* (New York: Harper and Row 1965) v–viii

A short biography of the Brontë family with attention given to the growth of *Jane Eyre* out of Angria and of *WH* out of Gondal.

A299 —— *The Brontës' Web of Childhood* (New York: Columbia University Press 1941)

This is the most authoritative study to date of the Brontës' childhood and their plays. EB: Chapters IX, XIII, XVII, XX, XXI, XXII, XXIII *et passim*. Appendix I is concerned with "Reconstructing Gondal," and Appendix III is "A List of Gondal Personal Names and Initials." A valuable aspect of this study of the juvenile manuscripts is that it points out their influence on the later writings. "Emily's one point of superiority was her full surrender to the creative spirit which Charlotte fought with all the strength of her tyrannical conscience." A bibliography of the Brontë manuscripts lists those of EB's poems, their location, and the location of the journal fragments and the birthday notes. *See* B143.

A300 —— "The Gondal Story" in C. W. Hatfield, ed *The Complete Poems of Emily Jane Brontë* (New York: Columbia University Press 1941) 14–19

Hatfield's presentation of the poems "reveals that the majority, perhaps all of them, pertain to...Gondal." This conclusion would discourage subjective interpretation of EB's poems. Accompanied by a chronological outline, there is an arrangement of the poems as an epic of Gondal.

A301 —— *Gondal's Queen: A Novel in Verse by Emily Jane Brontë* (Austin: University of Texas Press and Thomas Nelson 1955) 207 p

This well–known work is the formulation of the Gondal story from EB's poems and is based on the hypothesis that all the poems are related to Gondal. The author says, "the plot sequence of the poems and my own narrative prose links...are based on first–hand records, including all known literary remains of the four young Brontës." She presents a convincing case, although she does lean rather heavily on parallels in Gondal and Angria, in some instances, to support her premises. Gondal embodies "...on Emily's part a conscious and studied antithesis of philosophy and moral judgment advanced, no doubt, in protest against fallacies of the earlier creation [Angria]." The heroines of the Gondal poems are actually one heroine with several names.

A302 —— "Introduction" *Wuthering Heights* (New York: Harper and Row 1962) xi–xiv

This brief history of *WH* publication also mentions major criticism of the novel and traces the publications of EB's poems.

A303 ——— "Introduction and Notes" *Five Essays Written in French by Emily Jane Brontë* trans Lorine W. Nagel (El Paso: University of Texas Press 1948) 5–8

The essays, written in Brussels while EB was studying with M Heger "are in a very real sense autobiographical, sketching the fullest and clearest self–portrait we have of Emily." The introduction also gives the circumstances under which the essays were written and the dates of their composition. The essays are titled: "The Cat," "Portrait: King Harold on the Eve of the Battle of Hastings," "Filial Love," "A Letter from One Brother to Another," and "The Butterfly." See A122, B17, B109, B288, B289.

A304 ——— *Letters of Thomas J. Wise to John Henry Wrenn: A Further Inquiry into the Guilt of Certain Nineteenth–Century Forgers* (New York: Knopf 1944)

Thomas J. Wise, book collector and one of the editors of the Shakespeare Head Brontë, was discovered to be a forger. EB's manuscripts are not involved in the forgeries, but are concerned in Wise's collecting (p 23, 162–63, and 478).

A305 ——— *Two Poems "Love's Rebuke" and "Remembrance" by Emily Brontë: With the Gondal Background of Her Poems and Novel* (Austin, Texas: Charles E. Martin, Jr—Von Boeckmann–Jones 1934) (A limited, signed edition of 60 copies.)

In the section entitled "Gondal: The Background of the Poems" (25 p, unpaginated), the author asserts that they are the key to the whole of EB's writings. The first poem is a lover's accusation and the second is a sweetheart's answer. The nucleus of EB's life and genius was the Gondal story, and EB's poems are closely related to *WH*.

A306 RAYMOND, Ernest "The Brontë Legend, Its Cause and Treatment" in Joseph Bard, ed *Essays by Divers Hands, Being the Transactions of the Royal Society of Literature of the United Kingdom* n s 26 (London: Oxford University Press 1953) 127–41

"Almost every book on the Brontës is a fight . . ." and some of the people connected with the Brontës have been maligned by the biographers. This is a good defense of Mr Brontë, Aunt Branwell, and M and Mme Heger.

A307 ——— *In the Steps of the Brontës* (London: Rich and Cowan 1948) *passim*

This is a modern story of the Brontës, especially related to scenery and locale. The "Introductory" provides a full discussion of what biographers have written about the Brontës in the past. The family legends she heard at Law Hill probably gave EB her ideas for *WH*. EB's poems are quoted to give a picture of her character, personality, and mysticism.

A308 READ, Herbert "Charlotte and Emily Brontë" *Collected Essays in Literary Criticism* (London: Faber 1938) 280–98

This is a reprinting of Item B414.

A309 ——— "Charlotte and Emily Brontë" *Nature of Literature* (New York: Horizon Press 1956) 280–98

This is a reprinting of Item B414.

A310 ——— "Charlotte and Emily Brontë" *Reason and Romanticism* (London: Faber and Gwyer 1926) 159–85
This is a reprinting of Item B414.

A311 ——— "The Writer and His Region" *The Tenth Muse: Essays in Criticism* (London: Wyman and Sons 1957) 66–74 [69–71]
The universal and the particular are discussed as they are related to the moors and exemplified in *WH*.

A312 REED, Walter L. "Brontë and Lermontov: The Hero In and Out of Time" *Meditations on the Hero: A Study of the Romantic Hero in Nineteenth–Century Fiction* (New Haven: Yale University Press 1974) 85–137
Although Lermontov was influenced by Pushkin, Schiller, and Goethe, "...the greatest impact on his own writing was made by Byron. It is his preoccupation with Byron that gives him something in common with Brontë and provides some historical basis for a comparison of *A Hero in Our Time* with *Wuthering Heights*." Also, he, like EB, drew on Scott's *The Black Dwarf*, and they were both fascinated with "a Romantic hero's proximity to the Gothic villain." Reed goes far beyond these parallels into the philosophical ideas and writings of Pechorin, Goethe, Dostoyevsky, and Kierkegaard, among others.

A313 REEVES, James, ed *Five Late Romantic Poets: George Darley, Hartley Coleridge, Thomas Hood, Thomas Lovell Beddoes, Emily Brontë* (London: Heinemann 1974) 161–65 and *passim*
The minor poetry of the Romantic period is of little interest today. There is no collective Romantic poet, and no "school" of Romantic Poetry, yet these five poets represent significant minor poetry of the early nineteenth century worthy of attention. "... [T]hese poets were in a sense unfulfilled... but they were dedicated, and they had something to say...." Twenty–one of EB's poems were chosen to be printed here, with commentary and notes by Reeves. Her poems have "a Blake–like intensity and immediacy."

A314 REID, Stuart J. *Memoirs of Sir Wemyss Reid 1842–1885* (London: Cassell and Company 1905)
EB is mentioned several times, p 229–41, as Wemyss Reid's contribution to the interpretation of Brontë literature is reviewed.

*A315 RHYS, E. "Introduction" *Wuthering Heights* (New York: E. P. Dutton & Co 1907)

A316 ROBERTS, Mark "The Dilemma of Emily Brontë" *The Tradition of Romantic Morality* (New York: Barnes & Noble 1973) 156–97
The tragedy in *WH*, like that in so many Greek tragedies, moves from one generation to the next until it burns itself out. The core of *WH*, however, is a tension between Romantic "energy of the soul" and its opposite, a kind of "ecstasy of peace." Roberts attempts to show that EB endorses neither of these attitudes "...because she presents the strengths and weaknesses of the two opposing views with such imaginative power...." John Osborne must have had *WH* in mind when he wrote the play, *Look Back in Anger*; the two works are compared. The supernatural element in *WH* is also discussed.

A317 ROMBERG, Bertil "Who Narrates the First–Person Novel?" *Studies in the Narrative Technique of the First–Person Novel* (Stockholm: Almqvist & Wiksell 1962) 58–81 [65–66]; see also *passim*
WH is an example of the Chinese box as a narrative pattern. Mr Lockwood is the first–person narrator, but he is dependent on Nelly Dean, a secondary narrator, who is in turn reporting what was said or written by tertiary narrators (Isabella and Heathcliff). Reprinted: A283.

A318 ROMIEU, Emilie, and Georges Romieu *Three Virgins of Haworth: Being an Account of the Brontë Sisters* trans Roberts Tapley (New York: E. P. Dutton 1930)
According to this emotional and sentimental treatment of the traditional Brontë story, the sisters were unable to love and be loved because they were deprived of their mother in very early childhood.

ROMIEU, Georges *see* A318.

A319 ROSENGARTEN, Herbert J. "The Brontës" in George H. Ford, ed *Victorian Fiction: A Second Guide to Research* (New York: The Modern Language Association of America 1978) 172–203 [191–203]
Designed as a sequel to the Lionel Stevenson Guide (A58) which covers criticism of Victorian fiction before 1963, this volume covers the years 1962–1974. It is noted that since 1962, there has been a veritable "Victorian novel boom" in literary criticism. Rosengarten provides an excellent, comprehensive survey of recent criticism on EB and includes sections on manuscripts, editions, translations, and dramatic adaptations.

A320 ROWSE, A. L. "Afternoon at Haworth Parsonage" *The English Past: Evocations of Persons and Places* (London: Macmillan 1951) 143–64
An account of a personal visit to Haworth includes descriptions of the church and the weather and retells the Brontë story.

RUDOLF, Anthony *see* A18.

SAGAR, Keith *see* A344d.

A321 SAINTSBURY, George *The English Novel* (New York: E. P. Dutton 1913) 243
WH is mentioned as follows: "*Wuthering Heights* is one of those isolated books which, whatever their merit, are rather ornaments than essential parts in novel history." This is not true, however of the works of Charlotte Brontë. Both the sisters made a contribution to the history of the novel in that they kept the novel and romance together.

A322 SALE, William M., Jr, ed Wuthering Heights: *An Authoritative Text with Essays in Criticism* (New York: W. W. Norton 1963)
This edition of WH is based on the 1847 first edition and is a product of modern textual bibliography. The preface explains the edition, and the book also contains the following very helpful information: "Textual Commentary" 267–69; "Notes to the Text" 269–71; Appendix I, "A Note on Emily Brontë's Spelling and Capitalization" 271; Appendix II, "The Yorkshire Dialect" 272; Appendix III, "Emily Brontë's Copy of *Wuthering Heights*" 273–74; "Contemporary Reviews" 277–85; "Essays in Criticism" (see below) 286–378; and "Emily Brontë and

Wuthering Heights: A Selected Bibliography" 379–80. The essays, annotated under the individual entries, are as follows:

"The Structure of *Wuthering Heights*" by C. P. Sanger (A324)

"Emily Brontë and *Wuthering Heights*" [In part] by David Cecil (A51)

"The Genesis of *Wuthering Heights*" [From her book *The Genesis of* Wuthering Heights] by Mary Visick (A377)

"Theme and Conventions in *Wuthering Heights*" by Clifford Collins (B103)

"Nelly Dean and the Power of *Wuthering Heights*" by John K. Mathison (B332)

"The Narrators of *Wuthering Heights*" by Carl Woodring (B523)

"Fiction and the Analogical Matrix" [Originally "Fiction and the Matrix of Analogy"] by Mark Schorer (B439)

"Emily Brontë and Freedom" [From his book *Notable Images of Virtue*] by C. Day–Lewis (A82)

*A323 ——— ed, Wuthering Heights, *Revised; An Authoritative Text, with Essays in Criticism* (New York: W. W. Norton 1972) 382 p

A324 S[ANGER], C[harles] P[ercy] *The Structure of* Wuthering Heights (London: Hogarth Press 1926) 23 p

This work is one of the milestones in the progress of *WH* criticism. *WH* characters have "a pedigree of. . .absolute symmetry," and it is printed here to prove the point. Not only the dates in the pedigree, but all dates in the story (nearly one hundred) are accurately interrelated. Mr Sanger, a lawyer, is quite qualified to comment on the English points of law bearing on the plot, and he pronounces them flawless: The laws of entail and inheritance are strictly observed. A chronology is also printed with the essay. Reprinted: A104, A136, A220, A283, A322, A379. Partially reprinted: A10, A274. See: A238h, A238i, B102, B122, B354, B396.

A325 SCHORER, Mark "Fiction and the Analogical Matrix" and "Technique as Discovery" in J. W. Aldridge, ed *Critiques and Essays on Modern Fiction, 1920–1951* (New York: Ronald Press 1952) 83–98, 67–82

The first essay is a reprinting of Item B439 originally entitled "Fiction and the Matrix of Analogy." The second essay is a reprinting of Item B440.

A326 ——— "Fiction and the Analogical Matrix" *The World We Imagine* (New York: Farrar, Straus and Giroux 1968) 24–45

A reprinting of B439.

A327 ——— "Introduction" *Wuthering Heights* (New York: Rinehart and Company 1950) v–xviii

In writing *WH*, EB is emerging from her Gondal, a world of "unmoral passion," to the real world, which is a moral world. *WH* is a work of edification in which it seems the "cloddish" characters triumph at the end. The power of the book is that "yet the triumph is not all on the side of convention." The structure and the metaphors of the novel are also discussed. Reprinted: A220, A262.

A328 SCHWEIK, Robert C. "Introduction" [and appendix] *Wuthering Heights* (Bronxville, N Y: Cambridge Book Co 1968) i–viii, 365–72

A "significant index of Emily Brontë's ability as a novelist may be found in the unusual arrangement of the events of the story and in her choice of narrators." The appendix, "A Critical, Biographical and Illustrated Folio of Emily Brontë," contains short selected critical comments, a chronology, and several reproductions.

A329 SEAWARD, M. R. D. "Introduction" *Poems by the Brontë Sisters* (East Ardsley [England]): E. P. Publishing Ltd 1978) v–xii
(This edition is a reprint of that published by Smith, Elder in London in 1848 with the imprint date 1846.) The history of the first and second publications of the poems is recounted in detail, giving bibliographical descriptions of editions, printing costs, prices, other circumstances of publication, and a discussion of the problems involved in authentication of the original binding. See B184, B225.

SECCOMBE, Thomas *see* A271.

A330 SEDGWICK, Eve Kosofsky "Immediacy, Doubleness, and the Unspeakable: *Wuthering Heights* and *Villette*" *The Coherence of Gothic Conventions* (New York: Arno Press 1980) 104–53
Sedgwick uses Catherine's quality of "intense will toward directness" to begin a discussion of "the Gothic structure as it appears in the linguistic world of the novel and its characters." Catherine's use of language reflects her strong will; and in *WH* the faces of the characters have great significance. Also, the "reintegration" in the second half of the novel is discussed.

A331 SHARP, William "The Brontë Country" *Literary Geography* (London: Pall Mall Publications 1904) 106–24
This is a description of the Yorkshire area, interspersed with quotes from *WH* and Charlotte Brontë's novels.

A332 SHERRY, Norman *Charlotte and Emily Brontë* (London: Evans Bros 1969) 101–38
A short chapter on EB's poetry and two longer chapters on *WH* serve the aim of the "Literature in Perspective" series, which is to give a straightforward account of literature and writers.

SHERWOOD, Carole *see* A283.

A333 SHORTER, Clement "A Bibliographical Note" *The Complete Works of Emily Brontë* I *Poetry* (London: Hodder and Stoughton 1910) v–vi
Before the appearance of the Shorter volume, only thirty–nine of EB's poems had been published: twenty–two in *Poems by Currer, Ellis and Acton Bell*, and another seventeen in the poems printed by Charlotte Brontë after EB's death. One hundred thirty–eight additional poems are included in this volume.

A334 ———— *The Brontës and Their Circle* (New York: E. P. Dutton [1917?])
Material relating to EB is on p 132–63. This book contains letters of the Brontës that were not available to Mrs Gaskell when she wrote *The Life of Charlotte Brontë* — Charlotte Brontë's letters which refer to EB, two letters written by EB to Ellen Nussey, and some diary papers.

A335 ———— *The Brontës: Life and Letters* (London: Hodder and Stoughton 1908) *passim*

Subtitled "Being an attempt to present a full and final record of the lives of the three sisters, Charlotte, Emily, and Anne Brontë from the biographies of Mrs. Gaskell and others, and from numerous hitherto unpublished manuscripts and letters," this work contains primary source material such as the diary papers of 1841 and 1845, two of EB's letters to Ellen Nussey, and Charlotte Brontë's letters to Ellen Nussey and W. S. Williams concerning EB's illness and subsequent death. The emphasis, however, is on Charlotte Brontë. Reprinted: A84.

A336 ———— "Introduction" and ed *The Complete Works of Emily Brontë* II *Prose* (London: Hodder and Stoughton 1911) v–xvii
Charlotte Brontë was the center of the Brontë literary picture when Mrs Gaskell published her biography, and Charlotte used her popularity to bring EB to the front also. The author discusses at length his editing of EB's poems in Vol I and defends his policy of not correcting the poems. *WH*, as printed here, follows the first edition, and Joseph's dialect as amended by Charlotte Brontë is printed in footnotes. He suggests Patrick Brontë's early experiences in Ireland as a source for *WH*. Charlotte Brontë worked from models, but EB did not at all: her "genius was entirely introspective." The last part of the introduction discusses Mary F. Robinson's biography of EB.

A337 SHOWALTER, Elaine *A Literature of Their Own: English Women Novelists from Brontë to Lessing* (Princeton: Princeton University Press 1977) *passim*
"Coarseness" to Victorian readers could refer to "Damns" in *Jane Eyre* and the dialect in *WH*. *WH* is included in this treatment of English women novelists, but more attention is given to Charlotte Brontë because *WH* was not very widely read in the nineteenth century.

SILL, L. M. *see* A86.

A338 SIMPSON, Charles *Emily Brontë* (London: Country Life 1929) 205 p
This is one of the best biographies of EB, written "in the manner of a novelist," but he is not afraid to say "may have" instead of "must have." The biography is interwoven with local scenery and history—with Haworth, the moors, and the people concerned in EB's life. A family history and star–crossed romance at Law Hill, where EB taught, are suggested as partial sources for *WH*. This book is original in that the author attempts to reconstruct, chronologically, EB's life, not as it has always been supposed to have been, but—on the basis of the evidence—as it may have been. Mr Simpson argues convincingly that EB may have taught at Law Hill in Southowram a much longer period of time than has been believed, and that this experience could have had a great effect on her maturity and her writing. EB's poetry is compared with that of Ruysbroeck, St John of the Cross, Wordsworth, and Coleridge. *WH* is discussed with reference to C. P. Sanger's *The Structure of* Wuthering Heights (see A324). The contents of EB's desk (the early reviews of *WH* and Newby's letter) are described. This biography was reissued in 1977 by Folcroft Library Editions, Folcroft, Pennsylvania, and in 1978 by Norwood Editions, Norwood, Pennsylvania.

A339 SINCLAIR, May "Introduction" *Wuthering Heights* (London: J. M. Dent and Sons 1921) vii–xiii
This account of EB and her work is told in an admiring manner. EB is compared with Charlotte Brontë in terms of personality, fame, and authorship. EB's poems were precursory to *WH*, and it is in them that we see EB's "vision of life as she wishes it." Reprinted: A340.

A340 —— "Introduction" *Wuthering Heights* (London: J. M. Dent and Sons 1922) v–xi

This is a reprinting of Item A339.

A341 —— *The Three Brontës* (London: Hutchinson and Co 1912)

EB appears throughout this book, but she and her work are discussed in detail on p 165–240. The evidence supporting the author's conclusions about EB is authentic because it comes from Charlotte Brontë, Ellen Nussey, and the servants at the Parsonage. May Sinclair agrees with Maeterlinck's conception of EB as one whose "experience" took place in her heart if not in her life; she was a mystic with the power to weld love for earthly experience together with divine vision. EB's poems are discussed in relation to Gondal; the germs for *WH* are in them. There is a thorough treatment of *WH* that sees the roles of Nelly Dean and Lockwood as negligible and points out Heathcliff's relative passivity in "letting" evil occur. *WH* belongs to no school; it is on the same mystic plane as the poems. (See also A63.) Partially reprinted: A283.

*A342 —— *The Three Brontës* 2nd ed (London: Hutchinson and Co 1914)

This is a new edition of Item A341, with a new preface.

A342A SITWELL, Edith "Emily Brontë: 1818–1848" *English Women* (London: William Collins 1902) 35–36

A short biographical sketch emphasizing EB's retiring manner and quiet demeanor among people she did not know well.

A343 SKILTON, D. "Victorian Views of the Individual: The Brontës, Thackeray, Trollope and George Eliot" *The English Novel: Defoe to the Victorians* (Barnes & Noble 1977) 136–62 [136–38]

WH is described in terms of providing the fullest development of passions and impulses of the romantic individual.

A344 SMITH, Anne "Introduction: Towards a New Assessment" and ed *The Art of Emily Brontë* (New York: Barnes & Noble 1976) 7–29

The "new assessment" abolishes the earlier ideas that (1) *WH* is some kind of unique novel outside literary tradition, and (2) that EB's poetry is mere juvenilia with no value toward a study of *WH*. The new idea, supported by studies in the book, is "that Emily Brontë was a conscious artist, far ahead of her time." The characterizations of Lockwood and Nelly Dean are examined in depth, with their key roles seen as furthering the action and sharpening contrasts for the love story.

All the essays are published here for the first time:

A344a Grove, Robin " 'It Would Not Do': Emily Brontë as Poet" 33–67

EB, despite Charlotte's allegations to the contrary, did take responsibility for her own literary career and met the demands of publishing most admirably. Among other aspects of the poems discussed are the stance of defiance and the status of the persona. EB returned again and again to the pattern; the prison, love betrayed, the victor and the vanquished in the wars. An appendix lists the twenty–one poems contributed to the published *Poems*, shown by evidence to have been chosen, adapted, and titled by EB herself.

A344b Miles, Rosalind "A Baby God: The Creative Dynamism of Emily Brontë's Poetry" 68–93

Two sources are suggested for EB's enigmatic quality: (1) she was a determinedly private individual, and (2) the Gondal saga was of great importance in her life and poetry. Her poetic creations are compared briefly to works of Browning and Shakespeare, but the similarities are true only up to a point. "Hers was a ventriloquial gift, not a dramatic one...she played the 'baby god' with the inhabitants of her created world; and a tyrannical one, too...."

A344c Hardy, Barbara "The Lyricism of Emily Brontë" 94–118

"Just as the passions of *Wuthering Heights* prove and particularize abstractions, so too does her poetry...." Although EB did write love poetry, she usually wrote poetry expressing experiences of nature, religion, and death, and she joins these in an exploration of the nature of the Imagination.

A344d Sagar, Keith "The Originality of *Wuthering Heights*" 121–59

In this thorough investigation of *WH*, Sagar shows its originality by comparing an early passage with a similar one in *Adam Bede*, underscoring EB's "utter contempt for the proprieties of her sex, art and time." He also discusses the total absence in *WH* of any social community, the hostile reception the novel received from contemporary critics, and the striking modernity of *WH*.

A344e Goodridge, J. F. "A New Heaven and a New Earth" 160–81

WH is compared to Scott's novels and to the works of Byron, Hoffmann, Poe, and Dostoyevsky, leading to the point that such derivational theories are specious because they may limit our appreciation of the novel's range of meaning. The qualities of feeling in *WH* are universal. Goodridge also treats the concept of love in *WH* in relation to Platonism, Christianity, myth, and the European literature of courtly love.

A344f Tristram, Philippa " 'Divided Sources' " 182–204

Like William Blake, EB was convinced of the validity of "the innocent vision of childhood," a validity which adult experience cannot erase. "Both writers...glimpse, at least as vision, some further state of innocence in which these contraries are reconciled...."

A344g Apter, T. E. "Romanticism and Romantic Love in *Wuthering Heights*" 205–22

"*WH* is a study of romantic love undertaken by a Romantic imagination, but it contains a serious study of the destructive elements within the magnetism of anguish and passion...and projects a far more original and useful resolution of irrational passion and morality than death while nonetheless expressing sympathy with that old Romantic solution...." Apter goes on to show that "the reality of passion" is the central theme in *WH*.

A344h Wilson, Colin "A Personal Response to *Wuthering Heights*" 223–37

"...*Wuthering Heights* should be classified with *Le Grand Meaulnes*, as a piece of brilliant juvenilia.... Curiously haunting, perhaps, but only a rough sketch for the masterpiece that should have followed...." Wilson agrees with Margaret Lane that "Emily Brontë's view of mankind was...profoundly pessimistic..." and excludes her from the company of great novelists.

A345 SMITH, J. C. "Emily Brontë—A Reconsideration" in O. Elton, ed *Essays and Studies by Members of the English Association* (Oxford: Clarendon 1914) 132–52

The publication of EB's *Complete Poems* in 1910 sheds more light on the Gondal chronicle, but it is as yet unclear. The newly–discovered poems contain "A Farewell to Gondal"; thus it seems that at this point EB is ready to write *WH*. *WH* is clumsy, but its greatness lies in its mysticism.

———— *see* A138.

SMITTEN, Jeffrey R. *see* A4.

A346 SPACKS, Patricia Meyer "The Adolescent as Heroine" *The Female Imagination* (New York: Avon Books 1975) 171–90; see also *passim*
EB's complex perspective perceives the contradictory values and appeals of the two Catherines and recognizes the atmosphere of diminishment around the younger woman's development as well as the importance of that development. In this discussion of female adolescence, other novels examined are *Pride and Prejudice, Emma, Camilla,* and *The Bell Jar.* Esther in *The Bell Jar* is compared to Catherine Earnshaw; both heroines value themselves for their inability to adjust to an adult world.

A347 SPARK, Muriel "Introduction" *The Brontë Letters* (London, Nevill 1954) 11–26
The general background of the letters and manuscripts printed in the book is discussed here. The book contains EB's journal fragment, two birthday notes, and one of her letters to Ellen Nussey.

A348 ———— "Introduction" *A Selection of Poems by Emily Jane Brontë* (London: Grey Walls Press 1952) 9–19
Swinburne noted three of the most important factors in EB's work: her instinctiveness, her primitive nature–worship, and her passion. These factors are developed in this essay as they relate to EB's poetry.

A349 SPARK, Muriel and Derek Stanford *Emily Brontë, Her Life and Work* (London: Peter Owen 1953) 271 p
Part I, a biography of EB by Muriel Spark, deliberately separates fact from legend and relates the life story based on facts, not on conjecture. Part II by Derek Stanford logically and precisely reviews the criticism of EB, her poems, and *WH.*

A350 SPURGEON, Caroline F. E. "Philosophical Mystics" *Mysticism in English Literature* (Cambridge [England]: At the University Press 1913) 72–110 [80–84]
EB's poems portray her mysticism in two ways: "...her unerring apprehension of values, of the illusory quality of material things,...and a certain vision of the one Reality behind all forms...." She is placed with Blake and Wordsworth.

STANFORD, Derek *see* A349.

A351 STEVENSON, Lionel "Social Consciousness" *The English Novel* (Boston: Houghton, Mifflin 1960) 274–76
This is a brief discussion of EB's poetry and of *WH,* with attention to the point of view provided by the double narrative in *WH.*

———— *see* A68.

A352 STEVENSON, W. H. *Emily and Anne Brontë* (New York: Humanities Press 1968) *passim*

One of the "Profiles in Literature" series introducing the student or general reader to authors. Some aspects of *WH* investigated are the violence in the novel, and structure, characterization, speech, and recurrent imagery.

A353 STONE, Donald D. *The Romantic Impulse in Victorian Fiction* (Cambridge: Harvard University Press 1980) 41–44
WH is briefly compared to the works of Bulwer Lytton. The elements they have in common are supernatural occurrences, self–willed characters, charged romantic landscapes, and a love that transcends death. EB is perceived as "the Romantic novelist par excellence."

*A354 STONEMAN, P. M. "The Brontës and Death: Alternatives to Revolution" in Francis Barker, John Coombes, Peter Hulme, David Musselwhite, and Richard Osborne, eds *Literature, Society and the Sociology of Literature* (Colchester [England]: University of Essex 1977) 79–96

*A355 STORY, T. W. *Notes on the Old Haworth Registers* (A. E. Hall, Haworth Printing Works 1909) 45–49
The author is The Reverend T. W. Story, M. A., Rector of Haworth.

A356 STUART, Dorothy M. "Much Exposed to Authors" in N. Hardy Wallis, ed *Essays by Divers Hands: Being the Transactions of the Royal Society of Literature*, n s 30 (Oxford: Oxford University Press 1960) 19–35 [32–33]
The essay mentions the Duke of Wellington as he appeared in the Brontës' childhood plays.

A357 SUGDEN, K. A. R. *A Short History of the Brontës* (London: Oxford University Press 1929) *passim*
This history was written because "people are beginning to write fanciful tales" about the Brontës. The author delineates five problems related to the Brontës, including the theory that EB did not write *WH*, and the "enigma" of EB and her work.

A358 SUMNER, Chris *Reflections on the Brontës in Spen Valley & District* (C. Sumner [England]: 1973?) *passim*
Photographs, sketches, and maps are used to illustrate this local history of the valley.

A359 SUTHERLAND, J. A. *Victorian Novelists and Publishers* (Chicago: University of Chicago Press 1976) *passim*
A clear and detailed description of the kind of publishing world which existed in Victorian England at the time the Brontës were writing and trying to publish.

A360 SYMINGTON, J. Alexander *Catalogue of the Museum & Library, The Brontë Society* (New York: Burt Franklin 1968) *passim*
Originally published at Haworth in 1927, the catalogue lists manuscripts and books at the Museum, among them "Books owned by the Brontës." Also listed are dresses, furniture, crockery, drawings and watercolors, miscellaneous personal relics, and engravings and portraits.

——— see A416 and A417.

A361 SYMONS, Arthur "Emily Brontë" *Dramatis Personae* (Indianapolis: Bobbs, Merrill 1923) 45–51
This is a reprinting of Item B471.

A362 ——— "Emily Bronte" *Figures of Several Centuries* (New York: E. P. Dutton & Co. 1916) 109–14

A paean to the poetry of EB. Her poems are all outcries, and *WH* one long outcry. Similar to B471.

A363 ——— "Introduction" *Poems of Emily Brontë* (London: Heinemann 1906) v–x

Symons sees "a sense, not of delight, but of the pain and ineradicable sting of personal identity" in EB's poems. She is a tragic figure whose "every poem is as if torn from her."

TAPLEY, Roberts *see* A318.

A364 THOMAS, Edward "Emily Brontë" *A Literary Pilgrim in England* (London: J. Cape 1928) 269–74

This description of EB's "country" focuses on her love for it, a feeling which is supported by Charlotte Brontë's statements. The author also points out the moorland in her poetry and *WH*.

A365 TILLOTSON, Geoffrey "Charlotte and Emily Brontë" *A View of Victorian Literature* (Oxford [England]: Clarendon Press 1978) 187–225 [202–25]

EB's material for *WH* was strange, as she herself realized, and it therefore had to be mixed with the familiar to soften it. Tillotson emphasizes that it was not strange to a northerner, only to southerners. The beginning of the book is "southern" and familiar. Lockwood is a southerner, and EB uses him, Nelly Dean, and Isabella as screens so that she can maintain her own reserve as narrator. The characters in *WH* are measured against "Thackerayan truth," and Heathcliff is seen as existing "in essence in Thackeray's Barry Lyndon."

A366 TILLOTSON, Kathleen *Novels of the Eighteen–Forties* (Oxford: Oxford University Press 1954) *passim*

In the author's introductory chapter *WH* is used as an example of past–dating or past–setting employed in a novel to produce "aesthetic distance, underlining the distancing effect of Mr. Lockwood and Nelly Dean."

A367 TINKER, Chauncey Brewster "The Poetry of the Brontës" *Essays in Retrospect: Collected Articles and Addresses* (New Haven: Yale University Press 1948) 52–61

This is a reprinting of Item B483.

A368 TOBIN, Patricia Drechsel "*Wuthering Heights*: Myth and History, Repetition and Alliance" *Time and the Novel: The Genealogical Imperative* (Princeton: Princeton University Press 1978) 38–42

This is a section within a chapter titled "Subverting the Father: Some Nineteenth–Century Precursors." Among some others in the nineteenth century, the novels *WH*, *Pierre*, and *The Way of All Flesh* refuse the paternal narrative. "Although all three have the form of the generational novel, they nonetheless feature families irregular in nature and nurture, times that are negations of and alternatives to historical time, and narrative structures in which the endings somehow disconfirm the beginnings." *WH* could not possibly move linearly because Catherine and Heathcliff are the childhood of the race, and Cathy and Hareton the adults.

A369 TRAVERSI, Derek "The Brontë Sisters and *Wuthering Heights*" in Boris Ford, ed *From Dickens to Hardy: Pelican Guide to English Literature* VI (Baltimore: Penguin Books 1958) 256–73
The author emphasizes the imaginative qualities of Charlotte Brontë and EB. The spirit of concentration found in EB's poetry is also in *WH* and intensifies the "personal" or romantic theme. A second theme is "social" and is reflected in the contrast between Wuthering Heights and Thrushcross Grange. The second part of this essay is similar to the author's "*Wuthering Heights* after a Hundred Years" (B487). Reprinted: A379.

A370 TRILLING, Lionel "The Poems of Emily Brontë" in Diana Trilling, ed *Speaking of Literature and Society* (New York: Harcourt, Brace, Jovanovich 1980) 3–6
This is a collection of previously uncollected writings of Lionel Trilling; this chapter was written in 1924. EB's triumph in her poetry was that she broke through the barriers of a "...tough crust of triteness and...an idiom of poetic imagery worn to almost meaningless abstraction...." Her fame as a novelist is overshadowed by Charlotte Brontë.

TRISTRAM, Philippa *see* A344f.

TUCKER, Professor E. F. J. *see* A238i.

A371 TURNER, David R. *Emily Brontë's* Wuthering Heights (New York: Arco Books 1970) 59 p
A study guide.

TURNER, John R. *see* A424.

A372 TWITCHELL, James B. *The Living Dead: A Study of the Vampire in Romantic Literature* (Durham, N C: Duke University Press 1981) 116–22 and *passim*
Heathcliff is no vampire, but EB goes to considerable lengths to make vampirism a possible explanation for his aberrant behavior. The vampire reached an artistic peak in the figure of Heathcliff, a lineal descendant of the Gothic antihero whose antecedents were Milton's Satan and Blake's Devil. Twitchell's convincing explication of Heathcliff in the context of vampirism illuminates other facets of *WH*, such as the characters of Nelly and Catherine, and Catherine's death scene. "What such a reading does...is to return Heathcliff to the way he was viewed by the first generation of critics."

TYSON, Anne Jane *see* A277.

A373 UNTERMEYER, Louis *Makers of the Modern World: The Lives of Ninety–Two Writers, Artists, Scientists, etc. and Other Creators Who Formed the Pattern of Our Century* (New York: Simon and Schuster 1955)
In a chapter on Emily Dickinson (p 136–37) the author says Emily Dickinson has the "inner knowledge" of EB, and that a critic cannot tell how much of either author's works is based on experience and how much on imagination.

A374 VAN GHENT, Dorothy "On *Wuthering Heights*" *The English Novel, Form and Function* (New York: Rinehart 1953) 153–70
The strangeness of *WH* lies in its ethical attitude, its level of experience, and its great

simplicity (or lack of "the web of civilized habits.") Two "technical bulwarks" support the "uneasy tale": (1) the two narrators are both credible and commonplace, and (2) the story extends over two generations and ends with manners and morality. *WH* is related to EB's poetry, and the "window figure" and the "two–children figure," which are explicated in more detail in the author's essay of that title (see B494), are discussed. Reprinted: A10, A104, A220, A262, A375, A379. Partially reprinted: A274, A283.

A375 ——— "On *Wuthering Heights*" in Arnold Kettle, ed *The Nineteenth Century Novel: Critical Essays and Documents* (London: The Open University Press 1972) 108–26
A reprinting of A374.

A376 ——— "Problems for Study and Discussion: *Wuthering Heights*" *The English Novel, Form and Function* (New York: Rinehart 1953) 390–401
An example of the kind of problem posed: Only two animals in the story have plot significance. Why, then, is the Heights overrun with fierce dogs?

A377 VISICK, Mary *The Genesis of* Wuthering Heights (Hong Kong: Hong Kong University Press 1958, 1965) 88 p
This is a very thorough treatment of *WH* and the Gondal saga. EB's novel "arose . . . specifically out of the same material as her poetry," and both are discussed in great detail. This work is one that would be essential to any study of the relationship between *WH* and Gondal. There is an appendix of parallels and a short annotated bibliography. Partially reprinted: A10, A274, A283, A322. Reissued in 1980 with a Foreword by Edmund Blunden and an Author's Note to the 1980 edition (A36).

——— see A36.

A378 VIVANTE, Leone "Emily Jane Brontë 1818–1848" *English Poetry* (London: Faber and Faber 1950) 245–47
An objective, sensitive, and philosophical explication of EB's poetry.

A379 VOGLER, Thomas A. "Introduction" and "Story and History in *Wuthering Heights*" and ed *Twentieth Century Interpretations of* Wuthering Heights (Englewood Cliffs, N J: Prentice–Hall 1968) 1–13, 78–99
According to the introduction, there are two contradictory ways of "seeing" in *WH*. One is Lockwood's and Nelly Dean's way, embodying common sense and empirical vision, and the other is Catherine's and Heathcliff's way, vision beyond the limits of reality. "What both extremes overlook is the possibility that the novel is about the problem of contrasted vision itself, perhaps even about the impossibility of adopting decisively one or the other mode of vision." Vogler includes a chronology and a selected bibliography. The critical essays (annotated in the individual entries in most cases) are as follows:
"The Structure of *Wuthering Heights*" by Charles Percy Sanger (A324)
"Emily Brontë: *Wuthering Heights*" by Arnold Kettle (A192)
"Fiction and the Matrix of Analogy" by Mark Schorer (B439)
"The Brontë Sisters and *Wuthering Heights*" by Derek Traversi (A369)
"Preface to *Wuthering Heights*" by Albert J. Guerard (A140)
"The Circumambient Universe" [From his book *Emily Brontë*: Wuthering Heights] by J. Frank Goodridge (A129)

In a discussion of Nature in *WH*, the two rival houses, and worlds of heaven and hell, Goodridge says, "the exposed wilderness of unreclaimed nature is...the rock beneath the cultivated soil of human life...." The two houses show two possible ways of living. A number of private heavens and hells are contrasted, and in this connection, the author investigates Lockwood, Hindley, Heathcliff, Catherine, Cathy, Joseph, Isabella, and Edgar.

"Story and History in *Wuthering Heights*" by Thomas A. Vogler

A penetrating look at Lockwood and through Lockwood clearly demonstrates that any assumption of a resolution in *WH* is a repudiation of the essential theme of the novel, which consists of contraries, and the process of change is the reality behind the events in the novel.

"*Jane Eyre* and *Wuthering Heights*" by Virginia Woolf (A419)

"Emily Brontë and *Wuthering Heights*" by David Cecil (A51)

"On *Wuthering Heights*" by Dorothy Van Ghent (A374)

"Lockwood's Dreams and the Exegesis of *Wuthering Heights*" by Edgar F. Shannon, Jr (B445)

"Implacable, Belligerent People of Emily Brontë's Novel, *Wuthering Heights*" by V. S. Pritchett (B398)

"Introduction to *Wuthering Heights*" by David Daiches (A77)

"The Incest Theme in *Wuthering Heights*" by Eric Solomon (B455)

"Emily Brontë and the Metaphysics of Childhood and Love" by Irving H. Buchen (B78)

"Emily Brontë" by J. Hillis Miller (A251)

A380 WAGENKNECHT, Edward C. "Fire over Yorkshire" *Cavalcade of the English Novel* (New York: Holt 1943) 304–18; second edition (New York: Holt 1954)

The contributions of Charlotte Brontë and EB to English fiction are evaluated; there is also a thorough review of Brontë criticism to date and a bibliography. (The later edition, 1954, contains a supplementary bibliography of materials on the Brontës.)

A381 WAGNER, Geoffrey "Jane Eyre. With a Commencement on Catherine Earnshaw: Beyond Biology" *Five for Freedom: A Study of Feminism in Fiction* (London: George Allen and Unwin 1972) 103–37 [106–24]

EB's primary and overriding concern in *WH* is the exploration of the soul, of being, and existence beyond death. She investigates those aspects of life which are unaffected by time and place—and, significantly, by sex.

A382 WALKER, Hugh "The Brontës" *The Literature of the Victorian Era* (London: Cambridge University Press 1910) 723–24

EB was inferior to Charlotte Brontë as an artist, and even had she lived longer, "she might have proved an intractable pupil and have marred other novels as she marred *Wuthering Heights* by the very excess of the qualities which made her great."

A383 WALKER, Mrs J. R. "The Brontës" *Stories of the Victorian Writers* (London: Cambridge University Press 1922) 77–85

The author tells the traditional Brontë story and briefly discusses EB's poetry. She relates a legend about Hugh Brontë's adoption of an orphaned Welsh boy, similar to the story of Heathcliff in *WH*.

A384 WALTERS, J. Cuming *The Spell of Yorkshire* (London: Methuen and Co 1931)
On p 98–118 the author gives a depressing view of all the Brontës in the context of a gloomy geographical area.

A385 WARD, Mrs Humphry "Introduction" *Wuthering Heights* (New York and London: Harper and Brothers 1903) xi–xl
Mrs Ward opposes the opinions of George Saintsbury and Leslie Stephen regarding *WH* and says that the novel has not yet taken the place that rightly belongs to it. She wishes, however, for a more "flowing unity" in *WH*. It belongs to the "later Romantic movement." EB's genius is attributed to her Celtic blood, and she was influenced by German literature. EB's poetry is briefly discussed. Reprinted: B502. Partially reprinted: A10, A283.

A386 WATSON, Melvin R. "Form and Substance in the Brontë Novels" in Robert C. Rathburn and Martin Steinmann, Jr, eds *From Jane Austen to Joseph Conrad* (Minneapolis: University of Minnesota Press 1958) 106–17
WH and *Jane Eyre* survive as classics because their form and their substance are welded together; in the other Brontë novels form and substance are at war. EB excluded everything not pertinent to her theme in *WH*, and her timing is remarkable. *WH* is the greatest of the Brontë novels, he says, but for the most part he discusses Charlotte Brontë's work.

A387 —— "Tempest in the Soul: The Theme and Structure of *Wuthering Heights*" in Austin Wright, ed *Victorian Literature: Modern Essays in Criticism* (New York: Oxford University Press 1961) 86–97
This is a reprinting of item B503.

A388 WEST, Katherine "Early Victorian" *Chapter of Governesses, A Study of the Governess in English Fiction, 1800–1949* (London: Cohen and West Ltd 1949) 54–86 [71]
It is noted that the Brontës disliked children "...with the possible exception of Emily, whose little savages and spoiled darlings are always human beings...."

A389 WEYGANDT, Cornelius "The Spectacle of the Brontës" *A Century of the English Novel* (New York: Century 1925) 102–21
Jane Eyre and *WH* are books to be reread because of their intensity of emotion. *WH*'s "survival as a classic is assured despite its burden of absurdities." The lyricism in the novel contributes much to the enjoyment of rereadings of *WH*, and the reader tends to forget the brutalities of the story.

A390 WHEELER, Michael *The Art of Allusion in Victorian Fiction* (New York: Barnes & Noble 1979) *passim*
Use of allusion in the narrative of *WH* reflects the ambiguities of the implicit contract between the reader and narrators. There are few allusions in *WH*, but "...one is of crucial importance: the text of Branderham's sermon ("Seventy Times Seven") which Lockwood reads in the coffin–bed before he has his nightmares." The footnote to this suggests a secondary adopted text for the sermon.

*A391 —— "A Rude and Strange Production: Narrative Clues and Mysteries in *Wuthering Heights*" in Mario Curreli and Alberto Martino, eds *Critical Dimen-*

sions: English, German and Comparative Literature Essays in Honor of Aurelio Zanco (Cuneo: SASTE 1977?)

A392 WHITE, W. Bertram *The Miracle of Haworth: A Brontë Study* (London: University of London Press 1937)
This is a general study of the Brontë family, with a five–page bibliography. Chapter X, "Emily Is Changed," asserts that EB refused to return to Brussels with Charlotte Brontë because of the death of William Weightman. "This was undoubtedly the loss which completely altered Emily's whole outlook on life...." Mr Weightman is subsequently given credit for the passion found in some of EB's poems and for "a love that can triumph over death" in *WH*. EB's reading at Brussels probably included Ruysbroeck, St Therese, and St John of the Cross from whom she learned "the language of mysticism." Chapter XVII, *"Wuthering Heights,"* praises EB's acute observation of and use of the natural setting of the moors in her novel, but attributes the novel's greatness to the love of Catherine and Heathcliff, which was like that of Dante and Beatrice. The author also discusses Branwell Brontë's influence on *WH* and compares EB to many other female writers and poets.

A393 WHITEHEAD, Phyllis *The Brontës Came Here* (Halifax: Fawcett, Greenwood and Co 1965)
In this guide to most of the north–country places associated with the Brontës, an effort is made to connect sites and buildings with those in the Brontë novels, e.g., Wuthering Heights and Thrushcross Grange.

A394 WHITMORE, Clara H. *Woman's Work in English Fiction* (New York: Putnam 1910)
On p 249–57, *WH* and EB's poetry are discussed. Catherine is compared with Undine. During the three years of her marriage to Edgar Linton, Catherine's "better nature triumphs." Heathcliff is "capable of a love stronger than his hate."

*A395 WILKINS, Mary E. "Emily Brontë and *Wuthering Heights*" in Seymour Eaton, ed *The Booklovers Reading Club Handbook to Accompany the Reading Course Entitled, The World's Great Woman Novelists* (Philadelphia: 1901) 85–93

A396 WILKS, Brian *The Brontës* (New York: Viking Press 1975) *passim*
The Brontë story, published in folio, and handsomely illustrated with many colored plates. Among the reproductions are EB's painting of her tame merlin, "Hero," and her watercolor of the dog, "Keeper." Also included is a photograph of EB's writing box.

A397 WILLCOCKS, M. P. "Charlotte and Emily Brontë" *Between the Old World and the New* (London: Allen and Unwin 1925) 157–68
The author evaluates both EB and Charlotte Brontë; she points out the value of EB's escape into her inner world, the strength and mysticism of that world, and her absolute independence from the Victorian world and its creeds.

A398 WILLIAMS, A. M. "Emily Brontë" *Our Early Female Novelists and Other Essays* (Glasgow: J. MacLehose and Sons 1904) 65–85
The major influences on EB's work were the moors, her father, Miss Branwell, and Tabby. The promise of *WH* is in the delineation of character rather than the story. EB's poetry lacks

form and some of the poems have a "certain gloom," but attractive characteristics of them are a feeling for nature, pensiveness, and grandeur of thought.

A399 WILLIAMS, Harold "The Brontë Sisters" *Two Centuries of the English Novel* (London: Smith, Elder 1911) 214–33 [218–28]
EB "was pagan in temperament and creed" and felt "neither hope nor optimism. . . ." The characters in *WH* "are abnormal in an abnormal setting. . . ."

*A400 WILLIAMS, M. *Notes on the Clergy Daughters' School, Casterton* (Beverley [England]: Wright & Haggard 1935)

A401 WILLIAMS, Raymond "Charlotte and Emily Brontë" *The English Novel from Dickens to Lawrence* (New York: Oxford University Press 1970) 60–74 [64–69]
Jane Eyre and *WH*, although different from each other, are linked by an emphasis on intense feeling, a commitment to passion, which in the 1840s is very new in the English novel. *WH* is about relationships; more specifically, one relationship. Catherine and Heathcliff are defined by a "desire in" as opposed to a "desire for" another human being. Similarities and differences among *WH*, *Jane Eyre*, and *Villette* are discussed.

A402 WILLIS, Irene Cooper *The Authorship of* Wuthering Heights (London: Hogarth Press 1936) 94 p
The purpose of this book is to present the evidence against Branwell Brontë's authorship of *WH*. Part I discusses *WH*, pointing out the usefulness and value of the character Lockwood, and describing the effect achieved by the double narrative of the story. Part II, "Branwell Brontë's Writings," quotes his work and shows why he could not have written *WH*. Sections of this book are reprinted in A10, A104, A274, A283.

A403 ——— *The Brontës* (London: Duckworth 1933)
This is a short history of the Brontës. EB is discussed in Chapters V, VI, and VII. She was "difficult to live with," and wanted freedom from people; "freedom was the breath of her soul," but she was lonely. *WH* is evaluated in Chapter VII as primitive and realistic. The advantages and disadvantages of narration through Nelly Dean and Lockwood are discussed at length. Heathcliff was not monstrous in EB's eyes, and "Mrs. Dean's occasional inclination to see him as such has to be discounted"; after all, Lockwood at times enjoyed his company.

*A404 WILLY, Margaret *A Critical Commentary on Emily Brontë's* Wuthering Heights (London: Macmillan 1966) 79 p

A405 ——— "The Poetry of Emily Dickinson" *Essays and Studies 1957* n s 10 (London: John Murray 1957) 91–104
This is a comparison of Emily Dickinson's poetry with that of EB, with emphasis on EB's influence on Emily Dickinson.

A406 WILMOT–BUXTON, E. M. "Charlotte and Emily Brontë" *A Book of Noble Women* (London: Methuen and Co 1907) 247–73
The traditional, often told story of the Brontës, well written. Reprinted: A85.

*A407 WILSON, Barbara Ker "Foreword" *Wuthering Heights* (New York: Blackie and Son 1979)

WILSON, Colin *see* A344h.

A408 WILSON, Romer, pseud [Florence Roma Muir (Wilson) O'Brien] *All Alone: The Life and Private History of Emily Jane Brontë* (London: Chatto and Windus 1928) 298 p

This very personal interpretation of EB evaluates her life in an effort to explain her genius; therefore, most of the book is of necessity conjectural. The influence of the moors and EB's family environment are both seen as unhappy factors in her life, but they also created an individual capable of writing *WH*. Reflecting the tone of the rest of the book, Appendix IV is a list of EB's "poems of guilt."

A409 WINNIFRITH, Tom *The Brontës* (New York: Collier Books 1977) 46–65 and *passim*

Biography, juvenilia, and poetry are treated in the first three chapters. Winnifrith is refreshingly pragmatic and asserts that although the Brontë juvenilia and poetry are important to any Brontë study, they can be overemphasized. Of *WH*, he says, "It is...little help to know that Emily had her feet on the ground in describing what happened if we are still in the air about what these happenings mean, and the almost infinite variety of modern reading suggests that a definitive interpretation of *Wuthering Heights* is beyond our reach."

A410 ———— *The Brontës and Their Background: Romance and Reality* (London: Macmillan 1973) *passim*

"Most Brontë biographers, critics, and scholars have paid insufficient attention to the unreliability of the primary evidence on which they have based their theories...." Among other things, Winnifrith investigates the Brontës' religion, attitude toward literary conventions, and social views.

A411 WINTERICH, John T. "How This Book Came to Be" *Wuthering Heights* (New York: Heritage Press 1940) v–xv

A short introduction concerned with the publishing history of *WH*, and the possibility that Branwell Brontë may have had a part in the authorship.

A412 WISE, Thomas J. *The Ashley Library: A Catalogue of Printed Books, Manuscripts and Autograph Letters* (Edinburgh: Dunedin Press 1922)

On p 82 there is a descriptive bibliography of EB's holograph poems and editions of *WH* and *Poems* edited by Clement Shorter.

A413 ———— *A Bibliography of the Writings in Prose and Verse of the Members of the Brontë Family* (London: Clay and Sons 1917)

Part II, "Emily and Anne Brontë," is a descriptive bibliography. The fifteen corrections in the edition of *WH* owned by Clement Shorter, which are supposed to be in EB's own handwriting, are listed.

A414 ———— *A Brontë Library: A Catalogue of Printed Books, Manuscripts and Autograph Letters by the Members of the Brontë Family* (London: Dunedin Press 1929)

Part II, "The Writings of Emily Jane Brontë," is a descriptive bibliography.

*A415 ——— *Letters Recounting the Deaths of Emily, Anne and Branwell Brontë by Charlotte Brontë* [A pamphlet] 1913

A416 WISE, Thomas J. and J. Alexander Symington "Preface" and eds *The Brontës: Their Lives, Friendships and Correspondence* 4 vols [Shakespeare Head Brontë] (Oxford: Basil Blackwell 1932) I vii–ix
The brief mention of EB is as follows: "Emily Brontë is now recognized as affording one of the most interesting studies of womanhood, and her poetry ranks high in English literature."

A417 ——— "Preface" and eds *The Poems of Emily Jane Brontë and Anne Brontë* (Oxford: Shakespeare Head Press 1934) ix–xii
A survey of the history of the publication of EB's poems, with a bibliography of EB's and Anne Brontë's works.

A418 WOODBERRY, George E. "The Brontë Novels" *Studies of a Litterateur* (New York: Harcourt, Brace 1921) 253–60
A very perceptive evaluation of EB and Charlotte. The Brontës' "reputation remains side by side with Jane Austen's"; Mrs Humphry Ward's "Introduction" (see A385) is cited as the best criticism of the Brontës.

A419 WOOLF, Virginia "*Jane Eyre* and *Wuthering Heights*" *The Common Reader: First Series* (London: Hogarth Press 1925) 196–204 [201–4]
EB poses a question with her novel which she does not answer. Virginia Woolf paraphrases *WH*: ". . . not merely 'I love' or 'I hate,' but 'we, the whole human race' and 'you, the eternal powers. . . .' the sentence remains unfinished." EB could, however, "free life from its dependence upon facts." Reprinted A220, A379; partial reprinting: A10, A274, A283.

A420 ——— *A Room of One's Own* (New York: Harcourt, Brace and Co 1929) 112–16, 128–30 and *passim*
Virginia Woolf on the difficulties women novelists of the nineteenth century encountered when writing: ". . . What genius, what integrity it must have required in face of all that criticism, in the midst of that purely patriarchial society, to hold fast to the thing as they saw it without shrinking. Only Jane Austen did it and Emily Brontë. . . ."

A421 WRIGHT, J. C. *The Story of the Brontës* (London: Leonard Parsons 1925)
There are two chapters pertinent to EB: the first, "*Wuthering Heights*," reviews the past and present criticism of the novel, particularly that of J. Malham–Dembleby, who claims that Charlotte Brontë wrote *WH*; in the second, "Emily Brontë and Her Poetry," the author compares her poems with those of Wordsworth and Meredith.

A422 WYATT, A. J. and Henry Clay "The Brontës" *Modern English Literature 1798–1919* (London: W. B. Clive 1932) 130–31
A short summary asserting that an understanding of the Brontës' lives "is essential to an understanding of their work." *WH* is noted for "violence of the manners and eccentricity of the characters."

A423 WYATT, Edith "Brontë Poems" *Great Companions* (New York: Appleton–Century 1917) 191–97 [195–97]
". . . [T]he Brontë's lives are read into their work and their work into their lives until neither

has any distinct or integral value." Fragments of the Brontë poems are quoted to support the
theory that artistic creation need not be based upon experience.

A424 YABLON, G. Anthony and John R. Turner *A Brontë Bibliography* (London:
   Ian Hodgkins and Co Ltd; Westport, Conn: Meckler Books 1978)
   A descriptive bibliography covering 122 years, this is a list of books written about the lives
and works of the Brontë family and is confined to separately published monographs and
monographs on other topics which include a separate section on the Brontës. A full description
is given of each book in its first published form, arranged in alphabetical sequence by author's
name. "Each entry consists of a transcription of the title–page...date and place of publication...name of the publisher...." The transcription is followed by thirteen possible distin-
guishing characteristics, such as page size, description of the binding, and a designation of
the main theme of the book. The main theme categories are: biography, criticism, dramatization, fictional biography, topographical work (Haworth district), and miscellaneous. In addition, there are five useful indices.

A425 ZEMAN, Anthea *Presumptuous Girls: Women and Their World in the Serious
   Woman's Novel* (London: Weidenfeld and Nicolson 1977) 48–49, 97–99 and *passim*
   One of the problems EB works out through *WH* is her own concern about Christianity:
"...a Christian after–life, or the pagan wanderings of ghosts, fight out their battle through
Wuthering Heights...."

B   Articles
Anonymous

B1 "Another Brontë Discovery" *Literary Digest* 48 (Apr 4 1914) 759
   This article announces the discovery in Ireland of two Brontë portraits—one of EB and the
other of the three Brontë sisters—painted by Branwell Brontë.

B2 "Brontë Discoveries" *Bookman* (New York) 33 (May 1911) 228
   A report of J. Malham–Dembleby's discoveries of correlations between Charlotte Brontë's
[sic] *Wuthering Heights* and *Jane Eyre* accompanied by a Tourist's Guide to the Brontë country.

B3 "Brontës Are Earning a New Popularity" *Life* 15 (Nov 29 1943) 95–103
   The traditional story of the Brontës is told alongside photographs of the supposed farmhouse
model for Wuthering Heights, photographs of Haworth Parsonage, and engravings depicting
the story of *WH*.

B4 "Drawings by Emily Brontë of Geometrical Problems, Signed and Dated 'September the 9th 1837' " *BST* 14 (1962) Plate 11
   The drawings are reproduced without comment.

*B5 "Emily Brontë" *TLS* [pre Jan 30 1909]
   EB is the enigma in the Brontë family although we can know her to some extent through
her poems. The power of *WH* lies in its threadbare truth which is unadorned by any "romantic
beauty" of landscape. Reprinted: B6.

B6 "Emily Brontë" *Living Age* 260 (Jan 30 1909) 302–8
   This is a reprinting of Item B5.

B7 "Emily Brontë" *TLS* (Dec 18 1948) 713
   This centenary article about EB, her character, and *WH* concludes that "the unsolved
   mystery [of EB and *WH*] is the eternal one of genius."

B8 "Emily Brontë: A Diary Paper" *BST* 12 (1951) 15
   The diary fragment which was dated June 26 1837 is deciphered here; the frontispiece of
   this volume is a facsimile of the original.

B9 "A First Edition of *Wuthering Heights*" *BST* 14 (1964) 50
   A description of the Newby 1847 edition of *WH* with penciled corrections in the first volume,
   which was sold at auction in July 1964. The corrections are believed to be Charlotte Brontë's.

B10 "The Genius of the Moors" *Academy and Literature* 65 (Oct 3 1903) 333–34
   Regarding the controversy about Branwell Brontë's authorship of *WH*, this author asserts
   that *WH* was written by a woman and gives internal evidence: Mr Lockwood's point of view
   is never that of a man. Moreover, EB's poetry reveals her to be the only possible author of
   WH.

B11 "Landscape in the Brontë Novels" *The Academy* 71 (Sept 8 1906) 226–28
   EB's descriptions of scenery in *WH* are brief, but "extraordinarily effective" and essential
   to the plot.

*B12 "Notable Accessions to the Library 1963" *Newberry Library Bulletin* 6 (May
   1965) 127–62
   Among new editions acquired is a first edition of *WH*. [From mention in *Abstracts of English
   Studies*.]

B13 "The 150th Anniversary of the Birth of Emily Jane Brontë" *BST* 15 (1968) 201–
   5
   A description of the anniversary, which was marked by ceremonies in Haworth and at
   Westminster Abbey, with the commemorative addresses given by Naomi Lewis and Donald
   Hopewell.

B14 "Patrick Branwell Brontë and *Wuthering Heights*" *BST* 7 (1927) 97–102
   The article ascribing the authorship of *WH* to Branwell Brontë which appeared in *The
   Halifax Guardian* dated June 15 1867 is reprinted here because it is "too little known in its
   entirety and. . .difficult to obtain."

B15 "Pot–Shooting" *TLS* (Apr 30 1949) 281
   An article in which the *TLS* editor puts a stop to a controversy (see B237) about EB's poem
   "The Visionary," because of the excessive amount of conjecture. The writer mentions the
   Methodist influence on the Brontës emphasized by G. Elsie Harrison (see A150). See B166
   for a reply.

B16 "The 'Splendid Isolation' of Emily Brontë" *Current Literature* 40 (May 1906)
   512

This is a brief review of nineteenth–century criticism of *WH* with special attention to Clement Shorter's evaluation of the novel.

B17 "Three Essays by Emily Brontë" *BST* 11 (1950) 337–41

"The Cat," "The Butterfly," and "Letter from One Brother to Another," translated from the French by Lorine W. Nagel. These essays are in addition to the two French essays in the Bonnell Collection (see B109); all five are included in F. E. Ratchford's booklet (A303). See also A122, B288, B289.

B18 "Two Brussels Schoolfellows of Charlotte Brontë" *BST* 5 (Apr 1913) 25–29

This article recalls two schoolmates of Emily and Charlotte Brontë and reprints Miss Wheelwright's impression of EB, which was not flattering.

B19 "An Unrecovered Poetess" *TLS* (June 10 1915) 189

EB's courageous poetry is made timely by World War I. As a poet she is compared with William Blake. Unfortunately, she continually attempted to write an "English" poem and did not know where her true talent lay. She made the mistake of striving for a "conventional finish." Reprinted: B20.

B20 "An Unrecovered Poetess" *Living Age* 286 (July 24 1915) 216–22

This is a reprinting of Item B19.

B21 "Where the Brontës Borrowed Books: The Keighley Mechanics Institute" *BST* 11 (1950) 344–58

A discussion of the possible sources of the pseudonyms "Currer" and "Ellis," and a catalogue of the books available at the Institute in 1841.

*   *   *

B22 A., W. L. "An Emily Brontë Excursion, 1968" *BST* 15 (1968) 262

The Society's annual excursion was to Shibden Hall, Law Hill House, and the site of High Sunderland Hall. Donald Hopewell spoke about the scenic and architectural background of *WH*, designating High Sunderland Hall as the model for Wuthering Heights and Shibden Hall for Thrushcross Grange.

B23 ABERCROMBIE, Lascelles "The Brontës Today" *BST* 6 (1924) 179–200 [196–200]

A biographical and critical discussion of the Brontës. ". . .in the way the Brontës appear to us today [there is evident] the unquestionable supremacy of Emily." *WH* has "a perfect coherence of purpose." Partially reprinted: A10.

B24 ADAMS, Norman O. W., Jr "Byron and the Early Victorians: A Study of His Poetic Influence (1824–1855)" *Dissertation Abstracts* 16 No 2 (1956) 336–37

EB is one of the minor poets discussed in this study of the nature and extent of Byron's influence. For the minor poets Byron's influence was negative in value: the two themes most used were the Byronic hero, and passion and sentiment.

B25 ADAMS, Ruth M. "*Wuthering Heights*: The Land East of Eden" *NCF* 13 (June 1958) 58–62

Reverend Jabes Banderham's [sic] sermon on "Seventy Times Seven" establishes the fact that "no conventional morality prevails" in *WH*. Like Cain and his descendants, these people live outside God's law. The text for the sermon is Genesis 4 (see B445). Reprinted: A220.

B26 ADELMAN, Seymour "The First American Edition of the Brontës' Poems" *Book Collector* 9 (Summer 1960) 201
The writer comments (in answer to a query in a previous issue, B234) upon locations of first editions of the *Poems by Currer, Ellis and Acton Bell* and describes them. See also B405.

B27 AIKEN, Ralph "Wild–heart; An Appreciation of Emily Jane Brontë" *South Atlantic Quarterly* 34 (Apr 1935) 202–10
EB's Celtic nature impelled her to love sadness. She "gloried in the turbulent" and did not know fear, but she was not morbid. The only thing enigmatic about her was her genius.

B28 ALLEN, H. Merian "Emily Brontë—One Hundred Years After" *Education* 39 (Dec 1918) 225–30
The Brontë story, as it is retold here, depicts a loveless and lonely childhood out of which the growth of *WH* was natural. EB is compared to Edgar Allan Poe and *WH* to "The Fall of the House of Usher."

B29 ALLOTT, Miriam "Mrs. Gaskell's 'The Old Nurse's Story': A Link Between *Wuthering Heights* and *The Turn of the Screw*" *Notes and Queries* n s 8 (Mar 1961) 101–2
Mrs Gaskell's story in the 1852 Christmas number of Dickens' periodical, *Household Words*, was written two years after she read *WH*, is similar to it, and in turn inspired Henry James' *The Turn of the Screw*.

B30 ———— "*Wuthering Heights*: The Rejection of Heathcliff?" *Essays in Criticism* 8 (Jan 1958) 27–47
The author agrees with David Cecil about the storm and calm in *WH* (see A51), but she says this theme is more logical than he pictures it. EB translates the storm elements in the first half of *WH* into calmer, more humanized elements in the second half. EB also takes the calm to a "demoralizing extreme" in Linton Heathcliff, but there is no calm at the end of the story. EB does not answer her question; she only poses it. Partially reprinted: A274, A283. Reprinted: A10.

ALTROCCHI, John *see* B363.

B31 ANDERSON, Walter E. "The Lyrical Form of *Wuthering Heights*" *University of Toronto Quarterly* 47 (Winter 1977–78) 112–34
"Lyrical. . .is a general descriptive term to point up the radical formal difference between *Wuthering Heights* and those novels—Fielding's, Austen's, and Hardy's—shaped by a principle of logically progressive plots. . . ." Life in death is the supreme value in *WH*. EB "shifts the planes of reality to such a degree that ordinary life comes to seem less vital than death." Overriding all to express this value, EB defuses Heathcliff's cruelty, tempers his revenge, to sustain the reader's sympathy. She creates, in the second generation, non–memorable characters who merely remind of the monumental characters; Catherine and Heathcliff remain the central experience. The way EB works to achieve her transcendence of reality is the theme of this excellent essay.

B32 ANDREWS, W. L. [Letter to the Editor] "The Haworth Moors" *The Spectator*
190 (May 29 1953) 702
The writer disagrees with B. Scholfield (see B438) regarding the modernity of Haworth at
the time the Brontës lived there.

B33 ———— [Letter to the Editor] "The Miraculous Parsonage" *TLS* (July 31 1948)
429
Mr Andrews takes issue with a statement in a book review that the Brontë novels "have
escaped even a temporary eclipse," says that "there was a time when few people read them,"
and refers particularly to *WH*. See B433 for a reply.

B34 ———— "Our Greatest Woman" *BST* 10 (1945) 288–89
EB was esteemed by Alexander Woollcott, who recalled that James M. Barrie described
her, in an address, as "our greatest woman." Reprinted: A1.

B35 ———— "Ups and Downs of Celebrity" *BST* 11 (1947) 81–87
This is a one–hundred–year history of the readers of *WH* and *Jane Eyre*: the English reading
public. Reprinted: A1.

B36 ANKENBRANDT, Katherine W. "Songs in *Wuthering Heights*" *Southern Folklore Quarterly* 33 (June 1969) 92–115
Appearing in a key episode in the first part of *WH* is a stanza of a Danish folk ballad. Nelly
Dean is singing it to Hareton to quiet him after Hindley has dropped him over the staircase.
". . . If Emily Brontë needed a ballad on the themes of human cruelty and ghostly kindness
to children, the nearest was Jamieson's translation of 'The Ghaist's Warning.' " Two other
songs mentioned by name in *WH* are "Chevy Chase" and "Fairy Annie's Wedding." The
image of the song in *WH* suggests musical talent and musical awareness in EB. Moreover,
music may have an expressive function in *WH* as the songs appear at turning points in the
novel.

B37 ARNOLD, Helen H. "Americans and the Brontës" *BST* 10 (1940) 12–14
A survey of American reaction to the Brontë novels when they first appeared. *The American
Review*, June 1848: "It [*WH*] ought to be banished from refined society. . . ." Reprinted: A1.

B38 ARNOLD, J. V. "George Sand's *Mauprat* and Emily Brontë's *Wuthering Heights*"
Revue de Littérature Comparée 46 (Apr–June 1972) 209–18
It is likely that EB read *Mauprat*, since she read French, and Charlotte was lent many
French novels, which may have had a strong influence in her creation of *WH*. Arnold explicates
many parallels between the two novels. "Sand has shown us the positive, Brontë the negative
side of a unique and deathless love." See B479.

*B38A ASHDOWN, Dulcie "The Brontës" *The International English Journal* 2
(Feb–Mar 1982)

B39 ATHAS, Daphne "Goddesses, Heroines and Women Writers" *St. Andrews
Review* 3 (Fall–Winter 1975) 5–13
Although *WH* has the framework of a Persephone plot, it is the least Persephonic of all
nineteenth–century novels by women writers. Athas suggests that in this vein it is rather

"Satan–Psyche," reflecting chaste immortality in the love of Catherine and Heathcliff, and the demonic in Heathcliff as Milton's Satan.

B39A AUDET, Richard D. "Seeing into the Life of Things: The Imagination As Theme of Wordsworth's 'Lyrical Ballads' of 1798 and Emily Brontë's 'Wuthering Heights' " *DAI* 43 (Aug 1982) 449A

Although one work did not influence the other, both are key Romantic works, exploring the imagination as a sympathetic power. The Wordsworth–Dorothy and Heathcliff–Catherine unions affirm the imagination's ability to overcome human isolation, and both young Romantic writers trace the forces that either impede or foster such sympathetic unions.

B40 AUERBACH, Nina "Elizabeth Gaskell's 'Sly Javelins': Governing Women in Cranford and Haworth" *Modern Language Quarterly* 38 (Sept 1977) 276–91

The Brontë sisters are considered as a group, and EB is discussed in this Brontë family biographical context.

B41 BAILLIE, J. B. "Religion and the Brontës" *BST* 7 (1927) 59–69

EB's poetry, "the only revelation of her religious life which we possess," is discussed on p 66–68 from a religious angle.

B42 BAKER, Donald W. "Themes of Terror in Nineteenth Century English Fiction: The Shift to the Internal" *Dissertation Abstracts* 16 No 1 (1956) 118–19

"The influence of Gothicism...is particularly discernible in Scott, Bulwer–Lytton, the Brontë sisters, Dickens, Collins, and Le Fanu." Terror–fiction, employing psychopathological materials treated subjectively, was written late in the century; sadism, masochism, madness, neuroses, and psychoses are depicted by these authors.

B42A BAL, Mieke "Notes on Narrative Embedding" *Poetics Today* (Tel Aviv) 2 (Winter 1981) 41–59

Because the complex narrative embedding in *WH* is striking and significant, it is the example used in this essay on the subject. The study illuminates the novel, however: As we follow the way the image of Edgar is presented and developed, "it is noteworthy that the picture of Edgar should first be given directly by his antagonist" in a work where the narrative structure is full of mediations.

B43 BARKER, Ernest "The Inspiration of Emily Brontë" *BST* 12 (1951) 3–9

A discussion of "inspiration" in two senses—that which EB had, and that which she gave others. The three elements of her own inspiration are her Celtic blood, her Yorkshire environment, and—the least fortunate of the three—her mental diet and the books she read.

*B43A BARKER, Francis "*Wuthering Heights* and the Real Conditions" *Red Letter* 3 (Autumn 1976)

B44 BARROW, Marjorie Stuart [Letter to the Editor] "Emily Brontë Mysteries" *Poetry Review* 34 (Jan 1943) 59–60

Since Branwell Brontë had a studio in Bradford, the town could have played a part in EB's love life. EB could have visited there, and in this connection "L. Parensell" is mentioned. (See Item B178 for a reply.)

*B45 BAZZE–SSENTONGO, Emmanuel "Heathcliff's African Brothers" *Dhana* 4 (1974) 79–81

B46 BEBLINGTON, W. G. "Haworth Parsonage" *National Review* 123 (July 1944) 77–78
A visit to Haworth reveals the great change and modernization of the area. The threat of bombing caused the Bonnell Collection to be locked away in the musty Brontë Museum.

B47 BEETON, D. R. "Emily Brontë and Jan Christiaan Smuts" *BST* 15 (1968) 214–20
A comparison of an aspect of Field Marshal Smuts' philosophy, as it is expressed in his writings and speeches, with EB's philosophy as it is expressed in her poems and *WH*. (He had praised Olive Schreiner for being like EB.)

B48 BELL, Vereen M. "Character and Point of View in Representative Victorian Novels" *Dissertation Abstracts* 20 (Mar 1960) 3740–41
EB is one of six novelists treated in this study of the "introspective method of presenting character." "...[T]hey create an illusion of character...that we can be intellectually aware of, but not one that our senses can know."

B49 ———— "*Wuthering Heights* and the Unforgiveable Sin" *NCF* 17 (Sept 1962) 188–91
The author repudiates a theory put forth by Shannon (see B445) that the "First of the Seventy–first" sin is that of Catherine's marrying Edgar and traces in *WH* the "absence of forgiveness" theme, as seen in Lockwood's first dream.

B50 ———— "*Wuthering Heights* as Epos" *College English* 25 (Dec 1963) 199–208
The mode of double narration was the most expedient way of solving EB's problem of communication in *WH*. EB was affected by the oral tradition in her family: her father and her aunt told old Irish tales. EB, using Nelly Dean for the point of view and oral narrative as the medium, could "give full expression to her limited creative gift."

B51 BENSON, E. F. "The Brontës" *The Spectator* 146 (Feb 7 1931) 178–79
The author discusses the early misunderstanding of *WH* by the critics, by the public, and by Charlotte Brontë especially.

B52 BENTLEY, Phyllis [Letter to the Editor] "The Brontës and Methodism" *TLS* (May 20 1949) 329
The aspect of the influence of Methodism upon the Brontës sheds new light on their lives and works. Reprinted: B54.

B53 ———— [Letter to the Editor] "The Brontës and Methodism" *TLS* (June 10 1949) 381
The author presents evidence from the childhood plays that the Brontës in their childhood rebelled against Methodism. (See B228 for a reply.)

B54 ———— "Dr. Phyllis Bentley on the Brontës and Methodism" *BST* 11 (1949) 270
This is a reprinting of Item B52.

B55 ——— "Love Among the Brontës" *Contemporary Review* (London) 217 (Nov 1970) 225–30

After examining the real evidence of the kinds of relationships the Brontë sisters had with each other and with possible suitors, Bentley concludes: There was no love affair for Emily; she probably had a realistic view of her father and matched him in will power. As for the tradition that EB was deeply attached to Branwell, there seems to be no evidence for its origin. EB loved Charlotte with some reservation, but loved Anne altogether.

B56 ——— "New Brontë Devoirs" *BST* 12 (1955) 361–85

A French exercise written by EB (p 384–85) entitled "Letter" and corrected by M Heger is translated by the author, with the French original printed on the opposite page.

B57 ——— "A Novelist Looks at the Brontë Novels" *BST* 11 (1948) 139–51

The Brontë novels are discussed as novels in the light of (1) "kind...and (2) degree of impression they make...." which are the criteria by which to judge whether or not they are masterpieces (*WH*, p 147–49).

B58 ——— "The Significance of Haworth" *The Trollopian* 2 (Dec 1947) 127–36

This is an expansion of a chapter in her book, *The Brontës* (A26). The Haworth factor (landscape and ideology) supplied half the Brontë "mental equipment with which they molded these materials into art." Their Celtic heredity provided the other half. This is a thorough article on the background of the Brontë family.

B59 BEVERSLUIS, John "Love and Self–knowledge: A Study of *Wuthering Heights*" *English* 24 (Autumn 1975) 77–82

The traditional acceptance of the deathless love relationship of Catherine and Heathcliff is questioned. Nelly Dean correctly terms Catherine's "I am Heathcliff" speech "folly," because Catherine is deluding herself; she has strongly and repeatedly rejected Heathcliff.

B60 BLONDEL, Jacques "Imagery in *Wuthering Heights*" *Durham University Journal* n s 37 (Dec 1975) 1–7

"Imagery...is no ornament...but the very life of the book." Nature is an actor in *WH*; objects are animated with hidden violence. Some of the strong, rich images and verbs in *WH* are also found in EB's poems.

B61 BLOOMER, Nancy "Despair and Love in the Works of Emily Jane Brontë" *DAI* 37 (Feb 1977) 5135A–5136A

In *WH* EB reiterates the victory of faith over despair in the three generations of the Earnshaw family. Drawing on works of Nygren and Kierkegaard among others, the dissertation explores EB's central theme in the poetry and *WH*: unachieved selfhood.

B62 BLOOMFIELD, Paul "To Breathe Lightning" *Time and Tide* 29 (Mar 20 1948) 304

A modern book review of *WH*, written in a popular vein. Why do critics discuss what is meant by "Emily Brontë's poetical quality" in *WH* when Heathcliff is the central character? *WH* is seen in terms of "the personal struggle against possession by self–will—Heathcliff's struggle,...." and the author touches upon the social implications of this conflict.

*B63 BOSCO, Ronald A. "Heathcliff: Societal Victim or Demon?" *Gypsy Scholar* 2 (1974) 21–39

B64 BOWLIN, Karla J. "The Brother and Sister Theme in Post–Romantic Fiction" *DAI* 34 (Sept 1973) 1232A
"The plots of *Wuthering Heights, The Mill on the Floss,* and *The Sound and the Fury* revolve around the archetypal pattern that a brother and sister must grow up and part for the love of others. . .whichever of the pair deserts the other is blamed as if for a sin." Catherine and Heathcliff are considered siblings because they grew up in the same household together.

B65 BRACCO, Edgar Jean "Emily Brontë's Second Novel" *BST* 15 (1966) 29–33
In addition to Newby's letter, there is further evidence in favor of the existence of a second novel written by EB: Charlotte Brontë in one letter refers to "his second work" (Ellis Bell's), and in another she says EB is "too ill to occupy herself with writing." See B239, B295.

B66 BRADBY, G. F. "Emily Brontë" *Nineteenth Century* 108 (Oct 1930) 533–40
EB's poetry is compared with Shelley's. From her poetry, two characteristics of her personality can be derived: a sense of loneliness and a craving for some absorbing kind of love. Reprinted: A38.

B67 BRADNER, Leicester "The Growth of *Wuthering Heights*" *PMLA* 48 (Mar 1933) 129–46
One of the best and most comprehensive on the subject, this article explores sources of WH and influences on EB with regard to the novel, and includes a full consideration of sources mentioned by critics in the past. The development of EB's poems is traced with reference to the development of WH, because the poems were precursory to the novel. Wordsworth's possible influence on EB's poetry (through her childhood reading) is also discussed. Reprinted: A104. See B115.

B68 BRANTLINGER, Patrick "Romances, Novels, and Psychoanalysis" *Criticism* 17 (Winter 1975) 15–40
The romance form is regressive in the sense that romances "shadow forth and, at their best, examine 'primordial' or childlike mental processes." WH gains much of its strength from "the primitive, infantile quality of the rebellions which it depicts." The regressive nature of WH is demonstrated in a number of ways.

B69 BRASH, W. Bardsley "The Brontës of Haworth—Through Trials to Triumph" *London Quarterly and Holborn Review* 167 (Jan 1942) 57–66
An emotional retelling of the Brontë sisters' story, this article centers upon Charlotte Brontë, but the sisters are said to be "a triple cord which cannot be broken."

B70 ———— "Emily Brontë" *London Quarterly and Holborn Review* 160 (Oct 1935) 521–23
This review of EB's life refers to G. Elsie Harrison's connection of WH with William Grimshaw, the fanatical Methodist. Jabez Bunting, a Wesleyan preacher, is Jabes Branderham in the novel, and William Grimshaw is Mr Earnshaw. See A152.

B71 BRICK, Allan R. "Lewes's Review of *Wuthering Heights*" *NCF* 14 (Mar 1960) 355–59

An account of George Henry Lewes' 1850 Preface to *WH*, which was the first instance of an eminent critic's granting "the strange novel, which revolted many, its due regard," and of other nineteenth–century criticism of *WH*.

B72 ——— "*Wuthering Heights*: Narrators, Audience, and Message" *College English* 21 (Nov 1959) 80–86
"Emily Brontë's narrative form is deeply interfused with her essential message," in *WH*. The novel is compared with Coleridge's *Rime of the Ancient Mariner* wherein the wedding guest is the "personified audience" as is Lockwood in *WH*. Reprinted: A220, A283.

BRONSTEIN, Ethel *see* B204.

BROWN, Effie *see* B526.

B73 BROWN, Helen [Letter to the Editor] "Emily Brontë's Poems" *TLS* (Dec 21 1951) 821
The writer comments on "The Visionary" and EB's poems in general.

B74 ——— "The Influence of Byron on Emily Brontë" *Modern Language Review* 34 (July 1939) 374–81
EB's poetry has "resemblances of mood, and [of] the cadence and movement of the verse" to Byron's. The Byron influence would also explain her "tragic imaginings."

B75 BROWN, Helen and Joan Mott "The Gondal Saga" *BST* 9 (1938) 155–72
This is the first construction of EB's poems in an effort to find a continuous story in them. It precedes F. E. Ratchford's *Gondal's Queen* (see A301) and differs from her interpretation in pointing out three heroines instead of one.

B76 ——— "The Gondal Saga: Unpublished Verses by Emily Brontë" *TLS* (Feb 19 1938) 121. (See also *TLS* [Mar 19 1938] 188, which contains a slight correction of this article.)
The two unpublished poems are in the notebook entitled by EB "Gondal," which was presented to the British Museum in 1933. Although the other poems in it were previously published, this manuscript brought to light a considerable number of differences from the published versions.

B77 BROWN, T. J. "English Literary Autographs, XVII: The Brontës" *Book Collector* 5 (Spring 1956) 55–56
All four Brontës had a "microscopic" handwriting as well as a normal handwriting. This article gives the manuscript sources of both handwritings for each Brontë, describes them, and includes facsimiles (eight) of a sample of each handwriting.

B78 BUCHEN, Irving H. "Emily Brontë and the Metaphysics of Childhood and Love" *NCF* 22 (June 1967) 63–70
This is an excellent study of EB's metaphysics. Its purpose is "to read the poems in their own light and then to read the novel in the light of the poems." The love experience is related to childhood: "the second birth and death is that of love. . . ." *WH* is a story of childhood, and "paradise lost and regained" for the child and for the soul. Reprinted: A283, A379.

B79 ───── "Metaphysical and Social Evolution in *Wuthering Heights*" *Victorian Newsletter* 31 (Spring 1967) 15–20

There seem to be gaps between EB's "poetry and fiction, her metaphysics [See J. H. Miller, A251, which Buchen footnotes here] and sociology, and the two love stories in the novel." EB does integrate these, however, as the author points out.

B80 BUCKLER, William E. "Chapter VII of *Wuthering Heights*: A Key to Interpretation" *NCF* 7 (June 1952) 51–55

This chapter is a key to understanding the novel because in it Heathcliff's isolation becomes complete, Catherine sets her course, and the trustworthiness of Nelly Dean as a narrator is established.

B81 BUCKLEY, Vincent "Passion and Control in *Wuthering Heights*" *Southern Review: An Australian Journal of Literary Studies* 1 (1964) 5–23

The first half of this article is a careful and thorough investigation of the prose of *WH* and the controlled effects which are made stronger by a "commonsense realism." The second half is an excellent and original discussion of the nature of the Catherine–Heathcliff relationship in which the author rejects the widely–held idea that sexuality does not have a part in it. Partially reprinted: A274.

B82 BULLOCK, F. A. "The Genius of Emily Brontë" *BST* 9 (1937) 115–28

The writings of EB should be treated objectively, not subjected to psychoanalysis. Her quality of imagination is "an instrument and vehicle of knowledge...it tells us about the structure of reality," and should not be used to tell us about EB herself.

B83 BURKHART, Robert E. "The Structure of *Wuthering Heights*" *PMLA* 87 (Jan 1972) 104–5

In "Forum," a section of letters to the editor, R. Burkhart contends that D. Sonstroem (B457) could have made greater use of the structure of *WH* as a support for his argument. D. Van Ghent's view of the structure of *WH* (A374) is also discussed. (See B456 for a reply by Sonstroem.)

B84 BURNS, Wayne "On *Wuthering Heights*" *Recovering Literature* 1, No 2 (1972) 5–25

This is an earlier version of A42.

B85 BURROWS, Ken C. "Some Remembered Strain: Methodism and the Anti–Hymns of Emily Brontë" *West Virginia University Bulletin* 24 (Nov 1977) 48–61

A thorough, insightful exploration of EB's poems leads to a better understanding of her philosophy. "...Emily Brontë's mature response to the old Methodism of her childhood was to make lyrics out of hymns...so transformed that they might be called 'anti–hymns'...." She adapted evangelical forms to her own purposes, for example, to praise freedom of the imagination and the transcendence of the human soul.

B86 BUTTERFIELD, Herbert "Charlotte Brontë and Her Sisters in the Crucial Year" *BST* 14 (1963) 3–17

This is a modern evaluation of the Brontës' development toward literary careers. The crucial year was 1845 when the Brontë children came together again after being separated from each other and Haworth. From the dates of her poems, EB's creative period began in 1844.

B87 BYERS, David M. "An Annotated Bibliography of the Criticism on Emily
Brontë's *Wuthering Heights, 1847–1947*" *DAI* 34 (Nov 1973) 2611A–2612A
"Meyer Abram's division of critical approaches into the imitative, the expressive, the pragmatic and the objective is helpful, especially in the discussion of theories of meaning." The
bibliography contains accounts of all criticism on *WH* found in all published listings, excepting
only newspaper accounts and letters. The 262 entries were annotated from an examination of
original texts, covering sources in seven languages. The annotations vary from a few lines to
several hundred words.

B88 CARR, D. R. W. "The Sphinx of English Poetry" *Poetry Review* 34 (Mar–Apr
1943) 85–90
Personally, EB shared with Emily Dickinson an unconcern about publishing what she wrote
and about a posthumous fame. EB's poems reflect her self–containment and mysticism. Among
those her work has influenced are D. H. Lawrence and Charles Morgan.

B89 CARSON, Joan "Visionary Experience in *Wuthering Heights*" *Psychoanalytic
Review* 62 (Spring 1975) 131–51
"The novel's obscurities and its emotional resonance have suggested. . .that the reading of
this work in the light of. . .Jungian psychology might serve to clarify its apparent anomalies."
WH reveals an experience that can be read on three levels. The surface reading is that of
literal plot; the second level is psychological in portraying a regression to childhood; the third
"consists of the archetypal experience of the night sea journey. . . ."

B90 CARTER, Ann A. "Food, Feasting and Fasting in the Nineteenth Century
British Novel" *DAI* 40 (Sept 1979) 1479A
Food, feasting, and fasting are important literary devices used in the novels of Charlotte
and Emily Brontë and in the industrial novels of Mrs Gaskell. The novels discussed are *WH*,
Jane Eyre, *Villette*, *Mary Barton*, and *North and South*.

B91 CAUTLEY, C. Holmes "Old Haworth Folk Who Knew the Brontës" *Cornhill
Magazine* 29 (July 1910) 76–84
This is a record of conversations with the few people in Haworth who remembered the
Brontës.

B92 CECIL, Lord David "Fresh Thoughts on the Brontës" *BST* 16 (1973) 169–76
Upon re–reading *Jane Eyre*, *Villette*, and *WH* and his remarks made about them forty years
earlier, Lord Cecil makes some slight revisions in his original criticism of the first two books,
but makes no change in his view of *WH*. Re–reading *WH* intensified his impression that it is
not a pessimistic work. Moreover, he endorses Herbert Dingle's postulate in "The Origin of
Heathcliff" (B136).

B93 CHADWICK, Esther Alice "Emily Brontë" *Nineteenth Century* 86 (Oct 1919)
677–87
The author discusses Charlotte Brontë's characterization of EB as Shirley Keeldar in *Shirley*
and what past and present critics have said about EB and her work, in an attempt to depict
EB's personality.

B94 ——— "The Haworth Parsonage: The Home of the Brontës" *Nineteenth Century*
103 (Jan 1928) 133–44

Haworth Parsonage, which was to be converted into a Brontë Museum in the summer of 1928, was well known before the Brontës made it famous because Reverend William Grimshaw lived there. There is a description of the parsonage, inside and out, and a discussion of Brontë relics and manuscripts.

CHAMBERS, L. R. *see* B237.

B95 CHAMPION, Larry S. "Heathcliff: A Study in Authorial Technique" *Ball State University Forum* 9 (Spring 1968) 19–25

Heathcliff is seen, not as a devil or incarnation of supernatural forces, but as a "mortal, fallible man twisted and tortured by the evil which pervades his environment...." The characterizations of Joseph, Nelly, and Hindley are foils for the character of Heathcliff and help develop in the reader a critical attitude toward Christianity.

B96 CHASE, Richard "The Brontës: A Centennial Observance (Reconsiderations VIII)" *Kenyon Review* 9 (Autumn 1947) 487–506

Jane Eyre and *WH* are both considered, and EB's poetry is related to *WH*. These Victorian novels translated the social customs of the time into mythical art, whereas other Victorian novels were more concerned with society per se. "The Brontë novels are concerned with the neuroses of women in a man's society." The Brontë heroes and heroines are centers in an enclosed philosophy like A. J. Toynbee's, which gives a new interpretation to the novels. Reprinted: A55, A136, A220. See A283.

B97 CHILDE, Wilfred R. "The Literary Background of the Brontës" *BST* 10 (1944) 204–8

This article is chiefly evidence that much more is known about Charlotte Brontë's literary background than EB's, although some guesses are made regarding what EB read.

B98 CHITHAM, Edward "Almost Like Twins" *BST* 16 (1974) 365–73

A detailed examination of the relationship between Anne and Emily Brontë, as reflected in what we know of their Gondal collaboration and of their more mature poetry and prose.

B99 ——— "Emily Brontë and Shelley" *BST* 17 (1978) 189–96

EB copied her poems into two manuscripts, one titled "Gondal Poems," the other manuscript untitled. This is a close look at the poems in the untitled (A) manuscript; Edward Chitham compares them to the work of Shelley, who may have been a greater influence than has been hitherto supposed since EB had access to his poems in *Fraser's Magazine*.

B100 CHRISTIAN, Mildred G. "A Census of Brontë Manuscripts in the United States" *The Trollopian* 2 (Dec 1947) 177–99 through 3 (Dec 1948) 215–33

Many of the Brontë manuscripts are in the United States, and this is a "finding list" as well as a history of the manuscripts. They are arranged chronologically by date and separated as to author. *The Trollopian* 2 (Mar 1948) contains "Manuscripts of Poems by Emily Brontë" on p 243–53.

B101 ——— "III. A Guide to Research Materials on the Major Victorians (Part II): The Brontës" *Victorian Newsletter* 13 (Spring 1958) 19

This is a listing and discussion of the Brontë manuscript material available to students in the United States and in England. The author notes that no definitive bibliography of works of the Brontës yet exists.

B102 CLAY, Charles T. "Notes on the Chronology of *Wuthering Heights*" BST 12 (1952) 100–105

An excellent, fully–documented analysis of the intricate chronology of *WH* with a geneal-ogical table of the Earnshaw and Linton families. The genealogical table differs slightly from C. P. Sanger's table (see A324) in his *The Structure of* Wuthering Heights. See B396.

B103 COLLINS, Clifford "Theme and Conventions in *Wuthering Heights*" *The Critic* 1 (Autumn 1947) 43–50

Catherine and Heathcliff's love is a life–force relationship and is a principle because the relationship is of an ideal nature. The author touches on a comparison with D. H. Lawrence. Reprinted: A322.

B104 COOK, Davidson "Brontë Manuscripts in the Law Collection" *The Bookman* (London) 69 (Nov 1925) 100–104

The collection contains manuscripts of EB's poems and the manuscript of the 1841 "diary."

B105 ——— "Emily Brontë's Poems" *Nineteenth Century* 100 (Aug 1926) 248–62

Textual corrections of EB's poems and her unpublished poems are printed in this article for the first time. Especially interesting is EB's original poem printed alongside the poem as edited by Charlotte Brontë.

B106 COOPER, Dorothy J. "The Romantics and Emily Brontë" *BST* 12 (1952) 106–12

EB's similarity to the Romantics lies in her appreciation of the individual. She is compared with Keats, Shelley, Byron, Coleridge, Wordsworth, and others.

*B107 COPLEY, J. "The Portrayal of Dialect in *Wuthering Heights* and *Shirley*" *Transactions of the Yorkshire Dialect Society* 14 (1976) 7–16

B108 ——— "*Wuthering Heights* and *Shirley*—A Parallel" *Notes and Queries* n s 3 (Nov 1956) 499–500

The endings of the two novels are similar in their reference to ghosts. The author suggests that Charlotte Brontë in *Shirley* is "reaching out half–heartedly to the world of *Wuthering Heights*."

B109 CORNISH, Dorothy H. "The Brontës' Study of French" *BST* 11 (1947) 97–100

Two of EB's French compositions are translated by the author: "Portrait: Harold the Night before Hastings," and "Filial Love." (See A122, A303, B17, B288, B289 for other essays by EB.)

B110 COTT, Jeremy "Structures of Sound: The Last Sentence of *Wuthering Heights*" *Texas Studies in Literature and Language* 6 (Summer 1964) 280–89

This is an excellent linguistic analysis of the structural grammar in the last sentence of *WH*, relating it to EB's poetic sensibility.

*B111 COWHIG, Ruth M. *"Wuthering Heights—An Amoral Book?" Use of English* 17 (Winter 1965) 123–26

*B112 CRAIG, J. M. [A discussion of the legal problem in *WH*] *Saturday Westminster Gazette* (Sept 9 1916)

B113 CRANDALL, Norma "Charlotte, Emily and Branwell Brontë" *American Book Collector* 13 (Feb 1963) 21–22
The Brontës' "eccentric childhood produced odd lives and neurotic personalities," but "psychological disability in combination with innate gifts is a likely, fertile field for real and marvelous achievement."

B114 CROSS, B. Gilbert "A Brontë Reading List" *BST* 15 (1970) 424–26; 16 (1971) 52–54; 16 (1972) 146–50; 16 (1973) 228–31; 16 (1974) 299–302; 16 (1975) 402–5; 17 (1977) 141–44; 17 (1978) 222–26; 18 (1981) 43–45
These reading lists announce new publications on the Brontës, usually those appearing during the past year, including: new books, scholarly editions, selected reprints and reissues of books, sections in books, and articles. The articles are annotated in most cases. The lists by Cross span the years 1969 when the first list was published through 1981, excepting 1976 (B131), 1979, and 1980 (B279). The 1982 list is also B279.

B115 CROSS, B. Gilbert and Peggy L. Cross "Farewell to Hoffmann?" *BST* 15 (1970) 412–16
The extent of Hoffmann's influence on EB's work is discussed. Principal theories about the sources of *WH* from L. Bradner's essay (B67) are listed, among them Hoffmann's *Das Majorat*. This work is compared to *WH*, and it is established that there may be a link between the two tales, but *WH* is also linked to the Romantics, Scott, and the metaphysicals.

CROSS, Peggy L. *see* B115.

B116 CUNLIFFE, W. R. "The Brontës in Other People's Books" *BST* 11 (1950) 332–36
The Brontës are referred to in James Hilton's *Lost Horizon*, in Dorothy Sayers' *Gaudy Night*, and in other books.

B117 ——— "Emily Brontë: A Clue to Her Appearance" *BST* 13 (1959) 363
Charlotte Brontë, in a letter, describes EB's resemblance to George Henry Lewes. A pencil sketch of Lewes is in this issue of *BST*.

B118 CURRY, Catherine "Maria Brontë and the Brontës' View of Death" *Dublin Magazine* 10 (Winter 1973) 46–55
Although Maria Brontë, the oldest of the Brontë children, died at age thirteen, "she was to shape one of the major attitudes to appear in the later writings of her brother and sisters." EB and Maria were "close in character," and, like Maria, EB had no fear of death.

B119 CURTIS, Myra "Cowan Bridge School: An Old Prospectus Re–examined" *BST* 12 (1953) 187–92
EB entered this school in November 1824. The authenticity of the old prospectus manuscript

used by some Brontë biographers is questioned, and documents known to be genuine are reprinted here.

B120 ———— "The 'Profile' Portrait" *BST* 13 (1959) 342–46
This is a discussion about whether this portrait is of Emily Brontë or Anne Brontë, with the conclusion that it is Anne.

B121 DALEY, A. Stuart "The Date of Heathcliff's Death: April 1802" *BST* 17 (1976) 15–19
Heathcliff's final days set the tempo of the last major movement in *WH*, and the length of time covered matters, in that if it is weeks or months, the effect is subdued, but if it is days, the effect is more intense and dramatic. This essay shows, with strong supportive evidence, that Heathcliff's dissolution and death from beginning to end encompassed three weeks.

B122 ———— "The Moons and Almanacs of *Wuthering Heights*" *Huntington Library Quarterly* 37 (Aug 1974) 337–53
Charles Percy Sanger, in his classic essay on time in *WH* (A324) was puzzled by "the incongruity between the fictive dates and the actual dates of the years assigned to events in the novel." Close examination of the way EB featured the phases of the moon in major scenes shows this to be the principal key to the time sequences in *WH*. Pages of the English *Nautical Almanac* for 1827 are reprinted, and with evidence from the text of *WH*, support Daley's thesis. EB's coordination of time, space, light, and weather is also shown in her poems. See A238h.

*B123 DANIEL, John "*Wuthering Heights* and the Idea of Passion" *London Review* (Winter 1966)
Daniel asserts that the only way to describe the relationship of Catherine and Heathcliff is "incestuous." [From a quote in Cecil W. Davies' essay, B125.]

B124 DAVIES, Cecil W. "Art Within a Tradition: 'Wuthering Heights' and the German 'Novelle' " *BST* 17 (1978) 197–204
This essay seeks to demonstrate that *WH*—far from having no literary tradition—was written in a distinct literary tradition: that of the *Novelle* as it had developed in German literature.

B125 ———— "A Reading of *Wuthering Heights*" *Essays in Criticism* 19 (July 1969) 254–72
The dualistic construction of *WH* stems from the "web of childhood" plays. Heathcliff is no outsider; he is more of an Earnshaw than the Earnshaws themselves. The device of adoption is to make the love of Catherine and Heathcliff possible. Contending that this love is the core of *WH*, Davies discusses the critical views of Allott, Cecil, Kettle, and G. Moore, among others. The parson's daughter must have been familiar with the Pauline doctrine of adoption in Romans 8, 15–17, which may be important to an understanding of *WH* (the adopted son becomes the favorite son). Reprinted: A283.

DAY–LEWIS, C. *see* B303.

B126 DEAN, Christopher "Joseph's Speech in *Wuthering Heights*" *Notes and Queries* n s 7 (Feb 1960) 73–76
The author examines the accuracy and consistency of the West Riding dialect as it is written

in Joseph's speech in *WH*. Although it is judged not entirely scientifically accurate, EB achieved her literary purpose of creating a local atmosphere.

B127 DE GRAZIA, Emilio "The Ethical Dimension of *Wuthering Heights*" *Midwest Quarterly* 19 (Winter 1978) 176–95
A discussion of the structure and symbolism in *WH* which "define the nature of sin, account for the role of evil in the world, and point toward moral imperatives." Sin is the alienation of people from each other, and *WH* is filled with separation: gates, doors, bedchambers. Heathcliff is central to the moral theme as he experiences initiation, separation, and reunion.

B128 DE LAURA, David J. "Some Victorian Experiments in Closure" *Studies in the Literary Imagination* 8 (Fall 1975) 19-35
In this discussion of "a restrained, light 'Stylism'. . .that rose and fell quickly in the last fifteen years of the 19th century," EB is placed among the early- and mid-Victorians "in the restrained use of diction and metaphor and reliance upon 'symbolic' rhythm for intense and poetic effects."

B129 DELBAERE-GARANT, Jeanne "The Divided Worlds of Emily Brontë, Virginia Woolf and Janet Frame" *English Studies* 60 (Dec 1979) 699-711
A comparison of these three authors reveals "a continuity between romanticism, modernism and post modernism." There are parallels between *WH* and Woolf's *The Voyage Out* and *The Waves*, and Frame's *Owls Do Cry* and others of her works.

B130 DE SELINCOURT, Ernest "The Genius of the Brontës" *BST* 2 (Jan 1906) 234–55
The novels of Charlotte Brontë and EB are considered together. They are distinct from other nineteenth-century novels because "whatever their theme, we never get far away from their haunting presence." The novels have a poetic atmosphere. The Brontës are compared with Jane Austen.

B131 DEVERS, James "A Brontë Reading List 1976" *BST* 17 (1976) 62–65
Annotated for the most part, the list includes books, parts of books, reissues of books, plays, and articles. See B114 and B279 for other reading lists.

B132 DEVLIN, James E. "*Wuthering Heights*: The Dominant Image" *Discourse; A Review of the Liberal Arts* 5 (Summer 1962) 337–46
This essay shows very capably that "the motif of the novel, the frustration of psychic forces, is buttressed by a complex and skillful imagery which reflects. . .the main theme." For instance, action in *WH* is generated when a character moves from one house to the other because the houses represent two worlds. There is also a "thick web of imagery of restraint" throughout the novel.

B133 DICKINSON, A. "Spell of the Brontës" *London Quarterly and Holborn Review* 143 (Apr 1925) 256–59
The author's parents and their friends could remember the Brontë family, but knew surprisingly little about them. Here are accounts of some conversations with those who knew the Brontës.

B134 DICKSON, Sarah Augusta "The Arents Collection of Books in Parts and Associated Literature" *Bulletin of The New York Public Library* 61 (June 1957) 267–
80 [274]
The Brontë sisters are mentioned briefly, but none of the Brontë works is included in this
collection.

B135 DINGLE, Herbert "An Examination of Emily Brontë's Poetry from an Un-
accustomed Angle" *BST* 14 (1964) 5–10
Permeating EB's poetry are references to the weather, the time of day, the time of year,
and the light. Correlating the weather records of the Haworth area (the weather record
accompanies this issue) with the dates of her poems may be one yet-unexplored method of
determining which poems are Gondal (in which the Haworth weather probably would not
figure) and which are personal. Reprinted: A87.

B136 ———— "The Origin of Heathcliff" *BST* 16 (1972) 131–38
In a well–supported argument that Heathcliff is Earnshaw's illegitimate son, Herbert Dingle
maintains that this was EB's intent, as is clearly shown in the novel. Quotes from *WH* point
out the weak alibis Earnshaw employs to explain Heathcliff's origin and presence; further
credence is gained from the choice of his name, "...the name of a son who died in childhood...." See B92.

B137 DISKIN, Patrick "Some Sources of *Wuthering Heights*" *Notes and Queries* 24
(July–Aug 1977) 354–61
The possible relationship between *WH* and a number of tales and a novel published in the
Dublin University Magazine between 1835 and 1840 is examined.

B138 DOBSON, Mildred A. [Letter to the Editor] "Emily Brontë" *TLS* (Aug 24
1948) 471
Partly in answer to A. B. Hughes (see B257), the author refers to her article in BST (see
B139) regarding the definition of "mystic" as it applies to EB.

B139 ———— "Was Emily Brontë a Mystic?" *BST* 11 (1948) 166–75
A definition of "mystic" is given and it is pointed out that there is insufficient autobiographical
evidence to answer the question. There is, however, an exploration of EB's possible mystic
experience as reflected in her poems (see B138 and B257).

B140 DODDS, Madeleine Hope "George Hudson and the Brontës" *BST* 14 (1962)
36–37
Miss Branwell left her capital to the three Brontë sisters and a cousin. "On the initiative
of Emily Brontë she and her sisters invested the capital... in the York and the North Midland
Railway." George Hudson owned the railroad.

B141 ———— "The Gondal Poems and Emily Brontë" *Notes and Queries* 188 (May
5 1945) 189
This short article is in reference to poem fragments of EB's and Robert Bridges' interpretation
of them (A40). The poems concerned are "Tell Me, Tell Me, Smiling Child" and "The Inspiring
Music's Thrilling Sound," and they are related to Gondal.

B142 ——— "Gondaliand" *Modern Language Review* 18 (Jan 1923) 9–21
This is the first published attempt to connect EB's poems with her childhood Gondal chronicle. Both the chronicle and the poems contributed to her literary powers shown in *WH*.

B143 ——— "Heathcliff's Country" *Modern Language Review* 39 (Apr 1944) 116–29
Heathcliff's mysterious home, from which he came as a child and to which he returned to become wealthy, is not accounted for by the author's desire to avoid explanations, but was derived from Gondal. In this discussion of Gondal, the author differs with F. E. Ratchford's construction of the Gondal epic (see A299, *The Brontës' Web of Childhood*): there is no single dominating character in the story.

B144 ——— "A Second Visit to Gondaliand" *Modern Language Review* 21 (Oct 1926) 373–79
"The Twelve Adventurers," recently published by C. Shorter and C. W. Hatfield, contains stories written by Charlotte Brontë between the ages of twelve and twenty–one. These stories are shown to be closely connected with EB's poems.

B145 ——— "A Second Visit to Gondaliand" *Modern Language Review* 22 (Apr 1927) 197–98
A corrective note to her previous article (B144) taking into account the 1923 edition of *The Complete Poems of Emily Jane Brontë* and discussing changes of authorship of some of the poems.

B146 DOHENY, John "From *PMLA* to *Wuthering Heights*" *Paunch* 21 (Oct 1964) 21–34
John Doheny rejects the modern intellectual approach to *WH* (B476), arguing firmly for a recognition of the human sexuality of the characters in the novel. This begins a debate later including A. Efron, W. Empson, and W. Thompson, which is continued in later issues of *Paunch*. See B170, B477.

——— *see* B477.

B147 DOOLEY, Lucile "Psychoanalysis of the Character and Genius of Emily Brontë" *Psychoanalytic Review* 17 (Apr 1930) 208–39
This is a very interesting psychological evaluation of EB's character. A closed family circle, such as the Brontës had, "intensifies family relations and conserves emotions of infancy." EB's idea of "the doomed child" (her feeling about herself) is expressed in her poems and in *WH*. Nature was her "adopted mother," and her love of liberty came from her rebellion against her father. Reprinted: A91.

B148 DOYLE, Louis F. "Of Something That Is Gone" *America* 77 (June 14 1947) 297–98
EB's inexperience with the world enabled her to write a masterpiece, *WH*. Modern writers cannot imitate her because they will not melt their experience and imagination down "in the crucible of the creative faculty until it is workable. . . ."

B149 DRABBLE, Margaret "The Writer as Recluse: The Theme of Solitude in the Works of the Brontës" *BST* 16 (1974) 259–69

EB is included in this description of the Brontës as archetypal romantic writers, writing in and about a great solitude.

B150 DREW, Arnold P. "Emily Brontë and *Hamlet*" *Notes and Queries* n s 1 (Feb 1954) 81–82
Catherine Linton's mad scene, and her words while she is pulling feathers from her pillow are compared to Ophelia's flower speech in *Hamlet*, which the author suggests served as a model for Catherine's speech.

B151 DREW, David P. "Emily Brontë and Emily Dickinson as Mystic Poets" *BST* 15 (1968) 227–32
There are parallels between these two poets in character, environment, and poetry, but this article takes up in detail a common theme in their poetry: the expression of the mystical experience.

B152 DREW, Philip "Charlotte Brontë as a Critic of *Wuthering Heights*" *NCF* 18 (Mar 1964) 365–81
In her 1850 preface, Charlotte Brontë correctly evaluated the characters in *WH*: Nelly Dean is a moral force, and Heathcliff an evil force with whom we can sympathize as he works out his doom but whom we cannot call a hero. Reprinted: A10, A104, A136.

B153 DUGAS, Joseph Henry "The Literary Reputation of the Brontës: 1846–1951" *Dissertation Abstracts* 12 No 1 (1952) 61–62
This very thorough dissertation is "an attempt to describe and analyze the fame of the fiction written by Charlotte and Emily Brontë." As understanding of prose fiction grew, so did the popularity of *WH*. Although *Jane Eyre* was the more popular novel in the 1850s, *WH* is more popular in the 1950s. This dissertation has a twenty–seven page bibliography.

B154 DUNN, Richard J. "The Feeling of *Wuthering Heights*" *Research Studies* 45 (Sept 1977) 160–67
At the core of *WH* is the possibility of visionary experience and the impossibility of communicating it. Obviously the central characters are capable of visions and have difficulty explaining their feelings to others, but, as this essay shows, the same is true of the narrators in *WH*. One important instance, because "it presents a paradigm of the conditions for human communication throughout *Wuthering Heights*," is the conversation between Nelly and Catherine about her decision to marry Edgar Linton.

B155 DURBACH, Errol "The *Geschwister–Komplex*: Romantic Attitudes to Brother–Sister Incest in Ibsen, Byron and Emily Brontë" *Mosaic* 12 (Summer 1979) 61–73
Errol Durbach suggests that EB "in order to create a paradigm of the new Heaven—an immortal existence in which Love triumphs over time and change—imposes upon the fallible mortality of human desire the ideal–generating metaphors of incest."

B156 DURRELL, Lawrence "Dylan Thomas and Emily Brontë: The Only Woman I've Ever Loved" *BST* 14 (1963) 36
This is a reprinting of Item A100.

B157 EASSON, Angus "Two Suppressed Opinions in Mrs. Gaskell's *Life of Charlotte Brontë*" *BST* 16 (1974) 281–83
The manuscript of the book includes two opinions, one concerning EB's personality and the other Charlotte's, omitted by Mrs Gaskell from the printed text of 1857.

B158 EDGAR, Pelham "Judgments on Appeal: II. The Brontës" *Queen's Quarterly* 39 (Aug 1932) 414–22
EB and *WH* are discussed on p 418–22. There should be a detachment between a work of art and the personal life of the author. The writer says of *WH*: the character Nelly Dean's narration of the impassioned story is a formal flaw which the book survives. Her role is unbelievable, and there is a break in interest when the first Catherine dies. Reprinted: A102.

B159 EDGERLEY, C. Mabel "The Brontë Struggle against Illness" *BST* 10 (1944) 231–33
A description of the Brontës' illnesses and deaths, partly supported by data on the death certificates.

*B160 ———— "Causes of Death of the Brontës" *British Medical Journal* [pre 1934]
This article contains the certified cause of death of EB. Reprinted: A1, B161.

B161 ———— "Causes of Death of the Brontës" *BST* 8 (1934) 139–42
This is a reprinting of Item B160.

B162 ———— "Emily Brontë: A National Portrait Vindicated" *BST* 8 (1932) 27–32
The authenticity of EB's portrait in the National Portrait Gallery, London, is discussed.

B163 ———— "Ponden Hall and the Heatons" *BST* 10 (1945) 265–68
There is a possibility that the house, Ponden Hall, and the Heaton family were related to the setting of *WH* because EB visited there.

B164 ———— "The Structure of Haworth Parsonage" *BST* 9 (1936) 27–31
A description of the Parsonage accompanied by an architect's drawing of the floor plan and elevations.

B165 ———— "Tabitha Ackroyd" *BST* 10 (1941) 62–68
This is an account of "Tabby," the elderly woman who lived with the Brontës. She took care of the house and the children from 1824 until just before her death in 1855.

B166 EDWARDS, R. A. [Letter to the Editor] "Pot–Shooting" *TLS* (May 6 1949) 297
He comments on the article "Pot–Shooting" (B15), emphasizing that the Brontës did not only "know" Methodism; they were "soaked in it."

B167 EFRON, Arthur " 'Paunch,' 'Wuthering Heights,' and the Body" *Paunch* 40–41 (1975) 166–71
Efron takes exception to Wayne Burns' view (A42) of sexuality in the Catherine–Heathcliff relationship. He believes that what is projected, evoked, or enacted in their literal disembodiment is "a painful and original affirmation of the life of the body, including sexuality."

———— *see* B170.

B168 EGAN, Eileen M. "The Brontës and Catholicism" *The Magnificat* 91 (Feb 1953) 203–5
This is a discussion, from a sectarian point of view, of the reasons why the Brontës were not Catholic.

B169 ELLIOTT, W. Thompson "Atmosphere in the Brontë Works" *BST* 7 (1928) 119–36 [120–31]
EB's personality is seen as mystic, and the setting, characters, and story of *WH* as belonging to another world.

EMPSON, William *see* B477.

B170 EMPSON, William and Arthur Efron "Further Controversy on *Wuthering Heights*" *Paunch* 25 (Feb 1966) 68–72
A continuation of the debate about *WH* on the status of the characters and the theme of revenge, among other things, begun in October 1964. See B146, B477.

B171 EVANS, Margiad "Byron and Emily Brontë: An Essay" *Life and Letters* 57 (June 1948) 193–216
Byron, like EB, was a mystic—especially near the time of his death. This is a comparison of their poetry, their philosophies, their diction, and their religions. *Manfred* is compared with *WH*; Manfred is a Heathcliff with more humanity.

B172 FENTON, Edith M. "The Spirit of Emily Brontë's *Wuthering Heights* as Distinguished from That of Gothic Romance" *Washington University Studies* 8 (Humanistic Series) (1920) 103–22
This is a thorough study of the elements of similarity in *WH* and Gothic Romance. The dreams in *WH* are discussed in terms of Freudian theory.

B173 FIELD, W. T. "Catalogue of Objects in the Museum of the Brontë Society" *BST* 4 (June 1908) 43–72
Two items listed in the catalogue—a water color by EB and the printed circular for the Brontë sisters' proposed school—are both also reproduced.

B174 FIELDING, K. J. "The Brontës and 'The North American Review': A Critic's Strange Guesses" *BST* 13 (1956) 14–18
The review (Oct 1848) of *Jane Eyre*, *WH*, and *The Tenant of Wildfell Hall* is reprinted here and contrasted with Charlotte Brontë's letter in which she describes her sisters' reactions as she read it to them.

B175 FIKE, Francis "Bitter Herbs and Wholesome Medicines: Love as Theological Affirmation in *Wuthering Heights*" *NCF* 23 (Sept 1968) 127–49
The theological affirmation derives from the qualities of love portrayed in *WH*. The central Christian reality, as EB saw it, moves out of the lives of the nominally or neurotically religious characters into the keeping of those—Catherine and Heathcliff, and Cathy and Hareton—who embody Christian reality in their lives.

B176 FINE, Ronald E. "Lockwood's Dreams and the Key to *Wuthering Heights*" *NCF* 24 (June 1969) 16–30
"...My purpose is to demonstrate that the dreams are one of the novel's 'spasms of realism'.... The dreams provide the template for the narrative which they introduce. First, they contain certain elements which recur throughout the novel, such as books, blood, windows, wind, weapons, frustration, anger, terror.... Second, the actions of the dreams are archetypes for crucial narrative actions...." This is a clearly developed, well–written essay relying on the text of *WH* for support of the insightful contentions.

B177 FLAHIFF, Frederick T. C. "Formative Ideas in the Novels of Charlotte and Emily Jane Brontë" *Dissertation Abstracts* 27 (Sept 1966) 746A–747A
The second part of this thesis deals with EB and problems arising out of *WH*. EB resolved in her one novel many technical problems with which Charlotte Brontë struggled. *WH*'s narrative structure "balances involvement against detachment." *WH* is compared and contrasted to Charlotte's novels; *WH* is not like Charlotte's novels but has more affinity with *King Lear*.

B178 FLEMING, Edward V. [Letter to the Editor] "Emily Brontë and 'Louis Parensell' " *Poetry Review* 34 (May–June 1943) 190
This is a brief account of the "Louis Parensell–Love's Farewell" discovery, in reply to Item B44.

B179 FLITTERMAN–KING, Sharon "The Idea of Place: A Study of Setting in *Wuthering Heights, The Mill on the Floss*, and *Tess of the D'Ubervilles*" *DAI* 42 (July 1981) 225A
This study sees a writer's fictive places as existential patterns, or ontological designs. "Emily Brontë embodies her Romantic belief in the imagination's ability to transcend space and time by creating a fictional world that is not fixed to any facts."

B180 FORD, Boris "*Wuthering Heights*" *Scrutiny* 7 (Mar 1939) 375–89
"By common consent there is something wrong with *Wuthering Heights*...," but it has "rigid control and a clarity of execution that are truly remarkable." The texture of the prose is investigated, and the two themes (Catherine–Heathcliff and Catherine–Hareton) are traced and explicated. To be thought "terrible" and not "enjoyable" *WH* has to be stubbornly misread. Partially reprinted: A274.

B181 FOSTER, Amy G. "Brontë Society Publications" *BST* 15 (1966) 96–102
A listing of the contents of the *Transactions* Vol. 1 (1895–1898) through Vol. 14 (1961–1965), along with Parts (usually one appearing each year), and the principal contents of each Part. See A111.

B182 ———— "Brontë Society Publications" *BST* 15 (1967) 182–84
A listing of the contents of the *Transactions* Vol. 11 (1946–1950) through Vol. 15 (1966). See A111.

B183 FOTHERINGHAM, James "The Work of Emily Brontë and the Brontë Problem" *BST* 2 (June 1900) 107–34
EB's character is closely bound with *WH*. Her poems are discussed as they pertain to her character and genius. After presenting a critical history of *WH*, the author writes: "It has

faults of style, defects of construction." One fault is its double narrative; another is its narration by Nelly Dean. The theme is harsh. "It is a work that can never be popular...but it is a work of unquestionable depth, originality, and power, both in conception and execution." The "problem" of the title refers to sources for *WH*, which the author states are Yorkshire, EB's imagination, and the deterioration of Branwell Brontë.

B184 FOXON, D. F. "Binding Variants in the Brontë Poems" *Book Collector* 2 (1953) 219–21

Seven binding variants of the Brontë *Poems*, first and second editions, can be distinguished. Extant copies of the first issue with the original bindings are extremely rare. See A329, B225.

B185 FRANK, Albert J. von "An American Defence of *Wuthering Heights*—1848" *BST* 16 (1974) 277–80

"...[T]he one American review that has so far escaped the notice of Brontë scholars is also the only favourable American review.... It appeared in *Holden's Dollar Magazine* in June 1848...." The review, probably written by Charles F. Briggs, the magazine's editor, is reprinted here.

B186 FRANK, Katherine V. "The Empty Mirror: A Biography of Emily Brontë" *DAI* 40 (Nov 1979) 2694A

This study seeks to demystify previous legendary and static visions of EB's life and work. The biographical narrative focuses on the life events that engendered and confirmed EB's withdrawal from "the world without" and her retreat into "the world within." Her poetry and *WH* map out this interior existence.

B187 FRASER, J. "The Name of Action: Nelly Dean and *Wuthering Heights*" *NCF* 20 (Dec 1965) 223–36

Nelly Dean's conduct throughout *WH* is not only justified, but praised. "[Other] critical attacks [on *WH*]...seem to me symptomatic of a too–common sentimentality about wickedness...."

B188 FRIESNER, Donald N. "Ellis Bell and Israfel" *BST* 14 (1964) 11–18

This is a comparison of the lives and the poems of EB and Edgar Allan Poe.

B189 FULCHER, Paul M. [Letter to the Editor] "Emily Brontë" *Saturday Review of Literature* 5 (Sept 22 1928) 150

A brief comment called forth by a review of Romer Wilson's biography (see A408) of EB. He criticizes the reviewer's conjecturing because it is like that of Romer Wilson.

B190 GALLANT, Christine "The Archetypal Feminine in Emily Brontë's Poetry" *Women's Studies* 7, Nos 1–2 (1980) 79–94

In a plea for a more critical attention to EB's poems, Gallant says, "There is an authentic and haunting power to a number of poems which lifts them above their usual designation as 'minor poetry of a major novelist.' " The Gondal poems are seen as an affirmation of the archetypal Feminine, and the "personal" poems as a search for meaning in the individual self.

B191 GANNER, Heidemarie "*Wuthering Heights* in German Translation" *BST* 17 (1980) 375–78

German translation of *WH* began in 1851, together with the appearance of the English edition of the German publisher Tauchnitz in Leipzig. *WH* in Germany, however, did not have a lasting impact. A chronological list of German versions follows.

B192 GARBETT, Cyril "The Courage of the Brontës" *BST* 11 (1950) 327–31
This is a sermon preached at Haworth Parish Church on May 28 1950. "Their [the Brontës'] tragedy should shame those who...complain over smaller sorrows."

B193 GARRETT, Peter K. "Double Plots and Dialogical Form in Victorian Fiction" *NCF* 32 (June 1977) 1–17
WH forces us to shift from single to multiple focus, resulting in a tension between possible interpretations. Combined with the doubled narration of Lockwood and Nelly Dean, the reader must try alternate interpretations and thematic oppositions such as those between the houses, and between natural and supernatural forces and civilization.

B194 GATES, Barbara "Suicide and *Wuthering Heights*" *Victorian Newsletter* 50 (Fall 1976) 15–19
Eighteenth– and early nineteenth–century suicide law is summarized, and folk–belief regarding suicides seems consistent with some scenes in *WH*. "Heathcliff's claim to Wuthering Heights depends on his concealing his own conviction that Hindley's death is suicidal.... Catherine's burial place under the churchyard wall may have been determined by the nature of her death...."

B195 GÉRIN, Winifred "Byron's Influence on the Brontës" *Keats–Shelley Memorial Bulletin* 17 (1966) 1–19
(The frontispiece in this issue is "a water–colour by Emily Brontë of Lady Harley.") Four general characteristics of Byron's poetry are particularized and they sound remarkably like *WH* and *Jane Eyre*. *WH* and EB's poems are discussed on p 11–17. That Heathcliff is a very Byronic hero is shown by a comparison with Manfred.

B196 GILBERT, Ariadne "Children of the Moors" *St. Nicholas* 43 (May 1916) 646–50
A short informal history of the Brontës, containing a great deal of supposition about their personalities. EB's homesickness is related to one of her poems.

B197 GIRDLER, Lew "*Wuthering Heights* and Shakespeare" *Huntington Library Quarterly* 19 (Aug 1956) 385–92
EB was "so imbued with [Shakespeare's] plays that words and phrases from them sprang readily to her mind and often colored her writing." At two points in *WH*, EB refers directly to Shakespeare: to *Twelfth Night* and *King Lear*. These are the only evidences from her own pen that she knew Shakespeare. However, a comparison of *WH* with the plays Charlotte Brontë recommends in a letter to Ellen Nussey shows "striking parallels in theme, characterization, structure, and literary devices...." The plays considered are *Hamlet*, *Macbeth*, *Richard III*, *King Lear*, and *Taming of the Shrew*.

B198 GLECKNER, Robert F. "Time in *Wuthering Heights*" *Criticism* 1 (Fall 1959) 328–38
This is a perceptive essay by a student of William Blake. The time theme, central to *WH*, alone accounts for the character of Heathcliff. The past increasingly presses upon the present

in the narrative and in Heathcliff's mind. The key temporal images are the window and the mirror.

B199 GOLDSTONE, Herbert "*Wuthering Heights* Revisited" *English Journal* 48 (Apr 1959) 175–85
WH is now widely read and taught in senior high schools. This article, directed to high school teachers, rejects the analyses of *WH* by David Cecil (A51) and Dorothy Van Ghent (A374) and asserts that "the view of life in the book is direct, simple, very comprehensive, and clearly presented."

B200 GORDAN, John D. "What's in a Name? Authors and Their Pseudonyms" *Bulletin of The New York Public Library* 60 (Mar 1956) 107–28 [109]
The subtitle is "Notes on an Exhibition from the Berg Collection." *Poems by Currer, Ellis and Acton Bell* is included in this list of pseudonymous books. The real names of the authors are withheld until the end of the article.

B201 GOSE, Elliott B., Jr "*Wuthering Heights*: The Heath and the Hearth" *NCF* 21 (June 1966) 1–19
WH is seen on four levels: fairy tale, religion and the Bible, traditional elements of nature, and the process of initiation. Fire imagery is discussed. The "hearth" is synonymous with weak characters, i.e., the Lintons, and the "heath" with the strong characters, i.e., Heathcliff.

B202 GOSSE, Edmund "The Challenge of the Brontës" *BST* 2 (Feb 1904) 195–202
Although the focus is upon Charlotte Brontë and EB is generally included in statements about "the Brontë sisters," the article points out that pride, stubbornness, and imperviousness to public opinion were characteristics shared by the sisters. Reprinted: A131, A132.

B203 GOULD, Gerald L. "Emily Brontë's Relation to Gondal as Subject of *Wuthering Heights*" *DAI* 35 (Sept 1974) 1655A–1656A
"*Wuthering Heights* is an attempt to resolve the conflict between the death– and childhood–oriented . . . Gondal and the world of ordinary consciousness and adulthood." EB's compulsive attention to threshold and barrier imagery in *WH* is an expression of her ambivalence about Gondal.

*B203A GOWER, Edmund I. "The Sphinx of Our Modern Literature" *Friends Quarterly Examiner* 44 (Jan–Mar 1900) 251–61

B204 GRAZHDANSKAYA, Z. "Emily Brontë and Her Novel *Wuthering Heights*" trans Ethel Bronstein *BST* 17 (1976) 21–29
This is the prefatory essay in the first Russian edition of *WH* published in Moscow in 1956. Emphasis is on EB's social consciousness, e.g., "In Emily's creative powers can be heard an echo of the stormy events and advanced ideas of her time." See B299.

B205 GREEN, David Bronte "Portraits of the Brontë Sisters" *The Connoisseur* 120 (Sept 1947) 26–28, 66
The Brontë portraits are discussed, and the opinions of them held by Charlotte Brontë, Mrs Gaskell, and others are reprinted.

*B206 GREEN, Joseph J. "The Brontë–Wheelwright Friendship" *The Friends Quarterly Examiner* (Jan 1916)

B207 GREENWOOD, J. F. "Haworth" *BST* 2 (May 1901) 151–66
A history and description of Haworth, including quotes from the church registers regarding the Brontës' deaths; the Yorkshire weather and historical events are also included.

*B208 GRIMSHAW, Beatrice "Emily and Charlotte Brontë" *John O'London's Weekly* (Oct 1921)

B209 —— "First Love: A Glory That Is Never Forgotten" *John O'London's Weekly* (Oct 4 1924) 4
This sentimental investigation of "first love" includes Charlotte Brontë, Byron, and Keats, among others. EB "knew love," and her poem "Cold in the Earth" is quoted to prove it.

B210 GROVE, Robin "*Wuthering Heights*" *Critical Review* 8 (1965) 71–87
This is an investigation of the bond and relationship between Catherine and Heathcliff which is the "great fact and focus" of *WH*. EB is concerned with the unnaturalness of their love. The Hareton and Catherine Linton love is a kind of anti–masque or counterfeit of that of Catherine and Heathcliff.

B211 GRUDIN, Peter D. "*Wuthering Heights*: The Question of Unquiet Slumbers" *Studies in the Novel* 6 (Winter 1974) 389–407
Supernatural elements of *WH* ". . .are not. . .subject merely to the deranged perspectives of the novel's characters, but. . .create an objective context that is consistent and that has a bearing on the work's thematic emphasis. . . ."

*B212 GUTTELING, J. F. C. ["Emily Brontë"] *Students' Monthly* (Dec 1918)

B213 HADOW, W. H. "Education, As Treated by the Brontës" *BST* 6 (1925) 261–75
A bettèr title would be "the education received by the Brontës." Cowan Bridge School, Father Brontë (who as a father was not admirable), and the Brontës' reading matter are discussed.

B214 HAFLEY, James "The Villain in *Wuthering Heights*" *NCF* 13 (Dec 1958) 199–215
Nelly Dean is the villain. Frequently in a position to interfere with the actions of the characters and resentful and ambitious because of her station, Nelly manipulates people and events so that upon Catherine's death she finally becomes mistress of Thrushcross Grange. Reprinted: A220.

B215 HAGAN, John "Control of Sympathy in *Wuthering Heights*" *NCF* 21 (Mar 1967) 305–23
This is an analysis of the way in which EB accomplishes and sustains the reader's moral "double view" that allows him to disapprove of the actions of Heathcliff and Catherine, and yet never to lose sympathy with them. Reprinted: A136.

B216 HAGOOD, Patricia "Lancelot and Heathcliff: Obsessive–Compulsive Traits of the Hero" *DAI* 39 (Dec 1978) 3563A–3564A

In this parallel study of *WH* and Chretien's *Lancelot*, it is shown that both works are allegories with obsessive heroes. Both works employ dichotomous worlds, the abduction motif, and the Oedipus complex, among other devices, to work out oppositions and contraries.

B217 HALDANE, Elizabeth S. "The Brontës and Their Biographers" *Nineteenth Century* 112 (Dec 1932) 752–64

The biographers treated here are Mrs Gaskell and E. F. Benson. Various letters to and from people who knew the Brontës are discussed.

B218 HALDANE, R. B. "Emily Brontë's Place in Literature" *BST* 2 (May 1901) 142–50

Of the two sisters, Charlotte and Emily, Emily was the poet. "Emily must be placed not only above Charlotte, but with Shakespeare and Milton...."

B219 HALE, Norman L. "Views from Outside: Five Studies in Victorian Omniscience" *DAI* 37 (Dec 1976) 3641A–3642A

Each of the five novels studied, *WH*, *Little Dorritt*, *Pendennis*, *The Woodlanders*, and *Nostromo*, has a style of narration examining "human experience from a point of view outside it...as opposed to the inside treatment of character typical of the Jamesian novel."

B220 HALEY, William "Three Sisters" *BST* 11 (1947) 73–80

EB, Charlotte Brontë, and Anne Brontë had different personalities; they are compared with Chekov's Olga, Irina, and Masha Prozorov. Reprinted: A1.

B221 HALL, Henry C. "Early Victorian Portrait: Is It Emily Brontë?" *Apollo* 59 (Mar 1954) 68

An unsigned portrait, dated circa 1838–40, is thought possibly to be of EB, but there is no conclusive proof. An illustration of the portrait accompanies the article.

*B222 HANSON, T. W. "Emily Brontë's Footprints" *Municipal Libraries Readers' Guide* (Feb 1910)

B223 ———— "The Local Colour of *Wuthering Heights*" *BST* 6 (1924) 201–19

The author is a native of the moorlands of Yorkshire. He relates *WH* and some of EB's poetry to the country and to the climate.

B224 HARBOTTLE, A. [Letter to the Editor] "A Brontë Metre" *TLS* (Nov 26 1938) 755

The same metre that EB uses in "No Coward Soul Is Mine" was used by Dr Monsell in his hymn, "Birds Have Their Quiet Nests." (See also B344.)

B225 HARGREAVES, G. D. "The Publishing of *Poems by Currer, Ellis and Acton Bell*" *BST* 15 (1969) 294–300

An account of the initial publication and re–issues of the poems. Some examples of discrepancies between printed and manuscript readings of EB's poems are given. Binding variants and surviving manuscripts are discussed. Reprinted: B226. See A329, B184.

B226 ———— "The Publishing of *Poems by Currer, Ellis and Acton Bell*" *Library Review* 22 (Autumn 1970) 353–56
A reprinting of B225.

B226A ———— "Signatures and Dashes in Novels Printed by T. C. Newby in the Eighteen–Forties" *Studies in Bibliography* 34 (1981) 253–57
A bibliographical investigation of Thomas Cautley Newby's printing practices. His signature system appears in volume 1 of the 1847 edition of *WH*, although only volume 2 carries his name as printer. Further indication of his work appears in the occasional use of "..." for "—".

B227 HARRIS, Anne Leslie "Psychological Time in *Wuthering Heights*" *International Fiction Review* 7 (Summer 1980) 112–17
The focus of this discussion is on time as defined by and defining Catherine and Heathcliff. EB weaves layers of time, distancing the reader and, although less so, Nelly Dean and Lockwood. The narrators cling to the clock and calendar thereby contrasting their temporal time with the time of Catherine and Heathcliff, which is deep cyclical time.

B228 HARRISON, G. Elsie [Letter to the Editor] "The Brontës and Methodism" *TLS* (June 24 1949) 413
She makes the distinction that she is not, in her book *The Clue to the Brontës* (A150), trying to prove the Brontës Methodists, but is pointing out the enormity of the Methodist influence upon them. (This letter is possibly a reply to Letters to the Editor from P. Bentley [B53] and T. Olsen [B378]).

B229 HARTLEY, L. P. "Emily Brontë in Gondal and Gaaldine" *BST* 14 (1965) 1–15
WH presents "the dilemma of the soul in the most naked and uncompromising fashion." EB's essay on Harold on the eve of the Battle of Hastings "shows that in certain moods Emily was in love with defeat and possibly with death." Some of her poems are visions of lost happiness. This is a long, well–documented assertion of EB's unhappiness and possible misanthropy. Reprinted: A154.

———— *see* B237.

B230 HATCH, Ronald B. "Heathcliff's 'Queer End' and Schopenhauer's Denial of the Will" *Canadian Review of Comparative Literature* 1 (Winter 1974) 49–64
Many criticisms and interpretations of *WH* have slighted the ending of the novel, especially Heathcliff's death. The reader's sympathy for Heathcliff is deliberately maintained throughout so that Heathcliff can undergo a "redeeming process" at the end of the story. "In terms remarkably similar to those of Emily Brontë, Schopenhauer gives a full explanation of the type of 'suicide' which Heathcliff represents." This provocative essay also correlates Catherine's dying speech to the philosophy of Schopenhauer.

B231 HATFIELD, C. W. [Letter to the Editor] "Emily Brontë's 'Lost Love' " *TLS* (Aug 29 1936) 697
Mr Hatfield asserts that EB had no "lost love"; the letter is in response to a review of V. Moore's *The Life and Eager Death of Emily Brontë* (A258) entitled "Emily Brontë's 'Lost Love.' "

B232 HAWKES, Jacquetta "Emily Brontë in the Natural Scene" *BST* 12 (1953) 173–86
EB's Celtic inheritance was sufficiently alien to the moors to allow her to respond to them "with heightened force." EB's poetry contrasts dark and light, and the darkness is of the moors.

B233 ———— "The Haworth Moors" *Spectator* 190 (May 15 1953) 600
This is a personal description of Haworth and the moors. The contrast between the dark moorland and the light valley is related to EB's poetry and *WH*. (See B438 for a reply.)

B233A HAYNES, R. D. "Elements of Romanticism in *The Story of an African Farm*" *English Literature in Transition* 24, No 2 (1981) 59–79
Olive Schreiner's *The Story of an African Farm* has striking similarities to *WH*, "an indication of the extent to which Olive Schreiner consciously saw herself as a writer in the tradition of Emily Brontë and of the Romantic poets."

B234 HAYWARD, John [Letter to the Editor] "The First American Edition of the Brontës' Poems" *Book Collector* 8 (Winter 1959) 432
This is a query about the printing and publication of the *Poems by Currer, Ellis and Acton Bell*. (See B26 and B405 for replies.)

B235 HEDLEY, Arthur [Letter to the Editor] "Emily Brontë's Second Novel" *TLS* (Sept 6 1947) 451
In one of Charlotte Brontë's letters written in 1848 she states that EB is writing a novel. This letter asks what became of this "second novel." See B65, B239, B295.

B236 HENDERSON, Philip [Letter to the Editor] "Emily Brontë's Poems" *TLS* (Nov 30 1951) 765
He defends his edition of EB's poems and discusses the question of the authorship of "The Visionary," which has been argued before in *TLS* (B237).

B237 HENDERSON, Philip; Edwin Morgan; L. R. Chambers; L. P. Hartley [Letters to the Editor] "Emily Brontë's Poems" *TLS* (1949) (Jan 29) 73; (Feb 12) 110; (Mar 12) 169; (Apr 9) 233; (Apr 23) 270
This is a controversy about EB's poem "The Visionary," as to whether or not Charlotte Brontë wrote the last two verses. The editor put an end to the discussion with his article, "Pot–Shooting" (B15).

B238 HENNEMAN, John B. "The Brontë Sisters" *Sewanee Review* 9 (Apr 1901) 220–34
The Brontës' environment had more influence upon them than their ancestry. "Tabby," the Yorkshire woman who took care of the Brontë children, gave them insight into Yorkshire human nature and recounted the folklore. They were also strongly influenced by their father.

B239 HEWISH, John [Letter to the Editor] "Emily Brontë's Missing Novel" *TLS* (Mar 10 1966) 197
EB did not write a "missing" second novel. Newby, her publisher, referred to *The Tenant of Wildfell Hall* but was careless and mistakenly addressed the envelope to Ellis Bell instead of Acton Bell. (See B295 for a reply.) Reprinted: B240. See B65.

B240 ———— "Emily Brontë's Second Novel" *BST* 15 (1966) 28
This is a reprinting of Item B239.

———— *see* B402.

B241 HIGDON, David Leon "A Poetics of Fictional 'Time Shapes' " *Bucknell Review*
22 (1976) 50–68
WH and Conrad's novels "obtain much of their unique power from barrier time." By bringing
Lockwood and the reader to the scene after the main action has taken place, EB achieves the
same effect as that in a fairy tale. It is further pointed out that EB's meticulously exact dates
in *WH* are not at all the time experienced by the reader. Higdon also discusses "time shapes"
in the works of G. Eliot, Hardy, and Defoe, among others.

*B242 HIROTA, Minoru "A Comparative Study of *Wuthering Heights* and 'The Fall
of the House of Usher' " *Studies in English Language and Literature* (Fukuoka,
Japan) 27 (1976?) 115–36 (English summary, 143–44)

B243 ———— "The Elements of American Romance in *Wuthering Heights*: Concur-
rent Origin and Themes Found in *Wuthering Heights* and 'The Fall of the House
of Usher' " *Studies in English Language and Literature* (Fukuoka, Japan) 30 (Feb
1980) 57–75
WH is closer to the traditional American novel than it is to the English novel and has much
in common with the work of Edgar Allan Poe, as well as the traditional American novel forms
that can be traced in Hawthorne, Melville, James, and Faulkner. EB, like Poe, is concerned
with the spiritual conditions of the characters. Drawing upon Erich Fromm's *The Heart of
Man*, the works of Poe and EB are compared in the light of "incestuous symbiosis," and some
of the basic elements to link the two works are the images of sleep, mist, water, and descent.

B244 HIRST, J. C. "The Burial Place of the Brontës" *BST* 9 (1938) 181–85
The author, Rector of Haworth, gives an exact record of the Brontës' burial place. Reprinted:
A1.

B245 HOAR, Nancy Cowley "The Brontës' Floral Year" *BST* 16 (1971) 40–42
Flowers appear in profusion in Brontë novels and letters, but the flowers in *WH* are nearly
always wild.

B246 HOLGATE, Ivy "The Branwells at Penzance" *BST* 13 (1960) 425–32
"The Brontë juvenilia...abounds in sea–imagery and is set in foreign lands," due to the
influence of their aunt, Elizabeth Branwell, who told them stories of Penzance and the sea.
The article also gives a record of Branwell property and the family in Penzance.

B247 ———— "The Brontës at Thornton: 1815–1820" *BST* 13 (1959) 323–38
Thornton is the birthplace of Charlotte, Branwell, Emily, and Anne Brontë. The Brontës
lived there from 1815 to 1820. Inventories of the chapel are listed; the church records and
an old diary mention the dates Patrick Brontë preached.

B248 ———— "The Structure of *Shirley*" *BST* 14 (1962) 27–35
This article contains a description of EB as the heroine in Charlotte Brontë's novel *Shirley*.

B249 HOLLOWAY, Owen E. *"Wuthering Heights*: A Matter of Method" *Northern Miscellany of Literary Criticism* 1 (Autumn 1953) 65–74

The most interesting aspect of *WH* is the unique position it holds in novel literature. Its artistic strength lies in the method of narration: the protagonists are hardly presented directly at all. Since the story is not chronologically straightforward, the reader must participate and build the story for himself. The present is the appearance of things; that which is narrated of the past is the reality; and when reality has filled appearance, there is another great change to a new reality of the future.

B250 HOMANS, Margaret "Repression and Sublimation of Nature in *Wuthering Heights*" *PMLA* 93 (Jan 1978) 9–19

Most of *WH* takes place indoors, but Nature is a major element in the novel. Why did EB choose an indirect mode of the presentation of Nature instead of a direct one? Because Nature, or the destructive reality it represents, is so threatening that it must be repressed, while the figurative use of Nature is a sublimation, redirecting the dangerous force into a safe and constructive channel. Two keys to the analysis are Catherine's recollection of the lapwing story and the fragment of Cathy's diary found by Lockwood.

B251 ———— "Studies in the Feminine Poetic Imagination: Dorothy Wordsworth, Emily Brontë, and Emily Dickinson" *DAI* 39 (Oct 1978) 2229A

"This dissertation explores the ways in which three representative women poets, textually conscious of their femininity, respond to a literary tradition that depends on and reinforces the masculine orientation of language and of the poet."

B252 HOPEWELL, Donald "Cowan Bridge" *BST* 6 (1921) 43–49

This is an illustrated description of the school and the records of the school concerning the Brontës.

B253 ———— "The Misses Brontë—Victorians" *BST* 10 (1940) 3–11

The author discusses the extent to which the three Brontë sisters are "Victorian." *WH* is the only "perfectly constructed" Brontë novel. Reprinted: A1.

B254 ———— "A Westminster Abbey Memorial to the Brontës" *BST* 9 (1939) 236–38

The inscription on the Memorial (to be placed in The Poets' Corner) uses the last line of EB's poem "Old Stoic": "...with courage to endure."

B255 HOUSE, Roy T. "Emily Brontë" *The Nation* 107 (Aug 17 1918) 169–70

August 20 1918 would have been EB's one–hundredth birthday. "*Wuthering Heights* is nearly forgotten by the general public, while *Jane Eyre*...is still...widely read." He praises EB as the "poet turned novelist."

B256 HOWELLS, William Dean "Heroines of Nineteenth–Century Fiction. XIX: The Two Catherines of Emily Brontë" *Harper's Bazaar* 33 (Dec 19 1900) 2224–30

WH is compared, in some respects, with *Jane Eyre*. "Seldom has a great romance been worse contrived," he says, referring to the double narrative. However, he praises EB's non–intrusive authorship, and the "unfaltering truth of her scenes." Reprinted: A173.

B257 HUGHES, A. B. [Letter to the Editor] "Emily Brontë" *TLS* (Aug 7 1948) 443
The writer points out the reasons he believes EB was not a mystic. (See B138 for a reply.)

B258 HUGUENIN, Charles A. "Brontëana at Princeton University: The Parrish Collection" *BST* 12 (1955) 391–400
The collection contains early editions of the poetry of the three Brontë sisters and early editions of *WH*.

B259 INSH, George P. "Haworth Pilgrimage" *BST* 10 (1944) 209–13
The significance of Heathcliff is found in man's struggle against the moors. There are two important passages in the early chapters of *WH*: Lockwood's being attacked by the dogs and his encounter with the brindled cat, "Grimalkin." In the first *King Lear* is mentioned, and the second refers to *Macbeth*.

B260 IRWIN, I. H. "The Home of the Brontës" *The Woman's Journal* n s 15 (Nov 1930) 18–19, 44–46
This is a personal account of a visit to Haworth Parsonage, interwoven with the Brontë story.

B261 ISENBERG, David R. "A Gondal Fragment" *BST* 14 (1962) 24–26
This is the description and investigation of a 4 1/2″ × 3 1/2″ note (reproduced in Plate 4 of the issue) in EB's hand listing the heights and characteristics of Gondal characters. The young Gondal characters are compared with characters in *WH*.

B261A JACK, Ian "Novels and Those 'Necessary Evils': Annotating the Brontës" *Essays in Criticism* 32 (Oct 1982) 321–37
An editor and the annotator of the Oxford Clarendon editions of the Brontë novels, Jack recounts his bibliographical experiences with *Jane Eyre* and *WH*. He sees the principal duty of an annotator as an "attempt to enable his contemporaries to read a book as its original audience read it."

B262 JACOBS, Carol "*Wuthering Heights*: At the Threshold of Interpretation" *Boundary 2* 7 (Spring 1979) 49–71
Lockwood has many difficulties with the disparity between text and dreams at the beginning of *WH*; disparity between texts and dreams is at the center of the novel. Frank Kermode's essay (B275) is discussed, the function of names in *WH* is explored, and it is pointed out that there is a repetition of violent character displacement throughout the novel.

B263 JEFFERSON, Douglas "Irresistible Narrative: The Art of *Wuthering Heights*" *BST* 17 (1980) 337–47
The narrative of *WH* is irresistible in the same way as that in Coleridge's *Rime of the Ancient Mariner*. EB has not been given enough credit as an artist in the genre of the novel; to mention only one example, ". . . the subtlety and maturity of her characterization."

B264 JOHNSTON, Myrtle "The Brontës in Ireland" *Cornhill Magazine* 158 (July 1938) 76–87
The article refers to incidents recorded in William Wright's book, *The Brontës in Ireland* [1893], about the brothers of Patrick Brontë who lived in Ireland.

B265 [JONES, Joseph] "Rare Book Collections. I." *Library Chronicle of the University of Texas* 3 (Spring 1950) 224–25

Brontëana which is "a storehouse of secondary source material" was received by the University of Texas in September 1949. It was accumulated by Alex Symington in association with Thomas J. Wise. The collection includes: printed and typewritten bibliographies and catalogues of the Brontë family, several thousand magazine articles and newspaper clippings pertaining to the Brontës, transcripts of all letters by and to the Brontës known to the collector, facsimiles of Brontë manuscripts, scarce books and private prints including many of the Wise–Shorter pamphlets, and hundreds of photographs and slides of persons, places, and objects connected with the Brontës.

B266 JORDAN, John E. "The Ironic Vision of Emily Brontë" *NCF* 20 (June 1965) 1–18

Lockwood is "the city slicker in the haunted house." Opposed to David Cecil's view (see A51) that EB was innocent of irony, Jordan sees in *WH* "a fabric of ironies." Young Catherine, Nelly Dean, and Lockwood are major instruments of EB's irony—through their comments and narrations. The ultimate achievements of both Catherines are additional ironies. The significance of Zillah is discussed and the bird imagery pointed out.

*B267 JUNKIN–HILL, Margaret "Myths and Fallacies in *Wuthering Heights*" *Lakehead University Review* 3 (1970) 46–55

B268 JUSTUS, James "Beyond Gothicism: *Wuthering Heights* and an American Tradition" *Tennessee Studies in Literature* 5 (1960) 25–33

This is an investigation of the elements in *WH* "that make it vital in man's experience." *WH* is compared with the work of Hawthorne, Melville, Dreiser, and Faulkner.

B269 KATES, Bonnie R. "Novels of Individuation: Jungian Readings in Fiction" *DAI* 39 (Feb 1979) 4959A

"This work uses myth, psychoanalysis and literary criticism to trace the progress of a heroic myth of personality development through the fiction of the nineteenth century." *WH* is a successful novel of individuation. The other authors treated are M. Shelley, Hawthorne, and H. Rider Haggard.

B270 KAVANAUGH, James H. "Towards a Materialist Criticism: Explorations in Contemporary Critical Theory and Practice" *DAI* 38 (Mar 1978) 5461A–5462A

Analyzing recent trends in literary theory from the perspective of historical materialism, this study proposes an example of a materialist criticism with an interpretation of *WH*.

B271 KELLETT, E. E. "New Light on the Brontës" *London Quarterly and Holborn Review* 160 (Oct 1935) 519–21

Of all the Brontës, EB was especially influenced by the Methodism in Yorkshire.

B272 KELLY, Charlotte M. "What I Saw at Haworth" *Irish Digest* 78 (Oct 1963) 83–85

A personal description of the interior of the Brontë Museum at Haworth.

B273 KENNEY, Blair G. "Nelly Dean's Witchcraft" *Literature and Psychology* 18, No 4 (1968) 225–32

Nelly Dean is not so much a villain as "a witch, brought out of *Macbeth* to another heath, to prophesy doom to those modern murderers, Catherine Earnshaw and Heathcliff, who kill only themselves." The other two of the Shakespearean witch trio are Zillah and Cathy. Nelly is central to *WH*: "A close reading...suggests that Hindley was in fact the center of Nelly's emotional life, even though Hindley did not return her feelings, and suggests that sexual jealousies are the bases of Nelly's most puzzling acts...." The argument is well–supported by passages in *WH*.

B274 KENTON, Edna "Forgotten Creator of Ghosts; Joseph Sheridan Le Fanu, Possible Inspirer of the Brontës" *Bookman* (New York) 69 (July 1929) 528–34 [531–32]

The similarities between *The Purcell Papers* of Le Fanu and the Brontë novels are delineated. It was perhaps from Le Fanu's "occult" writings that EB derived Heathcliff. The tales were "Irish" or "ghostly."

B275 KERMODE, Frank "A Modern Way with the Classic" *New Literary History* 5 (Spring 1974) 415–34

In this discussion of what exactly constitutes a classic, Kermode has chosen *WH* as his example of a classic because "it meets the requirement that it is read in a generation far separated from the one it was presented to...." He addresses first the novel in isolation from its criticism, then some of its criticism, alluding to criticism of other classics such as *The Aeneid* and *King Lear*. See B262.

B276 KESTNER, Joseph "John Gibson Lockhart's *Matthew Wald* and Emily Brontë's *Wuthering Heights*" *Wordsworth Circle* 8 (Spring 1982) 94–96

Lockhart's final novel, *The History of Matthew Wald*, published in 1824, contains matter sufficiently like that in *WH* to be considered one of the possible sources of *WH*. Matthew's similarities to Heathcliff include not only his gypsy–like appearance, but also his oppression by his step–uncle and his contemptuous and unforgiving reaction to that oppression. Matthew and his Katherine share a close childhood and an enduring love for each other, and Matthew's life is concerned with inheritances, religious fanaticism, and revenge.

B277 KIERNAN, N. S. "The Moon in the Brontë Novels" *BST* 18 (1981) 36–38

In this short survey of mention of the moon in all the Brontë novels, it is noted that references to the moon appear only three times in *WH*; they are brief and realistic.

B278 KITE, J. E. [Letter to the Editor] "*Wuthering Heights*" *TLS* (Mar 16 1951) 165

He has a first edition of *WH* with penciled corrections in what Thomas J. Wise has identified as EB's handwriting. However, Charlotte Brontë did not make use of these corrections in subsequent editions.

B279 KLAUS, Meredith "A Brontë Reading List" *BST* 17 (1979) 302–6; 17 (1980) 382–86; 18 (1982) 152–56

Lists, for the current year: books, editions of Brontë works, reprints, sections in books, miscellaneous, and articles (articles annotated in most cases). See B114 and B131 for other Reading Lists.

B280 KLINGOPULOS, G. D. "The Novel as Dramatic Poem (II): *Wuthering Heights*" *Scrutiny* 14 (Sept 1947) 269–86

Two factors may explain a reader's dislike of *WH*: (1) *WH* is not a moral tale; nor is it a perfect work of art; (2) some of the passages are too insistent and deliberate. The tensions and conflicts in the novel are discussed. EB is "the first writer to have used the novel as a vehicle for that kind of statement which is contained in the finest of English dramatic poetry." *WH* is compared with her poem "Cold in the Earth," and is comparable to *Macbeth* although it does not have that play's coherence. See A283.

B281 KOLB, Eduard "An Exercise in Dialect Detection" *Transactions of the York-shire Dialect Society* 11 (1955) 11–17
Using excerpts from Joseph's speech in *WH*, the author demonstrates that dialect can be geographically placed by a process of elimination employing the lexical, morphological, and phonological features of dialect. See A284, A238j.

B282 KRIER, William J. "A Pattern of Limitations: The Heroine's Novel of the Mind" *DAI* 34 (July 1973) 277A–278A
Relying on an analysis of Descartes' *Discourse on Method* to polarize the mind and the world, the minds in the dissertation being those of heroines trapped in a powerless position, Krier investigates "the feminine situation." *Moll Flanders*, *Vanity Fair*, *Emma*, *WH*, *The Scarlet Letter*, and *Portrait of a Lady* are the novels studied.

B283 KRUPAT, Arnold "The Strangeness of *Wuthering Heights*" *NCF* 25 (Dec 1970) 269–80
Krupat discusses the technique of EB, the way she handles her materials. "The most prominent characteristic of the shared speech of Nelly and Lockwood is its fixity. The other characters are engaged in constant change with much at stake, but for the narrators, nothing is at stake. Both narrators also have a narrowness of emotional range...a diction of enforced limitedness...."

B284 LAMBERT, Diane E. "A Shaping Spirit: A Study of the Novels of Emily and Charlotte Brontë" *Dissertation Abstracts* 28 (May 1968) 4634A–4635A
A study of the five novels of EB and Charlotte Brontë, tracing (1) the literary and life experiences which shaped the Brontë imagination and (2) the way in which that imagination in turn shaped the novels.

B285 LANDOR, Mikail "Emily Brontë in Russia (On the 150th Anniversary of Her Birth)" *Soviet Literature* 11 (1968) 180–85
The first translation of *WH* appeared in Russia in 1956. It was an immediate success and the edition of 165,000 copies soon sold out. A Latvian translation came out in 1960 and a Lithuanian one in 1961. A critical history of *WH* in Russia follows.

B286 LANE, Margaret "The Drug–like Brontë Dream" *BST* 12 (1952) 79–87
The four Brontës escaped into a dream world which they had created as children, and each had his own manifestation of it. Charlotte Brontë broke out of it, but EB remained steadfastly in it and through this means achieved her novel and poems.

B287 ——— "Emily Brontë in a Cold Climate" *BST* 15 (1968) 187–200
EB does not attempt to humanize the natural world in *WH*; she knew that Nature is alien to Man, even when it is being kind. This modern discussion of *WH* considers some of the criticism the novel has attracted, settings in *WH*, the Gondal story, the characters, the poetic

prose, and several smaller points such as the books in *WH* and the number of deaths in *WH*. Reprinted A204.

B288 ——— "French Essays by Charlotte and Emily" *BST* 12 (1954) 273–85
On p 280–85 one essay by EB entitled "The Palace of Death" is translated by the author with the French printed on the opposite page. (See A122, A303, B17, B109, and B289 for other French essays.)

B289 ——— "The Palace of Death" *The Listener* 52 (Nov 11 1954) 803–4
This is a translation of EB's devoir "The Palace of Death," written for M Heger on October 18 1842, and a discussion of it, concluding that it is "macabre." The theme is supposed to have been EB's own choice. The author claims that EB saw civilization as a destructive force, and intemperance as the "Viceroy of Death." (See B335 for a criticism of this interpretation. For other French essays see A122, A303, B17, B109, and B288.) Reprinted A206.

B290 LANGMAN, F. H. *"Wuthering Heights" Essays in Criticism* 15 (July 1965) 294–312
The author attempts to "nail down some common faults in the criticism of this novel." The critics fall short on "the significance of the prose style and narrative method, the nature of the love between Catherine and Heathcliff, and the pervasive violence and cruelty." This is an excellent essay which should be read by anyone beginning work on *WH*. Reprinted: A104.

B291 LARKEN, Geoffrey "The Shuffling Scamp: Some Notes on Thomas Cautley Newby, the Original Publisher of *Wuthering Heights, Agnes Grey* and *The Tenant of Wildfell Hall*" *BST* 15 (1970) 400–407
A general history of Mr Newby, including his handling and mishandling of the publication of *WH* and *Agnes Grey*.

B292 LAVERS, Norman "The Action of *Wuthering Heights*" *South Atlantic Quarterly* 72 (Winter 1973) 43–52
In this essay, *WH* is read as drama, in terms of its actions. The governing action, to which all the smaller actions contribute, is: "To restore to power the Earnshaw family." A regular feature is that each character, after performing his own essential action, "goes from apparent health to immediate decline." Nelly Dean is the exception, but her motive is to preserve the status quo. EB's intention was to resolve the novel with a harmony of forces, and Lavers demonstrates that the various characters worked towards this conclusion.

B293 LAW, Alice "Branwell Brontë's Novel" *The Bookman* (London) 68 (Apr 1925) 4–6
The evidence is presented for Branwell Brontë's authorship of *WH*.

B294 LEMON, C[harles] H. "Balthus and *Wuthering Heights*" *BST* 15 (1969) 337–42
The Tate Gallery in London had an exhibition of the works of the artist Balthus toward the end of 1968, which included a number of pen–and–ink drawings and paintings illustrating scenes from *WH*. Four photographs of the drawings are reproduced here.

B295 ——— [Letter to the Editor] "Emily Brontë's Missing Novel" *TLS* (Mar 17 1966) 223

This letter is in reply to Letter to the Editor, B239. Hewish did not quote the full Newby letter (Newby refers to *WH* earlier in the letter). Nevertheless, it must be admitted that Newby's carelessness may be the only answer to the problem. Reprinted: B296.

B296 ——— "Emily Brontë's Second Novel" *BST* 15 (1966) 29
This is a reprinting of Item B295.

B297 ——— " 'An Exciting Chapter in the Society's History,' Purchase of Forty–four Autograph Letters by Charlotte Brontë and a Devoir by Emily Brontë" *BST* 17 (1980) 348–70
The devoir is a formal reply to a letter of invitation to a musical soiree and is reproduced in facsimile here.

B298 ——— "A Note on the Preface to the French Translation (of *Wuthering Heights* Published in 1892) by Theodore de Wyzewa" *BST* 17 (1976) 29–30
The Brontë Society recently purchased a copy of this edition, with the title translated as "L'Amant," reputedly the first French translation. T. de Wyzewa's preface (B526) is based largely on Mrs Gaskell's *Life of Charlotte Brontë* and rather inaccurate in some details. See B299.

B299 ——— "Russian and French Editions of *Wuthering Heights*" *BST* 17 (1976) 20–21
This is an introduction to the English translation of the prefatory essay by Z. Grazhdanskaya (B204) in the first Russian edition of *WH* (Moscow, 1956). It includes comments by the translator, E. Bronstein, and also mentions the French edition discussed more fully in B298 and B526.

B300 ——— "Sickness and Health in *Wuthering Heights*" *BST* 14 (1963) 23–25
The brief lives of the characters in *WH* and their many illnesses "would not have appeared unusual to Emily" because of her own experience with brief life and illness in the Brontë family.

B301 LESLIE, Shane "A Brontë Relic" *Time and Tide* 40 (June 13 1959) 683–84
A defense of Cowan Bridge School's reputation is contained in the account by the Reverend Benjamin Allen, of Philadelphia, of his visit there in 1828.

B302 LEVIN, Harry "Janes and Emilies, Or the Novelist as Heroine" *Southern Review* (Baton Rouge, La) n s 1 (Oct 1965) 735–53
EB is mentioned on p 742–44. This article is concerned with the feminine sex versus the masculine sex, as authors.

B303 LEWIS, C. Day "The Poetry of Emily Brontë: A Passion for Freedom" *BST* 13 (1957) 83–99
EB's poetry is related to *WH* and to her religious upbringing. Because of her struggle for freedom, the Gondal poems are full of prisoners and exiles. EB's morality in the poems and *WH* is discussed.

*B303A LILLINGSTON, Leonard W. "The Brontës and Their Books" *Connoisseur* 5 (Jan 1903) 47–50

B304 LITTELL, Philip "Books and Things" *New Republic* 16 (Aug 31 1918) 142
In a discussion of Emily and Charlotte Brontë, Littell says that inaccessibility to facts about EB has augmented her fame.

B305 LIVERMORE, Ann Lapraik "Byron and Emily Brontë" *Quarterly Review* 300 (July 1962) 337–44
WH is seen as a rewriting of Byron's *The Dream*. Heathcliff is Byron, Isabella is Byron's wife, and Catherine Earnshaw is Byron's half–sister. EB's poetry also was influenced by Byron.

B306 LOE, Thomas B. "The Gothic Strain in the Victorian Novel: Four Studies" *DAI* 35 (Oct 1974) 2231A
The first part of the study isolates and examines patterns recurring in the Gothic novel of the eighteenth and early nineteenth centuries. The rest of the study deals with individual Victorian novels containing the Gothic ideological and structural forms: *WH*, *Great Expectations*, *Heart of Darkness*, and *Tess of the D'Urbervilles*.

B307 LONGBOTTOM, John "*Wuthering Heights* and Patrick Branwell Brontë" *Yorkshire Notes and Queries* 1 (Feb 1905) 342–46
The author believes that Branwell Brontë was the real author of *WH* and supports his belief with a number of quotes he calls "Biographical Notes."

B308 LORD, Walter F. "The Brontë Novels" *Nineteenth Century* 53 (Mar 1903) 484–95
This article contains criticisms of all the Brontë novels, and "one yawns over *Wuthering Heights*." EB is not a great artist, but *Agnes Grey* by Anne Brontë "makes a great impression."

B309 LOXTERMAN, Alan S. "The Giant's Foot: A Reading of *Wuthering Heights*" *DAI* 32 (Jan 1972) 4007A–4008A
WH is an ambiguous novel with two different plots "complementary in structure yet contradictory in their philosophical implications." EB achieves calculated ambiguity of theme and design through these two plots.

B310 MacCARTHY, B. G. "Emily Brontë" *Studies: An Irish Quarterly Review* 39 (Mar 1950) 15–30
The story of the Brontës is told with careful adherence to the facts, centering upon EB and emphasizing environmental factors in her life. EB is defined as a "poet–mystic of the natural order," and is shown to reveal her feelings through her poetry.

B311 MacCARTHY, Desmond "The Brontës in Their Books" *BST* 10 (1945) 263–64
Any study of Brontë work should exclude a consideration of Brontë biography. EB is proof of the point because "there is an enormous gap which not only no records, but really no plausible conjecture can bridge."

B312 McCARTHY, Terence "The Incompetent Narrator of *Wuthering Heights*" *Modern Language Quarterly* 42 (Mar 1981) 48–64
Lockwood is not merely a narrative device; certain aspects of his character reflect some of the central issues in the novel. For example, he cannot bear isolation whereas the characters in *WH* are forced into isolation and separation from others. "Lockwood is almost a study in ineptitude, an object lesson in how not to read *Wuthering Heights*."

B313 McCAUGHEY, G. S. "An Approach to *Wuthering Heights*" *Humanities Association Bulletin* 15 (Autumn 1964) 28–34

This is an original essay which investigates *WH* from only one viewpoint: the trial of the Earnshaw family. As Hindley weakens over liquor, Catherine weakens over the Linton family, but at the end of the novel, an Earnshaw is master of Wuthering Heights.

B314 McCURDY, Harold Grier "A Study of the Novels of Charlotte and Emily Brontë as an Expression of Their Personalities" *Journal of Personality* 16 (Dec 1947) 109–52

This is a detailed psychological dissection of *WH* and the four novels of Charlotte Brontë. The characters in all five novels are closely examined and compared. The evaluation of the sisters' personalities, on the basis of this examination, is that "Charlotte Brontë is more defensive, Emily more aggressive." In the second half of the article McCurdy compares biographical information with his earlier inferences from the novels and his hypotheses are seemingly corroborated. Among them, regarding *WH* and EB's personality, *WH* "indicated a personality organized at the level of a child's, full of vitality and lacking in conscience, capable of decided alterations between strong aggression and moods of tenderness; and. . .it bespoke great self–absorption and little sociality in the author." The two sisters had a great influence upon each other, and this aspect of their personalities is also investigated.

B315 McINERNEY, Peter "Satanic Conceits in *Frankenstein* and *Wuthering Heights*" *Milton and the Romantics* 4 (1980) 1–15

Satanic personalities abound on the landscape of Romantic literature. "The nihilistic will S. T. Coleridge points to in Satan is the leading characteristic of his Romantic heirs" constituting a formula for the figure as he appears in *Frankenstein* and *WH*.

B316 MACKAY, Angus M. "The Brontës: Their Fascination and Genius" *The Bookman* (London) 27 (Oct 1904) 9–17 [14–15]

The author gives the reasons for the public's fascination with the Brontës and analyzes the Brontë genius.

B317 MacKAY, Ruth M. "Irish Heaths and German Cliffs: A Study of the Foreign Sources of *Wuthering Heights*" *Brigham Young University Studies* 7 (Autumn 1965) 28–39

Two principal sources for *WH* were the German "Das Majorat" and the Irish "The Bridegroom of Barna." This article shows how EB welded them together in *WH*. EB's source for the love of Catherine and Heathcliff was the love she and Branwell Brontë had for each other.

B318 MacKERETH, James A. "The Greatness of Emily Brontë" *BST* 7 (1929) 175–200

EB should not be analyzed or her works interpreted on a psychological level. She has transmitted in *WH* the idea that Man is "vaster than any temporal aspect or consciousness of himself." MacKereth also discusses *WH* in relation to other great literary works. See B504.

B319 McKIBBEN, Robert C. "The Image of the Book in *Wuthering Heights*" *NCF* 15 (Sept 1960) 159–69

". . .[J]ust as the window figure is primarily identified with the more tempestuous lovers, so the image of the book is the reflection of the stabilizing love of Cathy and Hareton." The article also contains an unusual interpretation of Heathcliff and connects a French essay written by EB, "The Butterfly," with *WH*. Reprinted: A136, A220.

*B319A McLEMORE, Joy Ellis "Edgar Linton: Master of Thrushcross Grange" *Re: Artes Liberales* 8, No 1 (1981) 13–26

B320 MacRAE, Elizabeth "Brontë Child Manuscripts at Harvard" *Horn Book Magazine* 17 (Mar–Apr 1941) 108–21
These are the manuscripts of Charlotte and Branwell Brontë only.

*B321 MADDEN, David "Chapter Seventeen of *Wuthering Heights*" *English Record* 17 (Feb 1967) 2–8
"Emily Brontë's *Wuthering Heights* repeats and anticipates in the transition between the two parts of the book. . . . This chapter [17] has more violence than the others . . . , and symbols have special power. . . ." [From an abstract in *Abstracts of English Studies.*]

B322 MADDEN, William A. "The Search for Forgiveness in Some Nineteenth–Century English Novels" *Comparative Literature Studies* 3 (1966) 139–53
In *WH* forgiveness is a central theme, as evidenced by Jabes Branderham's sermon. It is a "detached double parable of vengeance, hate, isolation, and death, on the one hand, and forgiveness, love, integration, and life on the other hand. . . ." The novel's message is that the only unforgivable sin is the refusal to forgive. The other novels discussed are *Vanity Fair, Heart of Midlothian, Pilgrim's Progress, Middlemarch, Tess of the D'Urbervilles,* and *Lord Jim.*

B323 ——— "*Wuthering Heights*: The Binding of Passion" *NCF* 27 (Sept 1972) 127–54
Lockwood's first dream in the novel—that taking place in the chapel involving Lockwood, Joseph, and Jabes Branderham and ending in violence—must be significant; its placement "suggests that Emily Brontë attached unusual importance to it." In this context, Madden examines Joseph's role in *WH*, analyzes the Cathy–Hareton story, and investigates the psychological and religious implications of the novel's double plot.

B323A MADEWELL, Viola D. "Emily Brontë's Word Artistry: Symbolism in *Wuthering Heights*" *DAI* 42 (May 1982) 4835A
EB used symbols "to develop her polarities and to unify them along the imaginatively rendered horizontal axis connecting Wuthering Heights and Thrushcross Grange, the vertical axis connecting the novel's several "heavens" and "hells," and the third dimensional axis connecting the spiritual and corporeal worlds." This study divides the more than seven hundred symbols into numerous categories and shows how they work to establish, enrich, and unify the concepts of *WH*.

B324 MAISON, Margaret "Emily Brontë and the Epictetus" *Notes and Queries* 25 (June 1978) 230–31
The stoicism in EB's verse may have derived from her reading of the Stoic masters, among them, Epictetus. A possible influence could have been Mrs Hester Chapone's *Letters on the Improvement of the Mind* (1773), probably read by EB.

B325 MALHAM–DEMBLEBY, J. "The Lifting of the Brontë Veil" *Fortnightly Review* 81 (Mar 1907) 489–505
The author alleges that Charlotte Brontë wrote *WH*.

*B326 MANLEY, Sandra M. " 'Pale T–Guilp Off' " *Transactions of the Yorkshire Dialect Society* 13 (1971) 25–28

B327 MARCHAND, Leslie A. "An Addition to the Census of Brontë Manuscripts" *NCF* 4 (June 1949) 81–84
Branwell Brontë's manuscripts and some letters written by Charlotte Brontë have been added to the Rutgers University Library. There is no mention of EB, but all of the collection (from the library of J. Alex Symington) has not yet been catalogued.

B328 ——— "The Symington Collection" *Journal of the Rutgers University Library* 12 (Dec 1948) 1–15
Although EB is not mentioned, p 2–3 describe the Brontë manuscripts in the collection, particularly Branwell's. Also mentioned are letters from Ellen Nussey to Charlotte Brontë.

B329 MARKS, William Sowell, III "The Novel as Puritan Romance: A Comparative Study of Samuel Richardson, the Brontës, Thomas Hardy, and D. H. Lawrence" *Dissertation Abstracts* 25 (Aug 1964) 1214
The author's purpose is ". . . to define and trace the Puritan ideals of love and marriage" in the English novel from Richardson to Lawrence. He discusses "the Brontës' greater sympathy with the demonic and a corresponding criticism of the society which represses it." There are parallels between *WH* and the songs and prophecies of William Blake.

B330 MARSDEN, Hilda "The Scenic Background of *Wuthering Heights*" *BST* 13 (1957) 111–30
The Law Hill area, a possible locale of *WH*, is described with map, pictures, and references to the novel.

B331 MARSHALL, William H. "Hareton Earnshaw: Natural Theology on the Moors" *Victorian Newsletter* 21 (Spring 1962) 14–15
Hareton sees Heathcliff as his deity, yet retains the native intelligence to effect his own regeneration. He is compared with Shakespeare's Caliban, and is like Browning's Caliban implicitly, although Browning allows his Caliban to work out his theological structure.

B332 MATHISON, John K. "Nelly Dean and the Power of *Wuthering Heights*" *NCF* 11 (Sept 1956) 106–29
This is an excellent treatment of Nelly Dean as an admirable woman whose point of view the reader must reject. The reader is forced to feel the inadequacy of Nelly's wholesome viewpoint, becomes himself an interpreter and judge, and feels "sympathy with genuine passions, no matter how destructive or violent." Reprinted: A104, A220, A322.

B333 MAUGHAM, W. Somerset "The Ten Best Novels: *Wuthering Heights*" *Atlantic Monthly* 181 (Feb 1948) 89–94
EB's almost morbid shyness and solitude are responsible for the method of narration in *WH*. "She hid herself behind a double mask," because she herself was Catherine Earnshaw

and Heathcliff. "I think it gave her a thrill of release when she bullied, reviled, and browbeat."
Reprinted: A243, A244, A245.

B334 MAURER, K. W. "The Poetry of Emily Brontë" *Anglia* 61 (1937) 442–48
Branwell Brontë was "particularly important in connection with Emily" because she was
the one most devoted to him. Her poetry is seen as barely escaping "insipidity and flatness"
because of the feeling in it of intense suffering, which is attributed to her involvement in
Branwell's tragic life.

B335 MAXWELL, J. C. "Emily Brontë's 'The Palace of Death' " *BST* 15 (1967) 139–
40
The essay is compared with the devoir of the same title written by Charlotte Brontë. The
author disagrees with Margaret Lane's interpretation (B289).

B336 ——— "A Shakespearean Comma in *Wuthering Heights*" *The Trollopian* 3
(Mar 1949) 315
This is a short textual note to the effect that the comma was commonly used for emphasis
in the nineteenth century. The *WH* example given here is, "Are you, Linton?" The sense is,
"Are *you* Linton?" This is young Catherine Linton's question when she first sees Linton
Heathcliff.

B337 MAYNE, Isobel "Emily Brontë's Mr. Lockwood" *BST* 15 (1968) 207–13
Lockwood is important to the structure of *WH* and also is a "skilful and realistic technical
device by which Emily Brontë communicates with her readers."

B338 MECKIER, Jerome "Some Household Words: Two New Accounts of Dickens's
Conversation" *Dickensian* 71 (Jan 1975) 5–20
Dickens mentioned that he had not read *WH* (giving no reason why) and that he would not
read *Jane Eyre*, as he "disapproved of the whole school."

B339 MEIER, T. K. "*Wuthering Heights* and Violation of Class" *BST* 15 (1968) 233–
36
Heathcliff, Nelly Dean, and Joseph are the three characters who upset traditional class lines
in *WH*. Moral decline accompanies class violation, and Linton Heathcliff is central to several
aspects of the decay.

B340 MELCHIORI, Barbara Arnett "The Windows of the Victorians" *English Miscellany* 25 (1975–76) 335–54
A discussion of window imagery as used by Victorian novelists, including EB.

B341 MELTON, James "The Brontë Parsonage Museum" *The Connoisseur* 135 (Apr
1955) 106–7
The Brontë Museum and some of the furniture and portraits are described and illustrated.

B342 MERRY, Bruce "An Unknown Italian Dramatisation of *Wuthering Heights*"
BST 16 (1971) 31–39
Beppe Fenoglio, an Italian writer, dramatized *WH* and accompanied the play with a critical
essay, both of which came to light in 1960. Merry summarizes the play and translates the
essay.

B343 MEW, Charlotte M. "The Poems of Emily Brontë" *Temple Bar* 130 (July 1904) 153–67

Primarily EB's poems, but also *WH*, are viewed as preamble to what she might have done had she lived. Her reputation "as a great artist and a repulsive woman" has been built upon *WH*, but the real EB is discoverable in her poems: "...sweeter and lighter fancies peer like stars between the masses of dark cloud...." This is a full and appreciative investigation of the poems.

B344 MEYERSTEIN, E. H. W. [Letter to the Editor] "A Brontë Metre" *TLS* (Nov 12 1938) 725–26

The similarity of metre in EB's "No Coward Soul Is Mine" and Felicia Herman's "The Hour of Death" (1824) is pointed out. (See B224 for another comparison of metre.)

B345 MEYNELL, Alice "Charlotte and Emily Brontë" *Dublin Review* 148 (Apr 1911) 230–43

This is a reprinting of Item A250.

B346 ———— "Charlotte and Emily Brontë" *Living Age* 269 (May 27 1911) 515–22

This is a reprinting of Item A250.

B347 MICHELL, Humfrey "Haworth" *Dalhousie Review* 31 (Summer 1951) 135–41

This is a personal and maudlin account of a visit to Haworth with a description of the town and the Brontë Museum.

B348 MIDGLEY, Wilson "Sunshine on Haworth Moor" *BST* 11 (1950) 309–26

This review of the Brontë history and genius is by a fellow Yorkshireman. The Brontës are briefly compared with Dorothy Wordsworth and Joan of Arc. There is some conjecture, but also some interesting material, about Yorkshire custom and reserve, e.g., "Even Nelly Dean only once kissed one of her charges."

B349 MILLER, J. Hillis "*Wuthering Heights* and the Ellipses of Interpretation" *Notre Dame English Journal* 12 (April 1980) 85–100

WH belongs to the "uncanny" as the term is used by Freud, and defined as "nothing else than a hidden, familiar thing that has undergone repression and then emerged from it." The dissatisfaction we feel for the "uncanny" and *WH* is "its failure ever to come together clear." The elements which produce this effect in *WH* are partly structural, and partly thematic, i.e., the presentation of violence, sexuality, and death. "The oscillation, bewilderment, or experience of alogical richness which cannot be mastered is the fundamental bearer of meaning in this work—fundamental, that is, in its lack of fundament."

B350 MIRSKY, Prince D. S. "Emily Brontë" *London Mercury* 7 (Jan 1923) 266–72

Charlotte and Emily Brontë are contrasted as to personality traits and first novels. *WH* is discussed with emphasis upon the characters, briefly compared with other European novels, and pronounced unique (with the possible exception of *Crime and Punishment*) in combining "in the same degree the two qualities of spiritual intensity and artistic efficiency."

B351 ———— "Through Foreign Eyes" *BST* 6 (1923) 147–52

EB is viewed subjectively through the author's "foreign eyes." There is an interesting comparison of Rochester and Heathcliff as they were conceived by their creators. EB and Heathcliff are both "outside nature," and EB's art is Latin and French because it is "of conscious and disciplined will." Reprinted: A1.

B352 MITCHELL, Giles "Incest, Demonism, and Death in *Wuthering Heights*" *Literature and Psychology* 23, No 1 (1973) 27–36
Although the character and behavior of Heathcliff are central to this psychological study, Catherine's psyche, motivations, and actions are also examined. Incest–repression is seen as part of the total design of symbolism in *WH*. "This is to describe nature, or the universe, as being in collision with itself."

B353 MOGLEN, Helene "The Double Vision of *Wuthering Heights*: A Clarifying View of Female Development" *Centennial Review* 15 (Fall 1971) 391–405.
The theme of *WH* is the development of the female personality from childhood to maturity. *WH* is Catherine's story, and "the second section of *Wuthering Heights* is not a parody of the first, nor is it merely a weakened restatement of it. It is rather a further, sophisticated development of the author's consideration of the maturation of the self." Richardson's *Clarissa* and Shelley's *Frankenstein* also investigated the self and "other" as does *WH*.

B354 MONTPENSIER STONE, Roy de "Re: 'Wuthering Heights' and re: 'Thrush-cross Grange.' Case for the Opinion of Counsel" *BST* 16 (1972) 118–30
Roy Stone, a retired barrister, writes a case to be submitted to Counsel to advise on the title to the properties of Wuthering Heights and Thrushcross Grange. See A324, A238i.

B355 MOODY, Philippa "The Challenge to Maturity in *Wuthering Heights*" *Melbourne Critical Review* 5 (1962) 27–39
This is a perceptive and thorough investigation of the central experience of *WH*, which is the love of Catherine and Heathcliff, accompanied by a discussion of the credibility of *WH* to the reader and the value of the intense emotion in it. The two narrators are also discussed briefly.

B356 MOORE, Charles L. "Another Literary Mare's–nest" *The Dial* 53 (Oct 16 1912) 277–78
Leyland, who said Branwell Brontë wrote *WH*, and Malham–Dembleby, who said Charlotte Brontë wrote *WH* are both proved wrong, with special attention to Malham–Dembleby. Emily and Charlotte Brontë differ in their poetry, their style, and their characters.

B357 MOORE–SMITH, Prof C. "Brontës in Thornton" *The Bookman* (London) 27 (Oct 1904) 18–22
The author's grandmother was acquainted with Patrick and Maria Brontë when they lived at Thornton.

B358 MOORE, T. Sturge "Beyond East and West: A Re–interpretation of Emily Brontë" *Asiatic Review* 37 (Oct 1941) 810–16
EB is discussed from an Eastern point of view, with special attention to her poetry. She is compared with William Blake.

*B359 MORGAN, Charles "Emily Brontë" *TLS* [pre 1932]
This is an objective discussion of EB's work. We have very few pieces of autobiographical

data on EB, and they did not reveal her inner self. The author briefly reviews the conjectural literature written about her. EB's life was on two planes: the one that Charlotte Brontë and Mrs Gaskell knew, and the mystic. An investigation of her poetry and *WH* reveal that EB was her mystic self in these. Reprinted: A259, A260. Partially reprinted: A283.

B360 MORGAN, Edwin "Women and Poetry" *Cambridge Journal* 3 (Aug 1950) 643–73 [648–56]
The article contains a thorough analysis of EB's poetry, along with a discussion of the poetry of Katherine Philips and Mrs Browning. EB is said to be the greatest of all women poets because she was not influenced by any literary world and her physical isolation allowed her to concentrate on her inner world. The Gondal saga as it relates to her poetry is also discussed.

——— *see* B237.

B361 MOSER, Thomas "What Is the Matter with Emily Jane? Conflicting Impulses in *Wuthering Heights*" *NCF* 17 (June 1962) 1–19
The author agrees with "the nineteenth–century view of *Wuthering Heights* as a powerful and imperfect book." He interprets it in a Freudian manner, and some of the Freudian aspects are very well–developed and supported. Reprinted: A262. See B377.

MOTT, Joan *see* B75 and B76.

B362 MOYNAHAN, Julian "Pastoralism as Culture and Counter–Culture in English Fiction, 1800–1928" *Novel* 6 (Fall 1972) 20–35
In this discussion of the pastoral tradition of the country in nineteenth–century fiction, *WH* "sets a standard against which all the other pastoral novels must be measured. *Wuthering Heights* is about the renaturing of society . . . or the realigning of society with the realm of wild nature."

B363 NADEL, Barbara S. and John Altrocchi "Attribution of Hostile Intent in Literature" *Psychological Reports* 25 (Dec 1969) 747–63
A selective literary analysis of works such as *Billy Budd, Othello, Crime and Punishment,* and *WH* attempts to show the types of people which attribute hostile intent to other types of people and the conditions or climate in which this happens. Edgar Linton and Heathcliff are the two illustrations from *WH*.

NAGEL, Lorine W. *see* B17.

B364 NELSON, Jane Gray "First American Reviews of the Works of Charlotte, Emily, and Anne Brontë" *BST* 14 (1964) 39–44
The first American reviews of the novels and the poems "varied . . . from disgust to perplexed enthusiasm." Ten magazines are quoted.

B365 ———"Sicily and the Brontë Name" *BST* 16 (1971) 43–45
The origins and evolution of the Brontë name from "Prunty" to "Brontë."

B366 NELSON, Lowry, Jr "Night Thoughts on the Gothic Novel" *Yale Review* 52 (Dec 1962) 236–57

WH is discussed on p 251–56. Heathcliff was an heir to the Gothic hero. *WH* is compared with *Moby Dick* and *Frankenstein*. All three novels are "without either God or devil."

B367 NEUFELDT, Victor A. "Emily Brontë and the Responsible Imagination" *Victorian Newsletter* 43 (Spring 1973) 15–21.
EB's poetry shows that she, "like Tennyson, fought a long battle over the question of the legitimate use of the creative imagination." Her imaginary world provided her with a sanctuary. "The writing of the novel and a change in the style of the last Gondal poems are the inevitable outcome of Emily's development as a self–aware artist."

B368 ———— "The Shared Vision of Anne and Emily Brontë: The Context for *Wuthering Heights*" *DAI* 31 (Aug 1970) 764A–765A
"Anne and Emily shared a bleak and pessimistic vision of human nature and the society in which they lived." EB saw dedication to the gratification of self as socially irresponsible; her characters in the land of Gondal, which she shared with Anne, were so dedicated, and she addressed this same problem in *WH*. "Heathcliff and Catherine were. . .errant human beings destroyed by their own wilfulness, and destroying others in the process."

B369 NICOLAI, Ralf R. "*Wuthering Heights:* Emily Brontë's Kleistian Novel" *South Atlantic Bulletin* 38 (May 1973) 23–32
Reappraisal of *WH* and a new appreciation for the work of Heinrich von Kleist set in at about the same time (1943?). Ralf Nicolai asserts they should be viewed jointly, particularly since internal evidence seems to point to a connection between *WH* and von Kleist's *Der Findling*. EB was probably familiar with von Kleist's work.

*B370 NICOLL, W. Robertson "Emily Brontë" *British Weekly* (Oct 1908)

B371 NIXON, Ingeborg "The Brontë Portraits: Some Old Problems and a New Discovery" *BST* 13 (1958) 232–38
The "pillar group" portrait of the three Brontë sisters "originally contained a fourth figure, almost certainly that of Branwell himself."

B372 ———— "A Note on the Pattern of *Wuthering Heights*" *English Studies* 45 (Supplement 1964) 235–42
This is one of the more thorough analyses of the structure of *WH*. The author points out that the action is "grouped round certain lyrical and dramatic passages. . . ." Reprinted: A283.

B373 O'BYRNE, Cathal "The Gaelic Source of the Brontë Genius" *The Columbia* 10 (July 1931) 12–13, 36
The story is told of the marriage of EB's paternal grandparents, with emphasis upon the Irish traits of the Brontë sisters. Hugh Prunty, their grandfather, was famous as a "shanachie" or story–teller. The author also discusses Catholicism in the family. Reprinted: A272.

B374 ODOM, Keith Conrad "The Brontës and Romantic Views of Personality" *Dissertation Abstracts* 22 (Dec 1961) 2004–5
Charlotte, Emily, and Anne Brontë are treated together in an investigation of the degree to which the Brontës employed views of personality held in the English Romantic period. The Romantic view is particularly seen in their attitudes toward childhood. Also Romantic is the fact that their good characters refer to the unity of Nature.

*B375 ODUMU, Ocheibi "Women Talk about Women: The Image of Women in the Novels of Jane Austen and Emily Brontë" *Horizon* (Ibadan) 9 (1972) 47–54

B376 OFFOR, Richard "The Brontës—Their Relation to the History and Politics of Their Time" *BST* 10 (1943) 150–60
The focus is upon Charlotte Brontë because of "the paucity of evidence" for Emily and Anne. However, this is an interesting account of historical events and trends during the lifetime of the Brontës.

B377 OHMANN, Carol "Emily Brontë in the Hands of Male Critics" *College English* 32 (May 1971) 906–13
WH has received biased critical treatment during its 120–year history. After examining contemporary reviews and two modern critical essays by Mark Schorer (B439) and Thomas Moser (B361), Ohmann concludes that *WH* "reveals a sophisticated awareness of the very kinds of sexual prejudice that have so often interfered with the understanding of it." The true subject of *WH* is freedom.

B378 OLSEN, Thomas [Letter to the Editor] "The Brontës and Methodism" *TLS* (May 27 1949) 347
This is a contradiction of the idea that EB was steeped in Methodism. (See B228 for a reply.)

B379 ORAM, Eanne "Brief for Miss Branwell" *BST* 14 (1964) 28–38
The biographers' comments on the Brontës' aunt, Elizabeth Branwell, and her influence upon the Brontë children have been perhaps unfair. Her contributions, religious and otherwise, are here more favorably evaluated.

B380 ——— "Emily and F. D. Maurice: Some Parallels of Thought" *BST* 13 (1957) 131–40
A comparison of Maurice's ideas to the philosophy in *WH* and EB's poetry.

B381 OVERTON, Grant "Do You Remember?" *Mentor* 17 (Dec 1929) 47–48
This is a brief retelling of the story of *WH* for popular consumption, with a few highlights of EB's family history. Neither is altogether correct.

B382 P.–G., M. E. "Tours Through Literary England: Through the Brontë Country" *Saturday Review* (London) 150 (Sept 13 1930) 310
The Brontë family's life story is told briefly in the context of the Yorkshire country, with map and descriptions.

*B383 PAGLIA, Camille "Sexual Personae: The Androgyne in Literature and Art" Unpublished doctoral dissertation, Yale University 1974.

B384 PARKINSON, E. M. "The Brontës' Domestic Servant Problem" *Saturday Review* (London) 150 (Aug 16 1930) 196–97
Both Charlotte and Emily Brontë "had no mercy on their servants." To support this theory, Nelly Dean in *WH* is given as an example: she is made to be lady's maid, nurse, housekeeper, fruit–picker, companion, and seamstress.

B385 PARRISH, M. L. "Adventures in Reading and Collecting Victorian Fiction" *Princeton University Library Chronicle* 3 (Feb 1942) 33–44

The author includes the Brontës in his discussion of his career as a book collector. *WH* "is one of the scarcest books in Victorian fiction."

B386 PASSOW, Emilie S. "Orphans and Aliens: Changing Images of Childhood in Works of Four Victorian Novelists" *DAI* 40 (Nov 1979) 2698A
In the works examined, among them *WH*, *The Mill on the Floss*, and *The Turn of the Screw*, two patterns emerge: the use of childhood as a metaphor for estrangement, and a movement from innocence to experience in the depiction of the child's range of awareness and responses.

B387 PAUL, David "The Novel Art. II." *Twentieth Century* 154 (Oct 1953) 294–301
WH is discussed on p 300–301. *WH* and *Jane Eyre* are compared in the context of EB's and Charlotte Brontë's "wish–fulfillment," a psychological motivation deprecated in the 1930s, but asserted by the author to be essential in any novelist.

B388 PEARSALL, Robert Brainard "The Presiding Tropes of Emily Brontë" *College English* 27 (Jan 1966) 267–73
This is a discussion and explication of EB's poetic language in *WH*. The speech of her central characters contains "bold metaphors." EB's "disguise [of misery] was the feverish intellectualization of her tropes. . . . Emily Brontë lusted to expose her troubled soul, and also lusted to cover it up."

B389 PEEL, Marie "Power and Pattern v. Morality 2: The Novel" *Books and Bookmen* 18 (Nov 1972) 48–52
In this study of the development of the English novel, Peel finds that where the power in a novel is greatest, there is a different kind of seeing and an honesty based on self–knowledge that exists on an instinctive level. *WH* has a kind of ". . . ur–morality rooted in the power of self. . . ."

*B390 ——— "Women's Lib in Lit" *Books and Bookmen* 17 (Nov 1971) 14–17

B391 PETYT, K. M. " 'Thou' and 'You' in *Wuthering Heights*" *BST* 16 (1974) 291–93
The dimensions of power and solidarity are reflected in the use of these pronouns in *WH*. EB uses them deliberately and in an unexpected manner to convey anger and lack of respect.

*B392 PHELPS, William L. "The Mid–Victorians" *The Bookman* [pre 1916]
WH is "more hysterical than historical in its treatment of human nature," but it "has the strength of delirium." EB's personal repression accounts for the passion in *WH*. Reprinted: A285.

*B393 PITTOCK, Malcolm "*Wuthering Heights* and Its Critics" *Critical Survey* (Summer 1971) 146–54
Three possible interpretations of *WH* are suggested. [From mention in *BST*.]

B394 PLATT, Carolyn V. "The Female Quest in the Works of Anne, Charlotte and Emily Brontë" *DAI* 35 (Jan 1975) 4450A
This discussion of the "active, questing heroine who strives for independence and self

development in a society in which women are encouraged to remain passive" concludes that
EB, more than her sisters, insisted on complete equality between men and women because
she believed that "people are androgynous, potentially fully human individuals."

B395 POLLIN, Burton R. "The Brontës in the American Periodical Press of Their
     Day: One Hundred and Ninety–three Reviews and Comments Annotated" *BST*
     16 (1975) 383–99
An annotated bibliography of criticism of EB and Charlotte Brontë in American periodicals
from 1846 through 1857, listed alphabetically by title of the periodical, this is an excellent
reflection of the American reception of the Brontë works. See B395A.

B395A ——— "More Contemporary Reviews of Books by the Brontës" *BST* 18 (1982)
     128–35
Eighteen reviews are added to Pollin's collection (B395), most of them concerned with
Charlotte Brontë's work.

B396 POWER, S. A. "The Chronology of *Wuthering Heights*" BST 16 (1972) 139–
     42
Power examines C. P. Sanger's chronology (A324) published in 1926 and Clay's essay (B102)
written in 1952 and concludes that Clay must have reached his conclusions independently of
Sanger.

B397 PRESTON, Albert H. "John Greenwood and the Brontës. The Haworth Sta-
     tioner Throws New Light on Emily" *BST* 12 (1951) 35–38
John Greenwood's notebook relates the doubtful incident of Mr Brontë's giving EB a lesson
in marksmanship.

B398 PRITCHETT, V. S. "Books in General" *New Statesman and Nation* 31 (June
     22 1946) 453
This is a modern review of *WH*. The Northern shrewdness and other Northern characteristics
are found in the "implacable and belligerent people" in *WH*. Heathcliff's ancestor in literature
is Lovelace, "the superb male in full possession of the powers of conspiracy and seduction,"
but Heathcliff is not so admirable a villain as Lovelace. Reprinted: A104, A220, A379.

B399 PRUNTY, Maura "Father of the Brontë Sisters" *Irish Digest* 73 (Dec 1961)
     52–54
This short history and character sketch of Patrick Brontë attributes the genius of his daughters
principally to their Irish ancestry. "Miss Ellen Nussey . . . was convinced that Emily got some
of her facts from her father's narratives."

B400 QUARM, Joan "Arming Me from Fear: Branwell Brontë's Contribution to
     Wuthering Heights" BST 17 (1979) 278–86
Branwell Brontë's degeneration greatly influenced EB's creation of character and plot in
WH, and his drug addiction is seen as central to Heathcliff's downward course toward the
grave.

B401 QUERTERMOUS, Harry Maxwell "The Byronic Hero in the Writings of the
     Brontës" *Dissertation Abstracts* 21 (July 1960) 191–92
The Byronic hero appeared early in the childhood writings of the four Brontës. In EB's

work "the Byronic hero, as depicted by the Brontës, reached its greatest realization." Catherine, as well as Heathcliff, is a Byronic hero; they are both incarcerated, and at the same time divine.

B402 RAINE, Kathleen [Emily Brontë's Poems] *New Statesman and Nation* 43 (Mar 8 1952) 277–78. Reply: J. F. Hewish 43 (Mar 29 1952) 375. Rejoinder: 43 (Apr 5 1952) 405
EB is pictured as a woman poet who is unafraid to deal with women as child–murderers and faithless lovers. J. F. Hewish resents this female angle. K. Raine replies, defending her assertion, and says that few women have written poems that would be memorable but for the fact that their authors were women.

B403 RAINWATER, Mary J. "Emily Dickinson and Six Contemporary Writers: Her Poetry in Relation to Her Reading" *DAI* 36 (Jan 1976) 4479A
Although Chapter IV analyzes scenes from *Jane Eyre* and *WH* in conjunction with a selected group of Emily Dickinson's love poems, the emphasis is on Dickinson's thematic affinities with the Brontë sisters' poetry. The other writers studied are Emerson, the Brownings, and George Eliot.

B404 RALLI, Augustus "Emily Brontë: The Problem of Personality" *North American Review* 221 (Mar 1925) 495–507
The biography of an author does relate to his work; we can see EB through *WH*. Her characters have a self–consciousness as Shakespeare's characters do, and this makes them psychologically real. Their sarcasm is bound up with EB's nature. She was not at peace with Man, but with Nature; she was a mystic. EB succeeded in depicting the soul and depicting eternity. Reprinted: A297.

B405 RANDALL, David A. "First American Edition of the Brontës' Poems" *Book Collector* 9 (Summer 1960) 199–201
He comments (in answer to a query in a previous issue, B234) upon the rarity of first editions of the poems and also mentions first editions of *WH*. (See B26 for another reply.)

B406 RATCHFORD, Fannie E. "An American Postscript" *BST* 11 (1947) 87–88
The contemporary reading public in America is discussed in relation to *WH* and *Jane Eyre*.

B407 ——— [Letter to the Editor] "The Brontës" *TLS* (Dec 11 1948) 697
There are references to the Brontës in letters written by their cousin, Elizabeth Jane Kingston, of Penzance. Among other things, Miss Kingston says that EB should never have written *WH*.

B408 ——— "The Brontës' Web of Dreams" *Yale Review* n s 21 (Autumn 1931) 139–57
This is an account of the Brontë childhood plays. EB is discussed on p 154–57, and her poetry is briefly related to the Gondal play.

B409 ——— "Correct Text of Emily Brontë's Poems" *BST* 10 (1942) 107–9
This is an appreciative discussion of C. W. Hatfield's (see A156) scholarly textual editing of EB's poems.

B410 —— [Letter to the Editor] "The Gondal Poems" *TLS* (Dec 4 1930) 1041–42

The author points out some heretofore unknown facts about Gondal which she derived from a study of EB's manuscripts in the Bonnell Collection.

B411 —— "The Significance of the Diary Paper" *BST* 12 (1951) 16–17

This diary paper is the second, in point of date, of four such pieces. Most significant in it is EB's statement that she is writing Augustus Almeda's life.

B412 —— "War in Gondal: Emily Brontë's Last Poem" *The Trollopian* 2 (Dec 1947) 137–55

EB's accounts of war in Gondal, in her poems, reflect her hatred of war with "vivid gory imagery."

B413 RAWLINGS, Carl D. "Prophecy in the Novel" *DAI* 34 (Nov 1973) 2575A–2576A

EB and *WH* are included in this discussion of prophecy in the novel, which takes as its starting point E. M. Forster (A110), and investigates his *A Passage to India*, Dostoyevsky's *Crime and Punishment*, and D. H. Lawrence and Herman Melville. "This fiction provides a sense of human intensity, of desire...pressing against a constraining pattern...."

B414 READ, Herbert "Charlotte and Emily Brontë" *Yale Review* n s 14 (July 1925) 720–38

This psychological view of the genius of both sisters considers their heredity, environment, possible childhood influences, and education in relation to their works. M Heger was not merely a schoolmaster, but "a master of the art of writing." *WH* has a "spirit of Romanticism" and at the same time it is a novel that reaches "the dignity of classical tragedy" in its evocation of pity and terror. Reprinted: A308, A309, A310.

B415 REED, Michael D. "The Power of *Wuthering Heights*: A Psychoanalytic Examination" *Psychocultural Review* 1 (Winter 1977) 21–42

Basic to the theory in Norman Holland's *Dynamics of Literary Response* is the idea that a reader's literary experience is oral. This essay explicates the operation of the theory in *WH*, designating counterpoint themes of denial, betrayal, and intrusion. A second part of the essay deals with the Victorian critics' reactions to *WH*, which were strong and negative.

B416 REILLY, A. J. "Celtic Elements in the Brontë Genius" *Ave Maria* 38 (Sept 23–30 1933) 393–96

One of the Brontë ancestors was the famous Gaelic poet, Padraic O'Prunta. "...[A] more rational explanation" of the Brontë genius is their Celtic heritage. Elements in this heritage are a duality of "aptitude at fighting and their subtle speech," a duality of orderly practicality and imagination, and an intense love of nature. EB's poetry follows the Irish mode rather than the English, and her highly–praised English in *WH* has the "colloquial directness found in English as it is spoken in Ireland."

B417 REILLY, Joseph J. "Some Victorian Reputations" *Catholic World* 145 (Apr 1937) 16–23

WH is discussed on p 20–22. Victorian writers are emerging now from the reactions of their age, and the author reviews EB's literary reputation from the 1850s to 1925 considering both *WH* and her poetry.

B418 REYNOLDS, Thomas "Division and Unity in *Wuthering Heights*" *University Review* (Kansas City, Mo) 32 (Autumn 1965) 31–37
This is an illuminating and coherent essay. The analogies, balances, and counterpointing in *WH* show the existence of love in hate and hate in love. Alienation leads to fusion, and annihilation to creation.

B419 RHODES, Margaret G. "A Brief Interlude...The Brontës at Silverdale" *BST* 14 (1964) 44–45
Charlotte and Emily Brontë spent one night in Silverdale in 1825 on a holiday from Cowan Bridge School. This is a description of the area and Cove House where they stayed.

B420 RHODES, Philip "A Medical Appraisal of the Brontës" *BST* 16 (1972) 101–9
"The tragedy of the Brontës resided in their isolation, begot by the peculiarities of their father and the the death of their mother when they were young." Dr Rhodes, a physician, takes the Brontës' psychological burdens into account along with their physical ones.

B421 RHYS, Ernest "The Haworth Tradition" *BST* 6 (1922) 88–96
"The power of the place [is] behind the power of the book," the author says of *WH*. The universality of *WH* is due to a selection of language that made it real. Reprinted: A1.

*B422 ROARKE, Jesse "The Poems of Emily Brontë: A Reflection" *Visvabharati Quarterly* 38 (1972–73) 108–19

B423 ROBERTSON, Charles G. "The Brontës' 'Experience of Life' " *BST* 9 (1936) 37–47
The question of whether or not the Brontë literature should be studied with biographical data in mind is considered. Knowing an author's biography can be misleading, as the author shows by a review of Brontë criticism. *WH* was not as popular eighty years ago as it is now because of the Victorian point of view.

B424 ROSENFIELD, Claire "The Shadow Within: The Conscious and Unconscious Use of the Double" *Daedalus* 92 (Spring 1963) 326–44
WH is one of the novels, in nineteenth– and twentieth–century fiction, illustrating the use of the double personality. Catherine and Heathcliff are doubles; they differ in sex alone and each possesses a complementary self in his choice of a mate. Only in the world of childhood or death, where the capacity for freedom is infinite, can they exist.

B425 ROSEVEARE, Austin "The Poetry of Emily Brontë" *Poetry Review* (London) 9 (Sept–Oct 1918) 257–67
The sentences in EB's poetry "lead one's thoughts literally towards infinity," yet her poetry is strikingly natural. Roseveare relates her poetry to many of the common human emotions, briefly compares it to Swinburne's, and discusses both form and content.

B426 ROSS, Ann M. "The Dreamer in the Landscape: A Critical Study of Emily Brontë's Poetry" *DAI* 41 (Oct 1980) 1617A
This study traces the development of EB's poetry, placing it in a social and historical context

and discussing relationships to the major Victorian landscape poems. Chapter I surveys 130 years of Brontë criticism, and Chapters IV and V contain Ross's grouping, evaluation, and explication of the poetry.

B427 ROUSSEAU, Kathleen G. "The Lyric Visualisation in 'Wuthering Heights': Selected Passages" *BST* 18 (1981) 30–35
WH has "an imbedded poetic quality" redefining itself over and over, and visualisation is the sustenance of the novel. Emily Dickinson is seen as successor to EB; she also dealt with love, death, and immortality and used "the sudden thrust of the unexpected word."

B428 ROWE, J. Hambley "The Maternal Relatives of the Brontës" *BST* 6 (1923) 135–46
The Branwell family tree, from 1605, is recorded here and includes the possible origin of EB's middle name.

B429 RUFF, William "First American Editions of the Brontë Novels: A Complete Bibliography" *BST* 8 (1934) 143–50
This is a brief account of the publication of the Brontë novels in America with a thorough descriptive bibliography.

B430 SAAGPAKK, Paul F. "A Survey of Psychopathology in British Literature from Shakespeare to Hardy" *Literature and Psychology* 18, Nos 2–3 (1968) 135–65
In this discussion of melancholy, remorse, grief, and insanity in literature, *WH* is seen as "a perfect psychopathological novel."

B431 SADLEIR, Michael "An Addendum to 'Enemies of Books' " *New Colophon* 1 (July 1948) 235–38
The article contains a short discussion of Thomas Cautley Newby, the first publisher of *WH*, and his handling of the publication of *WH*.

*B432 SAMAAN, Angele Botros "Themes of Emily Brontë's Poetry" in Magdi Wahba, ed *Cairo Studies in English* (1959) 118–34
The author "considers some themes in Emily Brontë's poems: whether they are Gondal or personal poems, 'there is a general feeling of desolation, loneliness, darkness, and gloom.' " [From an abstract in *The Year's Work in English Studies*.]

B433 SAN GARDE, W. A. S. [Letter to the Editor] "The Miraculous Parsonage" *TLS* (Aug 21 1948) 471
W. L. Andrews' (see B33) view of the earlier unpopularity of the Brontë novels is opposed by this writer, who remembers his mother's saying that the Brontë novels were "all the go."

B434 SCHARNHORST, Gary "*Wuthering Heights* and *The Portrait of a Lady*: A Dynamic Parallel" *Ball State University Forum* 19 (Winter 1978) 17–22
WH, as well as *Daniel Deronda* and *Madame Bovary*, may have served as one of Henry James' sources for *The Portrait of a Lady*. There is a correlation of setting, theme, and characterization between the two novels.

B435 SCHELLY, Judith M. "A Like Unlike: Brother and Sister in the Works of Wordsworth, Byron, George Eliot, Emily Brontë, and Dickens" *DAI* 42 (July 1981) 205A

An examination of the preoccupation of these five nineteenth–century English writers with the brother–sister relationship. "Claude Levi–Strauss offers an anthropological model which illuminates the conflict faced by these authors." The refusal to relinquish sibling for spouse represents "the permanent expression of a desire for disorder, or rather, counter–order."

B436 SCHEUERLE, William H. "Brontë's *Wuthering Heights*" *Explicator* 33 (May 1975) 1–2
EB used the Yorkshire superstition that "the presence of pigeons' feathers in the pillow or the bed of a dying person either prolongs that person's agonies of dying or even prohibits his death as he struggles in 'the most exquisite torture' " to intensify Catherine's suffering for her unforgivable sin of forsaking Heathcliff to marry Edgar Linton.

B437 SCHMIDT, Emily Tresselt "From Highland to Lowland: Charlotte Brontë's Editorial Changes in Emily's Poems" *BST* 15 (1968) 221–26
Charlotte Brontë made changes in EB's poems in 1846 with her approval. In 1850, after EB's death, Charlotte made changes in another group of Emily's poems. The 1850 alterations are compared with those made in 1846 and found to be more extensive.

B438 SCHOLFIELD, B. [Letter to the Editor] "The Haworth Moors" *Spectator* 190 (May 22 1953) 678
The writer disagrees with J. Hawkes (see B233): ". . . let the moorland stand for light." He also points out the modernity of Haworth when the Brontës lived there; e.g., they had a daily newspaper and a train to London. (See B32 for a reply.)

B439 SCHORER, Mark "Fiction and the Matrix of Analogy" *Kenyon Review* 11 (Autumn 1949) 539–60
The "matrix of analogy" is "that whole habit of value association." The novels treated are *Persuasion*, *WH*, and *Middlemarch*. *WH* is discussed on p 544–50. The novel is no tragedy; it is a "moral teething" for EB as well as for Heathcliff. The essay contains an explication of the animal imagery in *WH* and considers the verbs, metaphors, and epithets used. Reprinted: A322, A325, A326, A379; partial reprinting: A10, A274, A283. See B377.

B440 ———— "Technique as Discovery" *Hudson Review* 1 (Spring 1948) 67–87
WH has a "theme of the moral magnificence of unmoral passion," a theme impossible to sustain. Two aspects of EB's technique, however, objectify it: (1) Her narrative perspective has the two elements, conventional emotion (Lockwood) and conventional morality (Nelly Dean). (2) The perspective operates over a long period of time. Reprinted: A325.

B441 SCHREINER, Wilhelmina R. "The Criticism of Emily Brontë" *University of Pittsburgh: Bulletin of MA Theses* 34 (1937) 422
Criticisms of *WH* and EB's poems, examined from the time EB's work was originally published, show something of the literary temper of the times and of the personality of the critic.

B442 SCRIVNER, Buford, Jr "The Ethos of *Wuthering Heights*" *Dalhousie Review* 54 (Autumn 1974) 451–62
This essay on *WH* demonstrates that ". . . ethical concern determines the very structure of the novel." Man's existence as a kind of bridge between Being and Becoming forces upon him an ambivalence; he must act in this world, and yet find a way to give expression to the

essential part of himself. For example, Catherine marries Edgar to "aid Heathcliff to rise." Her error is that in trying to enhance their basic unity by the marriage, she is turning her back on that basic unity.

B443 SECCOMBE, Thomas "Place of the Brontës among Women Novelists of the Last Century" *BST* 5 (Apr 1913) 8–12
The title is a misnomer; the article discusses Charlotte Brontë only.

B444 SERLEN, Ellen "The Rage of Caliban: Realism and Romance in the Nineteenth Century Novel" *DAI* 36 (Aug 1975) 911A
The circumstances of nineteenth–century England created a need in readers to experience a more pleasing world than that in which they actually lived. *WH* is one of the examples, in that "...we are presented by Emily Brontë with the freedom of imagination represented by Heathcliff, and the humdrum reality of the rest of the inhabitants of the moors."

B445 SHANNON, Edgar F., Jr "Lockwood's Dreams and the Exegesis of *Wuthering Heights*" *NCF* 14 (Sept 1959) 95–109
Ruth Adams (see B25) asserts Branderham's sermon text to be Genesis 4; instead, it is Matthew 18. The author also repudiates Dorothy Van Ghent's dream interpretation. The thematic problem of the novel is the nature of Catherine's offense. In regard to Heathcliff: "In the terms of Emily Brontë's moral equation, there is no autonomous evil in the universe." Hate is a corollary of love, and "evil derives solely from separation—from the denial of sympathy and love." (See also B49). Reprinted: A220, A379.

B446 SHAPIRO, Arnold "*Wuthering Heights* as a Victorian Novel" *Studies in the Novel* 1 (Fall 1969) 284–96
The ethical and moral tradition in *WH* is that of the other great Victorian novels. EB and Charlotte Brontë both picture society as selfish, family life as open warfare for money and power, and religion as hypocritical, cold, and deflected from true Christian ideals.

B447 SHAPIRO, Michael D. "Sexual Conflict in the Victorian Novel" *DAI* 41 (Feb 1981) 3595A–3596A
"The admittance of the unconscious, irrational springs of sexuality in the Brontës' fiction was to a considerable extent undermined by Dickens' 'asexual' Happy Pairs and Thackeray's persistent misogyny." George Eliot, however, expanded and deepened the sexual implications of the "quest" theme in literary heroines begun by EB and Charlotte Brontë.

B448 SHUNAMI, Gideon "Giborim be–Kavlei Messaphrehem; Li–Shelat Emdat Hatatspit be–*Enkat Gvahim* Le–Emily Brontë" (Sum. in English: Characters in the Grip of Their Narrators: The Question of Point–of–View in *Wuthering Heights*) *Hasifrut* 3 (Sept 1972) 474–87
The unreliability of Lockwood and Nelly Dean serves to strengthen the credibility of the *WH* story. They also undermine the reliability of each other. See B449.

B449 ——— "The Unreliable Narrator in *Wuthering Heights*" *NCF* 27 (Mar 1973) 449–68
Critics of *WH* have seen Nelly Dean's role as many things, ranging from that of a reliable narrator to that of a villain. This essay attempts to prove Nelly an unreliable narrator. Not only is Nelly's view of characters and events misleading; she also withholds information from

the major characters at crucial times, thereby creating misunderstandings among them. A reprinting, in English, of B448.

B450 SIMPSON, Jacqueline "The Function of Folklore in *Jane Eyre* and *Wuthering Heights*" *Folklore* (London) 85 (Spring 1974) 47–61

Only those characters who have EB's fullest sympathy have a belief in folklore and the supernatural, e.g., Catherine and Heathcliff. Significantly, Zillah and Joseph have no folklore beliefs, and Nelly is steadfastly ambivalent about ghosts to the end. Imagery from folk–belief serves to express the "otherness" of Heathcliff.

*B451 SMITH, David "The Panelled Bed and the Unrepressible Wish of *Wuthering Heights*" *Paunch* 30 (Dec 1967) 40–46

Cathy's childhood bedroom and its panelled bed parallel the graveyard and its coffins. The bedroom is taboo to Heathcliff, and only in the grave can he and Catherine be reunited. [From an abstract in *Abstracts of English Studies*.]

B452 SMITH, David J. "The Arrested Heart: Familial Love and Psychic Conflict in Five Mid–Victorian Novels" *Dissertation Abstracts* 27, No 6 (1966) 1839A

The hypothesis of the dissertation is that principal characters in each of the novels (*Jane Eyre*, *The Mill on the Floss*, *Wuthering Heights*, *Pendennis*, and *The History of Henry Esmond*) are motivated by an unconscious mental conflict between an incest wish and an incest taboo. The conflict explains many aspects of the characters' inner and outer lives; it also illuminates the structure and the meaning of the novels.

B453 SNOWDEN, Keighley "The Brontës as Artists and as Prophets" *BST* 4 (Mar 1909) 78–92

This is a discussion of past and contemporary criticism of the novels of Charlotte and Emily Brontë.

B454 ——— "The Enigma of Emily Brontë" *Fortnightly Review* 124 (Aug 1928) 195–202

WH was written by a woman who had felt love, passion, and pain. Two sources for *WH* are suggested: Ruysbroeck's *The Heavenly Espousals* and EB's possible romantic attachment to the curate William Weightman. Three of her poems are connected with Weightman.

B455 SOLOMON, Eric "The Incest Theme in *Wuthering Heights*" *NCF* 14 (June 1959) 80–83

There is internal evidence in *WH* that Catherine and Heathcliff could possibly be half–brother and –sister. If the novel is read with this possibility in mind, the tragedy would be greater, the emotion heightened, and the inevitable separation of the two lovers more logical. Reprinted: A220, A379.

B456 SONSTROEM, David "The Structure of *Wuthering Heights* Continued" *PMLA* 87 (Mar 1972) 314

D. Sonstroem agrees that R. Burkhart's suggestion (B83) strengthens his own essay. However, Burkhart's symmetrical structure might suggest a "lucid, harmonious meaning" for *WH*, and Sonstroem's original schema argues that the patterns in *WH* are enigmatic.

B457 ——— "*Wuthering Heights* and the Limits of Vision" *PMLA* 86 (Jan 1971) 51–62

The reader of *WH* is clearly expected by EB to render verdicts. In this incisive essay Sonstroem argues that *WH* presents the spectacle of several limited and inadequate points of view—genteel, Christian, pragmatic, animistic—at indecisive war with one another. "...Emily Brontë addresses herself less to vision than to blindness: to man's refusal to overlook his prejudices, and his inability to discern what lies beyond his limitations." See B83.

B458 SPACKS, Patricia Meyer "Rebellions of Good Women" *Women and Literature* 6 (Fall 1978) 2–13

In this discussion of *WH* and *Villette* it is noted that both EB and Charlotte Brontë wrote of women who defied convention: "...[B]ehind the disguise of romantic fiction both authors can be seen to articulate fundamental feminist principles and the psychic forces that underlie them...."

B459 SPARK, Muriel "The Brontës As Teachers" *New Yorker* 41 (Jan 22 1966) 30–33

All four Brontës disliked teaching, but EB was the only one "to get out of the predicament with all speed."

B460 STARZYK, Lawrence J. "Emily Brontë: Poetry in a Mingled Tone" *Criticism* 14 (Spring 1972) 119–36

If EB's dialectic is, in fact, "a dialectic of becoming...it emphasizes dissolution rather than fusion, denial rather than affirmation...." The essay is an investigation into EB's philosophy as it seems to emerge from her essays in French, and focuses on her regard for the forces of nature, her separation of the "real" world from the world of flux and appearances, and her philosophy of death.

B461 ——— "The Faith of Emily Brontë's Immortality Creed" *Victorian Poetry* 11 (Winter 1973) 295–305

In a detailed analysis of "No Coward Soul Is Mine" EB's philosophy emerges: "The real genius of Brontë's poem resides in the fact that it not only transcends positivist systems in its elimination of death, but it does so by viewing creation's pervasive multiplicity as a blessing, not a bane...." Permanence is realizable in the world beyond, but it is nevertheless here with us now in the world of flux.

B462 STEDMAN, Jane W. "The Genesis of the Genii" *BST* 14 (1965) 16–19

The young Brontës based their Genii to a greater extent on *Tales of the Genii* by James Ridley than on *Arabian Nights*.

B463 STEPHENS, Margaret A. "Mysticism in the Works of Emily Jane Brontë" *DAI* 31 (Dec 1970) 2890A

Only with knowledge of EB's spiritual life can we interpret her works. One essay, "The Butterfly," gives her mystical conception of the world and provides the blueprint for *WH*.

B464 STEVENS, Joan "A Note on Mossmans" *BST* 16 (1971) 47–50

New material has been found revealing a closer connection than was previously known among the Mossmans, and the Taylors and Dixons, families instrumental in arranging for Charlotte and Emily to attend the school in Brussels in 1842.

B465 —— "Woozles in Brontëland: A Cautionary Tale" *Studies in Bibliography* 24 (1971) 99–108

As Mildred G. Christian has pointed out, the text of the Brontë letters published by Clement Shorter, and later by Wise and Symington in the Shakespeare Head Brontë, is imperfect and incomplete. This essay shows the extent of that unreliability, using as an example a letter from Charlotte Brontë to Mary Taylor in New Zealand dated 4 September 1848.

*B466 STOLLARD, M. L. "The Brontës and Their Visits to Leeds" *Yorkshire Evening Post* (May 7 1919)

B467 ——"The Brontës in Leeds" *BST* 13 (1959) 360–62

Leeds was the Brontës' shopping center. At Leeds Mr Brontë bought the famous wooden soldiers that began the plays, and "the children were. . .brought up on Leeds newspapers."

STONE, Roy de Montpensier *see* B354.

B468 STRACHAN, Pearl "Across the Moors" *Christian Science Monitor* (May 24 1947) 10

This article describes a personal walk across the moors and tells the Brontë story. The moors were the most powerful environmental influence on the works of the Brontës.

B469 SUCKSMITH, Harvey P. "The Theme of *Wuthering Heights* Reconsidered" *Dalhousie Review* 54 (Autumn 1974) 418–28

The Victorian context of *WH* should not be ignored, for an understanding of the Victorian view of marriage and sexuality adds considerably to an appreciation of EB's presentation. The typical marriage relationship is represented in the marriage of Catherine Earnshaw and Edgar Linton, but a very different form of sexual love from that approved by the Victorians is being presented here in the love of Catherine and Heathcliff.

B470 SUTCLIFFE, Halliwell "The Spirit of the Moors" *BST* 2 (Jan 1903) 174–90

"The outer world knew nothing of the storm and fret of Haworth Moor till *Wuthering Heights* was born." The characters in *WH* would not live without their surroundings.

*B471 SYMONS, Arthur "Emily Brontë" *The Nation* 23 (Aug 24 1918) 546–47

WH is called "one long outcry" from a woman who possessed "passion without sensuousness." The novel is praised for "the mystery of its terror," but it is not well–constructed. Furthermore, "her narrative is dominated by sheer chance and guided by mere accident." Reprinted: A361, B472.

B472 —— "Emily Brontë" *Living Age* 299 (Oct 12 1918) 119–21

This is a reprinting of Item B471.

*B473 T., M. "The Brontës of Haworth" *Public Library Journal* 5 (1932)

B474 TAYLOR, Robert H. "The Singular Anomalies" *Princeton University Library Chronicle* 17 (Winter 1956) 71–76

This is a discussion of the Parrish Collection at Princeton University which contains early editions of *WH* and *Poems by Currer, Ellis and Acton Bell.*

*B475 THIENE, John "Apparitions of Disaster: Brontëan Parallels in *Wide Sargasso Sea* and *Guerillas*" *Journal of Commonwealth Literature* 14 (1979) 116–32
Naipaul's *Guerillas* is similar to Rhys' *Wide Sargasso Sea* because, like EB, both authors portray a lost pastoral Eden. [From an abstract in *Abstracts of English Studies.*]

B476 THOMPSON, Wade "Infanticide and Sadism in *Wuthering Heights*" *PMLA* 78 (Mar 1963) 69–74
This is "...an interpretation of *Wuthering Heights* based upon the extraordinary sadism which underlies Emily Brontë's concept of emotional relationships...." Reprinted: A104, A283; partially reprinted: A274. See B146.

B477 ———, William Empson and John Doheny "Controversy on *Wuthering Heights*" *Paunch* 23 (Apr 1965) 79–94
A continuation of the debate on the status of characters and the theme of revenge in *WH* begun in October 1964. See B146.

B478 THOMSON, David T., Jr "*Wuthering Heights*: A Psychological Reading" *DAI* 37 (Apr 1977) 6517A
This study focuses on Lockwood, Nelly Dean, Catherine, and Heathcliff, and on the style and texture of each one's narrative. The psychological theories of Anton Ehrenzweig, Wayne Barker, and R. D. Laing are the basis for exploration of these four characters and their relationships with each other.

B479 THOMSON, Patricia "*Wuthering Heights* and *Mauprat*" *Review of English Studies* 24 (Feb 1973) 26–37
George Sand's *Mauprat*, published in 1837, was probably read by EB and became a part of her "imaginative store." Among the similarities discussed is a theme of "the civilizing influence of human love"; Bernard is tamed, and although Heathcliff is not, Cathy and Hareton, the second generation in *WH*, are. (For another comparison of *WH* with *Mauprat*, see B38.)

B480 THORBURN, Donald B. "The Effects of the Wesleyan Movement on the Brontë Sisters, as Evidenced by an Examination of Certain of Their Novels" *Microfilm Abstracts* 8 (1948) 109–11
Methodism affected the Brontës both consciously and unconsciously, and it is reflected in their "attitude toward liquor, toward dress, their anti–Catholic feeling, their sabbatarianism, their anti–High Church feeling, their attitude toward the sanctity of daily work...their use of the Bible for quotation and daily guidance, their humanitarianism, their belief in the worth of the common man, their belief in salvation through free choice, and their enthusiasm for the Evangelical type of religion and for missionary work." Their novels prove that they were "spiritual children of Methodism."

B481 THUR, Robert "Longing for Union: The *Doppleganger* in *Wuthering Heights* and *Frankenstein*" *DAI* 37 (Feb 1977) 4172B
"Ultimately, the *Doppleganger* in *Wuthering Heights* is an archetypal description of the psycho–sexual development of Woman from birth to a fully integrated, deeply creative personality." In contrast, the *Doppleganger* in *Frankenstein* describes the failure of integration.

B482 THWAITE, Anthony "Early Spring in Cwmdonkin Drive" *New Statesman* (May 28 1971) 738–39

The nature of the emotion in the poetry of Dylan Thomas is compared briefly to that of EB, Emily Dickinson, and A.E. Housman.

B483 TINKER, Chauncey Brewster "Poetry of the Brontës" *Saturday Review of Literature* 1 (Jan 10 1925) 441–42
This is a thorough analysis of EB's poetry. In spite of all the Brontë biography "the day will come...when...the literary work of the three sisters [will be] judged on its merits and not merely prized for the light it throws on their biography." All the Brontës lack discipline in their poetry; EB can "strike a false note," but she is the poetic genius of the family. There is "unchastened emotionalism," an "emphasis on freedom" and "intense self–confidence" in her poetry. Reprinted: A367.

B484 TOMBLESON, Gary E. "Alpha and Omega Recast: The Rhetoric of Cosmic Unity in Poe, Brontë, and Hardy" *DAI* 37 (Oct 1976) 2165A
Possibilities for reality, as cosmically unified, stem from the unconscious, which finds its fullest representation in fantastic art and literature. The works of Poe, EB, and Hardy are analyzed and compared, and also compared to examples of visual art, including works of Breughel the Elder and Gothic architecture.

B485 TOMPKINS, J. M. S. "Caroline Helstone's Eyes" *BST* 14 (1961) 18–28
The heroine of *Shirley* by Charlotte Brontë was, according to Charlotte, modeled on EB. This article discusses the likelihood that Caroline in the novel was modeled on Anne Brontë and discusses the relationship of the three Brontë sisters.

B486 TOUGH, A. J. "*Wuthering Heights* and *King Lear*" *English* 21 (Spring 1972) 1–5
The "sense of cosmic significance which pervades *King Lear* is created chiefly by six features...." The six, with the exception of astronomical comparisons, also appear in *WH*. Many parallels are drawn and supported by quotes from both works. One example: "...[T]he evil side of [Heathcliff 's] nature is revealed partly through animal imagery, just as the evil side of Goneril and Regan is...."

B487 TRAVERSI, Derek "*Wuthering Heights* after a Hundred Years" *Dublin Review* 222 (Spring 1949) 154–68
EB's models for *WH* may have been romantic melodramas, and *WH* could be called one too, but after this has been granted we must consider its dramatic intensity, morality, and mysticism. The two themes are the " 'personal' and 'social' aspects [which] stand in the closest relationship to one another." [The second half of this article is similar to the author's essay "The Brontë Sisters and *Wuthering Heights*" (A369).] Partially reprinted: A274. Reprinted A10.

B488 TRICKETT, Rachel "*Wuthering Heights*: The Story of a Haunting" *BST* 16 (1975) 338–47
By approaching *WH* in terms of a ghost tale, Trickett demonstrates the further subtleties of the novel, its similarities to, and differences from, a ghost tale.

B489 TURNELL, Martin "*Wuthering Heights*" *Dublin Review* 206 (Jan 1940) 134–49
This is a comprehensive, well–supported social analysis which assesses *WH* as "one of the

most tremendous indictments of contemporary civilization in the whole of nineteenth–century literature." The novel is a constructive social criticism and the real subject "is a conflict between two profoundly different ways of life. . . ."

B490 TWITCHELL, James "Heathcliff as Monomaniac" *BST* 16 (1974) 374–75
Monos for "one" and *mania* for "madness" combine to make "monomania," the term used by Nelly Dean at one point to describe Heathcliff's problem. "By 1833 the term. . .was still a medical word describing an observed state of deviation." Therefore, Heathcliff may have been meant to be, not a demon or ghoul, but "an artistic moulding of what was, in the 1840's, a relatively new category of aberrant personality."

B491 ———— "Heathcliff as Vampire" *Southern Humanities Review* 11 (Fall 1977) 355–62
"Heathcliff has risen from devil to tragic hero in three generations of critics. . ." and now he should be reconsidered to be perhaps a devil again. The popularity of vampirism in the folklore of the nineteenth century supports the theory that EB intended Heathcliff to be at least a metaphorical vampire.

B492 VAISEY, The Hon Mr Justice "*Wuthering Heights*: A Note on Its Authorship" *BST* 11 (1946) 14–15
Regarding the theory of Branwell Brontë's part in the production of *WH*: Chapters I, II, III, and the early part of Chapter IV differ from the rest of the book. "It is Branwell rather than Mr. Lockwood who is speaking."

B493 VANČURA, Zdeněk "The Stones of *Wuthering Heights*" *Philogica Pragensia* 13, No 1 (1970) 1–15
The manor house, Wuthering Heights, plays an important role in the story. For example, it is variously inaccessible and later more easily accessible to Lockwood. "The front door stood open, but the jealous gate was fastened. . . ." The manor house also serves as a departure point to evaluate *WH* and to explore its themes of love and forgiveness. Vančura makes the point that EB did not choose to destroy the manor house, perhaps in a conflagration similar to that of Thornfield Hall in *Jane Eyre*, or the House of Usher in *The Fall of the House of Usher*.

B494 VAN GHENT, Dorothy "The Window Figure and the Two–children Figure in *Wuthering Heights*" *NCF* 7 (Dec 1952) 189–97
This is an outstanding myth–and–symbol interpretation of *WH*. The Window Figure is well–supported by many instances in the novel. The Two–children Figure, which is related to several of EB's poems, also leads to interesting speculation. See A374.

B495 VANTREASE, Brenda R. "The Heroic Ideal: Three Views" *DAI* 41 (Nov 1980) 2106A
An exploration of the idea of individualism as a major component of the heroic ideal provides a means to examine the concept of the hero as developed in *WH*, Defoe's *Moll Flanders*, and Ayn Rand's *Atlas Shrugged*.

B496 VARGISH, Thomas "Revenge and *Wuthering Heights*" *Studies in the Novel* 3 (Spring 1971) 7–17
"What is the relation between the moral world in which personal revenge, at least, may

be condemned, and the worlds of Achilles or Hamlet or Heathcliff?" Heathcliff's revenge, examined in detail, becomes a margin of reference for the survival of the self, with "profound psychological and aesthetic significance" in *WH*, as it is in the greatest of English tragedy.

B497 VAUGHAN, C. E. "Charlotte and Emily Brontë: A Comparison and a Contrast" *BST* 4 (Apr 1912) 217–35

The sisters had in common passion, lyricism, and revolt, but EB was the more intense and Charlotte Brontë had more humor.

B497A VISICK, Mary "The Last of Gondal" *BST* 18 (1982) 75–85

The title refers to "the last that Emily Brontë had to say of her creation." The final disorder in the Gondal notebook seems to indicate that EB had outgrown her fascination with Gondal, and Visick believes that *WH* was the end result of this maturity. Yet, the question remains: Why did EB return to Gondal after she had finished *WH*?

B498 VISWANATHAN, Jacqueline "Point of View and Unreliability in Brontë's *Wuthering Heights*, Conrad's *Under Western Eyes*, and Mann's *Doktor Faustus*" *Orbis Litterarum* 29, No 1 (1974) 42–60

Three scenes are selected—one from each novel—in which a principal character reveals a hitherto unknown fact to the unreliable narrator. In *WH* the scene is the meeting of Catherine and Heathcliff just before Catherine's death. The narrators make mistakes of various kinds: They are deceived in their interpretation of what is going to happen, or documents written by the main characters open out perspectives which differ from the narrators' viewpoints, such as Cathy's annotations in the margin of her books and Isabel's letter to Nelly. The distance between the narrators and the main characters is a major factor of their fallibility, i.e., all the narrators stand on the side of the "average, balanced, peaceful 'good' citizen, with no gift for rebellion or originality."

B499 WADDINGTON–FEATHER, John "Emily Brontë's Use of Dialect in *Wuthering Heights*" *BST* 15 (1966) 12–19

EB uses dialect "in comparatively large amounts" on fifteen occasions in *WH* to "create character and mood." Her representations are quite accurate, though not always consistent. The emphasis in this article is upon EB's artistic use of dialect rather than the dialect itself.

B500 WAIDNER, Maralee L. "From Reason to Romance: A Progression from an Emphasis on Neoclassic Rationality to Romantic Intuition in Three English Woman Novelists" *DAI* 34 (Sept 1973) 1259A–1260A

The conflicts between reason and romance are examined in *WH*, Jane Austen's *Emma* and *Persuasion*, and Charlotte Brontë's *Jane Eyre*.

B501 WALBANK, Alan [Letter to the Editor] " 'The Visionary' and 'The Eve of St. Agnes' " *TLS* (June 18 1954) 393

EB's poem "The Visionary" and Keats' "The Eve of St. Agnes" are compared, and their similarity in theme and expression is noted.

B501A WALLACE, Robert K. "Emily Brontë and Music: Haworth, Brussels, and Beethoven" *BST* 18 (1982) 136–42

Wallace discusses the music EB was known to have studied at Haworth and that which she was likely to have studied and heard in Brussels. "...[T]he music of Beethoven, in particular, may well have been a catalyst in the artistic growth that resulted in *Wuthering Heights*."

B502 WARD, Mrs Humphry "*Wuthering Heights*" *BST* 2 (Jan 1906) 227–32
This is a reprinting of Item A385.

B502A WARD, Marcella L. "Anguish and Resolution: A Study of Myth in the Work of Emily Brontë" *DAI* 42 (May 1982) 4835A
A reading of *WH* with an awareness of the Victorian mores leads to a premise that EB's main concern was "the mediation between tensions of embitterment and conciliation." The Gondal epic of Notebook B and the poems of Notebook A lend credence to EB's devotion to the resolution of these opposites.

B503 WATSON, Melvin R. "Tempest in the Soul: The Theme and Structure of *Wuthering Heights*" *NCF* 4 (Sept 1949) 87–100
WH is analogous to Elizabethan drama. Heathcliff is "a Hamlet without Hamlet's fatal irresolution," and the novel is structurally organized like a five–act tragedy. The author concludes that *WH* is the product of a mature artist. Reprinted: A220, A387.

B504 ———— "*Wuthering Heights* and the Critics" *The Trollopian* 3 (Mar 1949) 243–63
This is an excellent and detailed review of one hundred years of criticism of *WH*. Earlier criticism was, for the most part, derogatory and confused. "Since 1920 more rational, sensible criticism on *Wuthering Heights* has appeared than during the seventy–odd preceding years...." Noted as worst are the parallel school, the autobiographical school, and the Freudian school. J. A. MacKereth and David Cecil (see B318 and A51) are credited with the most competent interpretations. Reprinted: A104.

B505 WEIR, Edith M. "Contemporary Reviews of the First Brontë Novels" *BST* 11 (1947) 89–96
The 1848 English reviews are reprinted here.

B506 ———— "New Brontë Material Comes to Light; A Picture Attributed to Emily; Letters from the Hegers" *BST* 11 (1949) 249–61
A watercolor is discovered which is supposed to have been painted by EB when she was in Brussels. It is reproduced on the frontispiece of this issue and is judged by the author to be genuine.

B507 WEISSMAN, Judith " 'Like a Mad Dog': The Radical Romanticism of *Wuthering Heights*" *Midwest Quarterly* 19 (Summer 1978) 383–97
The true link between *WH* and the works of other Romantics is that it is a redefinition of the elemental feelings of human beings—the instincts. Of the plentiful animal imagery in *WH*, dogs are the most important animal, for EB is stressing that humans share with dogs instincts of fidelity to person and place. *WH* is a "declaration that we are capable of living more passionately and simply than we do."

B507A WEST, Carol L. "Aspects of Time in *Wuthering Heights*" *DAI* 41 (June 1981) 5112A–5113A
This study focuses on nonlinear time in *WH*, "unconventional beginnings, inconclusive

endings, simultaneity, and especially repetition, the novel's most characteristic mode of temporality." EB depicts human experience as resisting chronological order and the conventional distinctions between past, present, and future.

B508 WEST, Rebecca "The Role of Fantasy in the Work of the Brontës" *BST* 12 (1954) 255–67
The emphasis is upon *WH*, which has a triple significance: it is a novel in which the truth is told about the characters; it is a critical work exposing the English society to which Lockwood belonged; and it is a poetical work because it interprets the universe.

B509 WIDDOWSON, Peter "Emily Brontë: The Romantic Novelist" *Moderna Språk* 66 (Feb–Mar 1972) 1–19
WH is seen as a statement of the Romantic view of life. Nature in *WH* suggests "a sense of liberty from the corruption and meanness of 'civilisation'. . ." and childhood, too, is seen as free from civilization, embracing truth and purity of response. Another Romantic idea reflected in *WH* is the opposition of Passion and Sense, and EB is also interested in the supernatural and strange states of mind. These Romantic characteristics are bound together by simple and poetic language. Finally, Heathcliff is the embodiment of Life itself as a deity, ". . . particularly when made manifest in the free individual human soul. . . ."

B510 WILKINS, Mary E. "Emily Brontë and *Wuthering Heights*" *Booklover's Magazine* 1 (May 1903) 514–19
EB is evaluated as an author. Although *WH* has "the repulsiveness of power," EB is intent upon the truth and handles brutality and coarseness "like another woman would a painted fan."

*B511 WILKS, Brian "Through the Eyes of the Brontës" (London) *Sunday Times Magazine* (Mar 14 1976) 32–41
Drawings and paintings by the Brontë children, some never before published. [From mention in *BST*.]

*B512 WILLIAMS, Gordon "The Problem of Passion in *Wuthering Heights*" *Trivium* 7 (May 1972) 41–53.
At times the love of Catherine and Heathcliff seems Gothic, but it is actually more suggestive of modern Freudian psychology, Shakespeare, and the Faustian tradition. [From an abstract in *Abstracts of English Studies.*]

B513 WILLIS, Irene Cooper "The Authorship of *Wuthering Heights*" *The Trollopian* 2 (Dec 1947) 157–68
The claim that Branwell Brontë wrote *WH* was first made twenty years after the novel was published. Evidence is presented here against the allegations of those who say they were witnesses to events which tend to support Branwell's partial or complete authorship of *WH*.

B514 WILLSON, Jo Anne A. " 'The Butterfly' and *Wuthering Heights*: A Mystic's Eschatology" *Victorian Newsletter* 33 (Spring 1968) 22–25
This is a good correlation of one of EB's essays with *WH*. "It is the purpose of this paper to suggest that the 'why' of *Wuthering Heights* may be found in one of the five seldom-discussed essays written by Emily Brontë while she was a student at. . . Brussels, in 1842." These essays were EB's first attempts at formulating a philosophy, and the essays, like *WH*,

appeal more to perception than to reason. "The Butterfly" is especially a philosophical pred-ecessor of *WH* in its examination of the forces of good and evil, and the reason for evil on earth. EB writes in the essay: "...each suffering of our unhappy nature is only a seed for that divine harvest which will be gathered when sin...[and] death...will leave their former victims to an eternal realm of happiness and glory."

B515 WILLY, Margaret "Emily Brontë: Poet and Mystic" *English* 6 (Autumn 1946) 117–22
This is a discussion of EB and her poems. The influences upon EB were the solitude of her life, the stimulus of the Brontë childhood composition, her brother Branwell, and the moors. The author suggests that EB felt a death–wish that struggled with her love of life, and that both impulses are reflected in her poems.

B516 WILSON, Angus "Evil in the English Novel" *Kenyon Review* 29 (Mar 1967) 167–94
WH is briefly discussed on p 181–83 as the author traces "transcendent good and evil"—especially evil—in the English novel. Heathcliff is a fallen angel, a representation coming directly from the Gothic. Even though he is not redeemed by Catherine's love, as Rochester is redeemed by Jane Eyre's, yet their love transcends the rest of the events of the book.

B517 WILSON, David "Emily Brontë: First of the Moderns" *Modern Quarterly Miscellany* 1 (1947) 94–115.
The proletarian novel may have had its beginning one hundred years ago in EB's *WH*. Far from being isolated, as she is often pictured, EB was very much a part of the birth of modern industrial England. She is believed, by Wilson, to have been very sympathetic with the common people of her time and place. The strife and turbulence in Gondal is seen as a projection of her own real environment, and the third chapter of *WH* reflects the authoritarianism and clerical violence of official Methodism towards the restless common people. In an atmosphere of uncouth roughness synonymous with the Pennine character, "the story of Heathcliff and Catherine Earnshaw works itself out as a metaphor of the social struggle of [EB's] own time, with all its cruelty and hatred...."

B518 WILSON, F. A. C. "The Primrose Wreath: The Heroes of the Brontë Novels" *NCF* 29 (June 1974) 40–57
The Brontë novels are related to the concept of the androgyne. Each of the Brontë sisters fuses androgynous characteristics to obtain the image of the true hero. Charlotte Brontë's characters alternate between "masculine," or controlling, and "feminine," or responsive roles. In *WH*, however, the man is subordinate and the woman becomes the regulator. This essay investigates the Brontë novels in the frame of Jungian demonstrations that the human psyche is androgynous.

B519 WILSON, The Hon Lady "The Brontës as Governesses"*BST* 9 (1939) 217–35
Since very little is known about EB as a governess, the discussion centers upon the other Brontës.

B520 WINSOR, Dorothy A. "The Continuity of the Gothic: The Gothic Novels of Charlotte Brontë, Emily Brontë, and Iris Murdoch" *DAI* 40 (May 1980) 5882A
This essay discusses Gothic conventions, defining the unspoken assumptions expressed by use of them, and determining the world view Gothic conventions imply. "Since the Brontës

and Murdoch wrote in different centuries, examination of the work of all three also shows how the use of Gothic conventions has changed or remained the same as the novel has changed, as society has changed, and as women's lives have changed." Examined are: *WH*, *Jane Eyre*, *Villette*, *The Bell*, *The Unicorn*, and *The Time of the Angels*.

B521 WOOD, Butler "Influence of the Moorlands on Charlotte and Emily Brontë" *BST* 6 (1922) 79–87
There was a strong influence of the moorlands on the Brontë characters; EB's nature–worship is reflected in *WH*. Reprinted: A1.

B522 —— "Some Bibliographical Notes on the Brontë Literature" *BST* 4 (Mar 1911) 189–98
This article discusses current Brontë biography and some of the events connected with publication of the Brontë novels.

B523 WOODRING, Carl "The Narrators of *Wuthering Heights*" *NCF* 11 (Mar 1957) 298–305
The author points out the further value—in addition to those values mentioned by other critics—of Mr Lockwood, the stranger, and Nelly Dean, the intimate. Nelly Dean adds much warmth to the novel without interfering with the actions of the main characters. Reprinted: A220, A322.

B524 WORDSWORTH, Jonathan "Wordsworth and the Poetry of Emily Brontë" *BST* 16 (1972) 85–100
EB's poetry was perhaps influenced by Scott, Byron, and Shelley; nevertheless, her poems show an affinity to the work of Wordsworth.

B525 WORTH, George J."Emily Brontë's Mr. Lockwood" *NCF* 12 (Mar 1958) 315–20
Lockwood deludes himself (but not the reader) about his own character and personality, which was deliberately drawn by EB not only to act as a foil to Heathcliff, but also to be an ordinary man through which the reader might see and believe the events and people of *WH*. Reprinted: A220.

B526 WYZEWA, Theodore de "Emily Brontë: 1818—19th December, 1848" trans Effie Brown *BST* 17 (1976) 30–34
M Emile Montegut, writing about EB and *WH* in 1857, is quoted. He says EB was a genius who produced the most remarkable works of the three sisters. The French people in 1857, however, were not looking for a novel like *WH*; they liked Mrs Gaskell's domestic scenes. See B298.

B527 YSKAMP, Claire E. "Character and Voice: First–Person Narrators in *Tom Jones*, *Wuthering Heights*, and *Second Skin*" *DAI* 32 (June 1972) 6948A
"Analyzing tension that exists between the first–person narrator as a character (i.e., a real fictional person) and the first–person narrator as a voice (i.e., as an observer, a reporter, and a commentator) suggests a method of interpretation of how the novelist uses the first–person narration to communicate with the reader." The method used in *WH* is extrapolation.

B528 ZANDVOORT, R. W. "Recent Literature on the Brontës" *English Studies* 25 (Dec 1943) 177–92

Essentially a review of the literature written about the Brontës within the past twenty years, this article is of special value because it contains reviews of many foreign books, articles, and dissertations.

C Books and Articles in Foreign Languages

C1 ALFEROVSKAJA, L. G. "Nekotorye problemy izučenija poèzii Èmilii Brontë" *Vestnik Leningradskogo Universiteta. Serija Istorii, Jazyka i Literatury* 20:64–71 (c. 1979)

C2 ANDREANI, Patrizia "L'altra morte: *Cime tempestose* di Emily Brontë" *Lettore di Provincia* 43:36–44 (c. 1979)

C3 AOYAMA, Seiko "Ai to Kodoku to Kuno to: Brontë Shimai" in Yoshinobu Aoyama, ed *Eibungaku no Heroine–tachi* (Tokyo: Hyronsha 1977) 187–228

C4 BATAILLE, Georges "Emily Brontë et le mal" *Critique* 13 No 117 (Feb 1957) 99–112

C5 ——— "Emily Brontë et le mal" *La Littérature et le Mal* (Paris: Gallimard 1957) 11–31 (See A18a, A283 for English translations.)

C6 BAY, André "Les soeurs Brontë à la recherche de bonheur" *Nouvelles Littéraires* (April 1972)

C7 BENGTSSON, Frans S. *Folk som sjöng* (Stockholm: Norstedt 1956)

C8 BERGGREN, Kerstin " 'I Am Happiest Now When Most Away' av Emily Brontë" *Studiekamraten* 57 (1975) 108

C9 BJRNESTAD, Ellen *Brontë–Kvartet* (Kbenhavn: Hernov 1980)

C10 BLAYAC, Alain "A Note on E. Brontë's Romanticism in *Wuthering Heights*" *Cahiers Victoriens et Edouardiens* 3 (1976) 1–6 (Revue du Centre d'Etudes et de Recherches Victoriennes et Edouardiennes de l'Université Paul Valéry, Montpellier.)

C11 BLEIKASTEN, André "La Passion dans *Les Hauts de Hurlevent*" *Bulletin de la Faculté des Lettres de Strasbourg* 36 [pre 1958] 357–64

C12 BLONDEL, Jacques "Cent ans de critique autour d'Emily Brontë" *Les Langues Modernes* 42 (1948)

C13 ——— *Emily Brontë: Expérience spirituelle et création poétique* (Paris: Presses Universitaires de France 1956) (See A10, A262, A283 for partial translations.)

C14 ——— "Emily Brontë: Récentes explorations" *Études anglaises* 11 (Oct–Dec 1958) 323–30

C15 ——— *Emily Brontë*, Wuthering Heights: *The Main Episode* (Paris: Didier 1951) 70 p

C16 ——— "Nouveaux regards sur Emily Brontë et *Wuthering Heights*" *Annales de la Faculté des Lettres et Sciences Humaines d'Aix* 1961

C17 ——— and Jean–Pierre Petit *Études Brontëenes* (Paris: Editions Ophrys 1970)
The collection includes:
"La Mort dans *Wuthering Heights*" by Jean–Pierre Petit, 7–18
"Emily Brontë and Emily Dickinson, A Study in Contrasts" by Jacques Blondel, 19–29 (In English. See A34A for annotation.)
"Le Sacré et le Profane dans *Wuthering Heights*" by N. Lecarme, 31–42
"Gothique et Surnaturel dans *Wuthering Heights*" by J. Rancy, 43–53

C17A BOLTON, Françoise *"Les Hauts de Hurlevant*: Superposition de Genres" *Le Genre du Roman—les genres de romans* (Paris: PU de France 1980) 105–11

BONITZER, Pascal *see* C59.

C18 BRAMANTE–TEDESCO, Luciana "Emily Brontë poetessa e romanziera" *Revista Letteraria per i Licei Classico Scientifico, Artistico e per l'Istituto Magistrale* 2 (1969–1970) 421–42

C19 CARRÈRE, Félix *"Les Hauts de Hurlevent* d'Emily Brontë, histoire d'amour?" *Annales de la Faculté des Lettres d'Aix* 32 (1958) 75–89

C20 DAHM, Hildegard "Die Technik der Charakterdarstellung und das Künstlerische Gesamtbild der Charaktere im Roman *Wuthering Heights* von Emily Brontë" Innsbruck 1955 (Dissertation)

C21 DEBU–BRIDEL, Jacques *Le Secret d'Emily Brontë* (Paris: Ferenczi 1950)

C22 DEXANT, B. "Originalité de *Jane Eyre* et des *Hauts de Hurlevant* par rapport au roman féminin anglais dans la première moitié du XIXᵉ siècle" *Annales du Centre d'Enseignment Sup. de Brazzaville* 4 (1968) 13–22

C23 DIMNET, Ernest *Les Grands Ecrivains Etrangers, Les Soeurs Brontë* (Paris: Blond & Cie 1910) (See A86 for English translation.)

C24 DUPONT, V. "Trois Notes sur les Brontës" *Études anglaises* 6 (Feb 1953) 1–27

C25 EAUBONNE, Françoise d', ed *Emily Brontë. Choix de textes, bibliographie, portraits, fac–similés* (Paris: P. Seghers 1964) 185 p

C26 ELLISIV, Steen "Problemet Emily Brontë" *Edda* 49 (1949) 161–78

C27 ESCOMBE, Lucienne *Emily Brontë et ses démons* (Paris and Clermont: Fernand Serlot 1941)

C28 FRÉCHET, René "Emily Brontë et son élan mystique" *Foi education* 27 (1957) 95–103

C29 FROESE, Fritz "Untersuchungen zu Emily Brontë's Roman *Wuthering Heights*" Königsberg 1920 (Dissertation)

C30 GASQUET, E. "Structure et Point de Vue dans *Les Hauts de Hurlevent*" *Études Anglaises et Americaines* 3 (1966) 115–28

C31 GIARTOSIO DE COURTEN, Maria Luisa *Il Mondo Infernale di Emily Brontë* (Sagep. 1975)

C32 HAN, Soon–ok "Emily Brontë's Family Background Reflected in *Wuthering Heights*" *Yonsei Review* (Seoul) 5 (1978) 153–66

C33 JALOUX, Edmond "Le Mystère d'Emily Brontë" *D'Eschyle à Giraudoux* (Librairie universelle de France 1947)

C34 KELLNER, Leon "Charlotte Brontë und Ihre Schwestern" *Die Englische Literatur im Zeitalter der Königen Viktoria* (Leipzig: Bernhard Tauchnitz 1909) 243–58

C35 KOLJEVIĆ, Svetozar "Tragom *Orkanskih visova*" *Letopis Matice Srpske* 416 (1974) 986–1004

C36 KOVAČEVIĆ, Marko "Funkcija prirode u strukturi romana *Orkanski Visovi*" *Izraz* 22:838–54 (c. 1978)

C37 KUHLMANN, Rudolf *Der Natur–Paganismus in der Weltanschauung von Emily Brontë* (Bonn: Schloppe 1926)

C38 KUHNELT, Harro Heinz *Emily Brontë* (Innsbruck: Institut für Sprachwissenschaft der Universität 1976)

C39 LAS VERGNAS, Raymond "Powys, l'homme tranquille du Dorset" *Revue de Paris* (September 1965) 98–103

LECARME, N. *see* C17.

C40 LUSTOSA, Stella Maria *As Irmãs Brontë* (Brazil 1948)

C41 MAACK, Annegret "Die Literaturkritische und Literarische Rezeption von Leben und Werk der Brontë–Sisters" *Literatur in Wissenschaft und Unterricht* (Kiel: West Germany) (c. 1979)

C42 MAURAT, Charlotte *Le Secret des Brontë ou Charlotte Brontë d'Après les Juvénilia, ses Lettres et Ceux qui l'ont Connue* (Paris: Buchet/Chastel 1967) (See A246 for English translation.)

C43 MESSIAEN, P. "Les Hauts–de–Hurle–Vent" *Revue des Cours et Conférences* 40 (1938) 189–92

C44 MIYAGAWA, Shizue *Brontë Kenkyu* (N.p.: Gakushobo 1979) 290 p

C45 MOORE, Virginia *La Vie d'Emily Brontë* (trans. from English by Mireille Hollard) (Paris: Gallimard 1939) 251 p (In English, A258.)

C46 NAGANORI, Hajime "Emily Brontë no *Arashi ga Oka*: Heathcliff to Catherine no Shocho-teki Imi" *English Literature and Language* (Tokyo) 14 (1978) 13–33

C47 NAKAOKA, Yo *Emily Brontë Ron* (Tokyo: Kokubunsha) (c. 1974)

C48 NONAKA, Ryo *Brontë Shimai: Kodoku to Chimmoku no Sekai* (Eibei Bungaku Sakkaron Sosho 3) (Tokyo: Tojusha 1978)

C49 ——— "Brontë Shimai no buntai" *Eigo Seinen* 125 (1979) 150–53

C50 OCAMPO, Victoria *Emily Brontë: (Terra incognita)* (Buenos Aires: Sur 1938)

C51 PETIT, Jean-Pierre *L'Oeuvre d'Emily Brontë: La Vision et les Thèmes* (Lyon: Editions L'Hermes 1977)

C52 ——— "Temps et Récit dans *Jane Eyre* et *Wuthering Heights*" Actes du Congrès de Dijon (1968) in *Formes du roman anglais du XVIe au XXe siècle* (Marcel Didier 1972) 37–52

——— see C17.

RANCY, J. *see* C17.

C53 RAUTH, Heidemarie *Emily Brontë's Roman* "Wuthering Heights" *als Quelle für Bühnenund Filmversionen* Veröffentlichungen de Universität Innsbruck, 84 (1974)

C54 RÉBORA, P. "Emily Brontë" [I Libri del Giorno] (November 1926)

C55 ROMEIN-VERSCHOOR, Annie "Lezend en denkend over Emily Brontë" *De Gids* 137 (1973) 87–95

C56 ROMEIU, Emilie and Georges Romieu *Vies des Hommes Illustres—No. 35. La Vie des Soeurs Brontë* (Paris: Librarie Gallimard 1929) (See A318.)

ROMIEU, Georges *see* C56.

C57 SONNINO, Giorgina "Il Pensiero Religioso di una Poetessa Inglese del Secolo XIX. Emilia Giovanna Brontë" *Nuova Antologia* 5th Ser. 39:122–31 (c. 1904)

C58 ———— *Tre Anime Luminose Fra le Nebbie Nordiche: Le Sorelle Brontë* (Florence: G. Civelli 1903)

C59 TECHINE, Andre and Pascal Bonitzer *Les Soeurs Brontë. Scenario Original avec huit Pages d'Illustrations* (Paris: Editions Albatross 1979)

C60 TORIUMI, Hisayoshi *Brontë Shimai no Sekai* (Eibei Bungaku Ser. 19) (Tokyo: Hyronsha) (c. 1978)

C61 ———— "Brontë Shimai no Shosetsu ni tsuite no Note" *Oberon* 17(1): 10–23 (c. 1978)

C62 TRAZ, Robert de *La Famille Brontë* (Paris: A Michel 1938)

C63 ———— "L'Enfance des Brontës" *Revue de Paris* 45 (1938) 579–605

C64 USADA, Akira "*Wuthering Heights* e no Shikaku" *Eigo Seinen* 125 (1979) 109, 160, 223, 273, 312, 367, 408, 456, 512, 560.

C65 VERES, Grigore "Emily Brontë" *Iasul Literar* 19 (1968) 68–70

C66 VESTDIJK, S. "De Geheimen van *Wuthering Heights*" *Criterium* [The Hague] 2 (1941) 358–76

C67 VIEBROCK, Helmut "Emily Brontë: *Wuthering Heights* in Paul Goetsch, Heinz Kosok and Kurt Otten, eds *Der Englische Roman im 19. Jahrhundert: Interpretationen* (Berlin: E. Schmidt 1973) 346 p

C68 WELLS, Augustin *Les Soeurs Brontë et l'étranger* (Paris: Rodstein 1937)

Index of Chapter and Article Titles

Index of Book Titles

Index of Introductions to *Wuthering Heights* and the Poetry

Index of Bibliographies and Anthologies
of Criticism

Emily Brontë:

A10, A17, A104, A162, A220, A262, A283, A322, A344, A379, B87, B426, B441, B504.

The Brontës:

A1, A4, A8, A9, A20, A58, A73A, A85, A111, A136, A216, A274, A277, A280, A319, A424, B37, B114, B131, B153, B181, B182, B279, B364, B395, B395A, B429, B505, B528.

Chronological Index

1981	A48, A177, A221, A224, A372, B42A, B179, B226A, B233A, B277, B312, B319A, B427, B435, B447, B507A
1982	A31A, A73A, A252, B38A, B39A, B261A, B276, B323A, B395A, B497A, B501A, B502A
No Date	A142, B5, B160, B359, B392